PRAISE FOR *BOUNDARY SPANNING LEADERSHIP*

Understanding boundaries so organizations can successfully explore and push into new frontiers is a challenge for every leader in almost all undertakings. Ernst and Chrobot-Mason help us better understand the power of teams working collaboratively together.
—*Vice Admiral Cutler Dawson (USN Ret.), President and Chief Executive Officer, Navy Federal Credit Union*

Many colleges and universities are searching for new, innovative, inter-disciplinary ways to teach students and develop knowledge, making the ability to work effectively across boundaries more crucial than ever. Ernst and Chrobot-Mason offer smart, practical insights that can greatly enhance how educators work together to create future generations of leaders.
—*Thomas W. Ross, President, University of North Carolina School System*

This book helps you build the essential boundary spanning capabilities you need to lead people fractured by strongly held values, beliefs, feelings, and practices that seem impossible to reconcile. The authors share wisdom and experiences from around the globe in a book rich with examples, tools, tactics, and cautionary pitfalls—stories that touch your heart and boost your leadership potential.
—*Victoria J. Marsick, Ph.D., Professor of Education and Co-Director J.M. Huber Institute, Columbia University*

I have had the privilege to apply the authors' practical thought leadership in my business roles since 2005. Now Ernst and Chrobot-Mason have created a next-generation classic to share what will quickly become a must-read guide to leading in the global economy.
—*Greg Pryor, Vice President, Leadership and Organization Effectiveness, Juniper Networks*

Our deepening interdependence with each other is an undeniable reality, a frightening challenge, and a remarkable opportunity. This book boldly guides us into this rapidly emerging new global reality, showing us the simplicity on the other side of the complexity, illuminating insights and skills each of us can use to lead powerfully in the 21st century.
—*Max Klau, Ph.D., Director of Leadership Development, City Year, Inc.*

The globally diverse backgrounds and multiple stakeholder groups that comprise today's organizations demand the innovative leadership approaches espoused in *Boundary Spanning Leadership*. The authors' timely toolset draws from extensive, deep experience and research, and describes in detail how to overcome the numerous challenges that dissimilar teams pose to leaders.
—*Norty Turner, Vice President and General Manager, EMEA and India, Hertz Equipment Rental Corporation*

The biggest challenge in a matrix organization is connecting the dots to unlock value. *Boundary Spanning Leadership* provides practical tools to constructively remove silos, neutralize negative politics, and put in place the conditions to achieve outstanding results.
—*Kevin Dooley, Global Head of HR Communications and Employer Brand and Marketing, Deutsche Bank*

Working across boundaries is key to successfully running a global business. The authors have written a superb book which provides today's leaders with the necessary insights and tools to steer successfully through times of transition.
—*Guy Kempfert, Global Head Learning and Development, Syngenta Crop Protection AG*

This book articulates a concept we believe is critical to our success at Lenovo: Businesses that transform cultural differences into organizational strengths, that focus intensely on building a unified global team, and that make their culture a top priority at every level have the best chance to succeed and build an enduring, winning company.
—*Kenneth DiPietro, Senior Vice President HR Lenovo*

For too long organizations have struggled with how best to nurture important collaborations across boundaries of time, space, expertise, and hierarchy. Ernst and Chrobot-Mason identify and make actionable critical practices to help any leader obtain a multiplier effect from their talent. A must read!
—*Rob Cross, Ph.D., Associate Professor, University of Virginia McIntire School of Commerce and author of* Driving Results Through Social Networks *and* The Hidden Power of Social Networks

Boundary Spanning Leadership brings elusive concepts to life with practical processes illustrated by inspiring stories and action tips. It's a common-sense approach to navigating the complex world we experience every day. Timely and timeless—read it now!
—*Ernie Turner, President, LIM (Leadership in International Management), author of* Action Reflection Learning: Solving Real Business Problems by Connecting Earning with Learning.

Silos, stovepipes, and narrow conceptions of role and identity beware: This groundbreaking book helps people work together more constructively despite your efforts!
—*Richard Hughes, Ph.D., senior author of bestselling textbook* Leadership: Enhancing the Lessons of Experience

Ernst and Chrobot-Mason distill the transformational power of boundary spanning leadership into an intuitively sound and inspirationally coherent practice. This book is as valuable as anything we've seen before in conflict transformation and bridging communities of all kinds: deceptively simple solutions to profoundly complex issues of building cultures of peace.
—*Mark Johnson, Ph.D. Executive Director, Fellowship of Reconciliation*

Boundary Spanning Leadership reminds leaders of the critical need to connect with diverse stakeholders by finding common ground as individual human beings.
—*Shalini Mahtani, Founder, Community Business Asia*

Few of us know how to work in a world where everything influences everything else. Finally, we have a guide. Grounded in a persuasive philosophy, Ernst and Chrobot-Mason's new book offers the pragmatic skills we have been searching for, but, until now, have eluded us.
—*Nancy Adler, Ph.D., S. Bronfman Chair in Management, McGill University, Canada, author of the bestseller,* International Dimensions of Organizational Behavior

Boundary Spanning Leadership offers a wealth of insights on how to lead effectively across differences. It is sure to be an invaluable resource to anyone who wants to be a better leader.
—*David V. Day, Ph.D., Woodside Professor of Leadership and Management, University of Western Australia Business School*

At last, a practitioner-oriented book based on solid research, that enables leaders, regardless of the country where they are employed, to inspire culturally diverse teams.
—*Gary Latham, Ph.D., Secretary of State Professor of Organizational Effectiveness, Rotman School of Management, University of Toronto.*

Leading difference is one of the most important cross-sector challenges that leaders encounter. Through hands-on practical advice, illustrated by compelling stories of success, Ernst and Chrobot-Mason have fashioned a multidimensional framework for spanning boundaries and leading across groups.
—*Nick Barker, Ph.D., Director, Asia Pacific Leadership Program, East-West Center*

BOUNDARY
SPANNING
LEADERSHIP

BOUNDARY SPANNING LEADERSHIP

Six Practices for
Solving Problems, Driving Innovation,
and Transforming Organizations

CHRIS ERNST
DONNA CHROBOT-MASON

New York   Chicago   San Francisco   Lisbon   London
Madrid   Mexico City   Milan   New Delhi   San Juan
Seoul   Singapore   Sydney   Toronto

The **McGraw·Hill** *Companies*

4 5 6 7 8 9 0   QFR/QFR   1 9 8 7 6 5 4 3 2

ISBN: 978-0-07-163887-6
MHID: 0-07-163887-3

This publication is designed to provide accurate and authoritative information in regard to the subject matter covered. It is sold with the understanding that the publisher is not engaged in rendering legal, accounting, or other professional service. If legal advice or other expert assistance is required, the services of a competent professional person should be sought.

—*From a Declaration of Principles Jointly Adopted by a Committee of the American Bar Association and a Committee of Publishers and Associations*

McGraw-Hill books are available at special quantity discounts to use as premiums and sales promotions, or for use in corporate training programs. To contact a representative, please visit the Contact Us pages at www.mhprofessional.com.

This book is printed on acid-free paper.

This book is dedicated to our families.

To our children, Madeleine, Wilson, Alex and Emmarie—may you find the courage and compassion to build bridges wherever there are borders.

To our parents and siblings for encouraging and inspiring us to discover new frontiers—Emery, Chris, Andy, Sara, Dick, Carol, Larry, Winifred, Agustin, Lia, and Mary.

And to our spouses, Dave and Winifred, for your boundless love and support.

CONTENTS

FOREWORD

In the traditional hierarchy of modern organizations, information flows vertically up and down the chain of command in a controlled way. Groups are differentiated and bounded. Organized by location or functions, group members have a high degree of similarity. We use organizational hierarchies for our benefit: to control flows of different kinds, for example, information and resources. We have learned how to coordinate work with those above and below us. We know what to expect from people in particular functions, locations, or positions. Technological, geopolitical, and social transformations, however, have introduced many additional ways that information can flow—laterally, diagonally, and in spirals— disrupting organizations by creating new communication channels, changing long-standing practices, and diffusing the distribution of power based on "who knows what." This change in organization means that in addition to understanding how to work vertically, people in leadership roles need to understand how to work in all directions and with all people regardless of occupation, level, location, ancestry, nationality, religion, or a variety of other characteristics and beliefs. Today, the leadership advantage goes to the people who are most closely linked to others and can work with a great variety of people from differing positions, backgrounds, and locations. This requires new practices, which Ernst and Chrobot-Mason describe as *boundary spanning leadership*. Leaders can put these practices to work, knitting together disparate sources of information and perspectives and creating what the authors call the *Nexus Effect*—the limitless possibilities and inspiring results that groups can achieve together above and beyond what they can achieve on their own.

Boundary Spanning Leadership provides the reader with an understanding of the critical skills necessary to lead in this changed environment. That understanding has its origin in an ambitious project, organized by Maxine Dalton and myself and conducted by several social scientists at the Center for Creative Leadership, called the "Leadership Across Differences" (LAD) project. Our original goal was to focus on the need for groups historically in conflict to learn to collaborate. We recognized that modern organizations were putting people who had a history of conflict or tension into close contact with one another and were asking them to work together. We wanted to develop a model for how people in organizational leadership roles could welcome, accept, and coordinate people of differing views and perspectives. Working with several noted experts (most importantly Donna Chrobot-Mason) and partners across the globe, the LAD team sought to understand the twenty-first-century leadership skills required to bring people together in organizations to commit to a particular direction or purpose. Our goal was to develop case studies about leadership in light of the common work of people who had different backgrounds and identities, which may have caused significant conflicts for previous generations. The journey took us to studying organizations in Spain, Hong Kong, Scotland, South Africa, Brazil, France, the United States, Jordan, India, Japan, Singapore, and Germany. We felt that by learning the stories of organizations in a variety of different countries, we could distill knowledge that could help people in positions of leadership reach across once formidable divides to bring people together. So did our sponsors and funders: large multinationals, government agencies, universities, and NGOs.

Boundary Spanning Leadership is a product of this study. The authors have synthesized data from 25 different organizations collected by a team of social scientists, distilling it into useable tactics and practices for leading across differences. Further, as the work developed, they realized that the tactics and practices identified could be used to bridge several different kinds of gaps in human relationships in organizations, in addition to those caused by the mixing of people with very different histories, perspectives, values, and cultures. In a subsequent CCL study, the "Leadership at the Peak" project, they queried senior-level executives about boundary spanning more generally and learned that the tactics and practices identified earlier were useful, not just for cases where there were deeply rooted conflicts of identity, but also for the more common, less entrenched identity conflicts between people from different functions or from different organizational locations—typical situations in the contemporary, ever-changing organizational world.

This volume is especially well timed. With every passing day, the leadership advantage seems to go to the person or organization who can best integrate disparate pieces of information and groups of people. As individuals transition to leadership roles that require greater degrees of boundary spanning, the collaborative and connecting approaches shared in this book are becoming more important. Leaders in the current environment must understand how to lead across the variety of boundaries in organizations. This is true both in the sense of building productive organizations among people who were once bitter enemies as well as encouraging people who were formerly competitors in business to work together to move an organization forward. Everywhere people have to move out of their comfort zones and learn to work outside vertical and local channels to engage a much larger and better informed community.

Although there are many books on leadership, the practical advice in this book stands out. *Boundary Spanning Leadership* offers a research-based approach. It is not based on assumptions or hopeful logic. Rather it has its basis in rigorous research, both that of CCL and others, focused on identifying the principles that govern healthy human interaction in the face of difference. Ernst and Chrobot-Mason have taken this body of work and broken it down into understandable tools and frameworks that individuals in organizations can employ. Further, they provide the reader with questions, activities, and opportunities for reflection in which to apply these practices and tactics to their own lives. *Boundary Spanning Leadership* offers a practical approach to understanding how identity and other human characteristics interact with the goals of organizations. The volume offers a way to build the leadership capacity that enhances the creativity and productivity of people operating in today's multi-cultural, information-rich environment.

Marian N. Ruderman
Senior Fellow, Center for Creative Leadership
Greensboro, North Carolina

PREFACE

In a twist to current thinking about our global, interconnected society, we believe that the world is indeed boundless and flat, but that human relationships are still bounded and confined by powerful limits.

Since Thomas Friedman's bestseller, *The World Is Flat*, was published in 2005, the world of business has felt anything but flat—the global financial crisis, climate change, energy crisis, and political and religious unrest. Why do things feel bumpier than ever? Of course there's no single answer, but we believe that the connections in our physical world have now outstripped the connections in our relational world. What is happening is that advances in Internet and collaboration technologies have dismantled many of the boundaries that once prevented people from working together. Yet as physical boundaries were removed, the boundaries that still exist in human relationships remain, in sharp and jagged relief. In a flat world, bridging boundaries between groups is the new and critical work of leadership.

The most important challenges we face today are interdependent—they can only be solved by groups working collaboratively together. For businesses, governments, organizations, and communities to solve current problems and realize new opportunities, leaders must think and act beyond group boundaries and identities.

Boundary spanning leadership is the capability to create direction, alignment, and commitment across group boundaries in service of a higher vision or goal. It begins with a new understanding of vertical, horizontal, stakeholder, demographic, and geographic boundaries. It can be accomplished through six practices: Buffering, Reflecting, Connecting, Mobilizing, Weaving, and Transforming. And it results in today's limiting borders being transformed into tomorrow's limitless frontiers.

Along with our colleagues at the Center for Creative Leadership (CCL), we have learned that where disparate groups collide, intersect, and link there is significant potential for a nexus to be created that unleashes limitless possibilities and inspiring results. At the nexus between groups resides greater direction, alignment, and commitment to solve pressing problems. At the nexus between groups lie new levels of collaboration to drive innovation. At the nexus between groups awaits the opportunity to transform your work, your businesses, and your communities.

How did we reach this conclusion? How did we come to see boundaries not just as borders that limit and constrain, but also as frontiers where the most advanced, breakthrough thinking resides? We arrived by taking a journey that required us, as authors, to reach across, bridge, and collaborate across boundaries ourselves. It's taken us a decade of hard work to get here. Along the way, we've confronted our own fair share of limitations and constraints—within ourselves and within our own efforts to work with a vast network of colleagues around the world. As part of a collaborative team conducting a research project across six world regions (Africa, Asia, Europe, the Middle East, North America, and South America), we know from experience that spanning boundaries is an arduous task. Yet we've also experienced firsthand the novel ideas and exciting possibilities that emerge at the nexus between groups.

Most of all, however, we've learned from people like you—leaders who are striving to think and act beyond boundaries. It has been our privilege to work with leading individuals and their organizations around the world. And it has deeply shaped our thinking, both as researchers and as practitioners.

As researchers, we were struck by the data. Along with our colleagues at CCL, we created a database of over 2,800 survey responses and nearly 300 interviews. The research project involved multiple methods across multiple countries, allowing us to draw more powerful and comprehensive conclusions than would have been possible using any one method or country alone. In analyzing the data and integrating it with research and theory from other fields and disciplines, we can now say with a degree of confidence that when leaders need to span boundaries to accomplish a larger goal—across a wide variety of contexts and cultures in the world—the six practices described in this book will help.

As practitioners, we were inspired by the stories. We came to realize that the stories we heard from leaders all over the world held important lessons of experience. They were signposts pointing the way toward a new approach to leadership. The data collected by the

CCL team and our review of existing theory and research gave us the foundation to write this book. The stories, however, convinced us that we could write a book that was not only meaningful, but had the potential to inspire action. We realized, both individually and collectively, that these stories challenged us to think and act beyond our own boundaries, to go beyond the status quo, and to try new approaches. And we began to envision how these stories would inspire others to do the same.

Donna was particularly moved by the stories from South Africa, where she learned about the persistent borders that exist between black and white groups within a large insurance firm. Employees at companies like *Insurance Incorporated** are still trying to come to terms with the radical changes that occurred in 1994 when Nelson Mandela was elected president, signaling the end of apartheid and nearly five decades of legally sanctioned racial segregation. As you'll learn in Chapter 4, a shift in political power happened literally overnight, yet leaders and employees in the company continue to find it takes much longer to change hearts and minds to reflect these new laws.

Donna says, "I was moved by the pain that leaders at Insurance Incorporated seemed to be experiencing and how poorly equipped they were to span these deep divisions within their organization. Although my research, writing, and teaching over the past 10 years had largely been about how leaders should view differences as a benefit and competitive advantage, the stories from South Africa helped me to truly understand, perhaps for the first time in my

---

*Throughout the book, we use pseudonyms for some people and their organizations. These pseudonyms are italicized the first time they are used in their respective chapters.

career, just how challenging it was to collaborate across differences. It became clear to me that today's technology is an enabler for collaboration, but not the answer. The answer lies much deeper. We will continue to be limited in our potential to work effectively together across boundaries until we develop new capabilities to address the more relational and psychological aspects of the borders that keep us apart in our minds and our hearts. I realized that I could do more, as a scholar and an educator, to help my students and the leaders I work with to develop their capacity to overcome these borders and to take advantage of the potential that resides at the intersection of groups working collaboratively together."

Chris will never forget the leaders of Child Relief and You (CRY), a nonprofit organization in India, and the stories they shared with him. He says, "In a whirlwind two weeks, I conducted interviews with CRY staff in a number of regional offices across vast India—Bangalore, Delhi, Kolkata, Mumbai, and outlying regions. As the organization locates its offices in impoverished parts of Indian cities to be near the children they serve, I traveled using nearly every form of transportation imaginable—plane, train, bus, 'deluxe taxi,' 'econo taxi,' moped, *tuk-tuk*, and bicycle rickshaw. Arriving at various regional offices, I immediately observed that each office had its own unique energy and vitality. Yet in the interviews, I saw and felt a tremendous sense of interconnection across the various regional groups. Each group was distinct, with unique experiences, backgrounds, and expertise. Yet as you'll read about in Chapter 8, CRY was able to collaborate creatively across regional boundaries to realize a new and exciting strategic frontier.

"The stories that leaders shared with me in India inspired me in my work. At the time, I was serving in an expatriate role in CCL's office in Singapore. My job was to help launch CCL's research and innovation unit in the Asia Pacific. This required managing a small team of researchers that hailed from China, India, and Southeast Asia, while also staying connected to CCL's global research efforts in Europe and the United States. Over a three-year period, our team (like CRY) was able to realize new possibilities by integrating different areas of experience and expertise. Routine team practices such as sharing personal 'cultural incidents,' offering our 'begs, brags, and what-ifs' to the team, and conducting 'deep dive' sessions on topics of shared interest often led to new insights and valuable outcomes. Yet, as I will be the first to admit, leading across such widely different cultures, levels of experience, and areas of expertise was hard work. There were times where I felt at a loss for what to do, frustrated by my own limitations, and unsure of how to proceed. In these moments, the stories from India encouraged me. These stories, along with the many successes our team experienced, convinced me of what is ultimately possible at the nexus between groups."

As both researchers and practitioners, the two of us have been on a 10-year journey that has given us a bird's-eye view of the many challenges leaders face in a world that proves to be more jagged and bumpier than ever. In this book, we will share with you what we have learned along the way—the pitfalls to avoid as well as the practices for success.

Boundary spanning leadership resides within and across individuals, groups and teams, and larger organizations and systems. Our focus is you and how you can develop the collaborative skills, mindsets, and behaviors of boundary spanning leadership. You may be a CEO, a middle manager, or a project manager. You may be working in a nonprofit organization or as a community organizer. You may be a human resource professional, educator, or consultant. You could be working in Brazil, China, Germany, or the United States, or in all four countries during the course of a year. Regardless, our core message to you is this: through six boundary spanning practices, you can turn limiting borders into limitless frontiers to solve mission-critical problems, create innovative solutions, and change and transform your organization to thrive. In short, this book is about helping you achieve inspiring results at the nexus between groups.

Let's be clear—boundary spanning leadership is not for the faint of heart. It's not easy to lead outside your box in the organizational chart, across the lines of stakeholder interests, beyond the borders of the division or groups you represent. It's a constant challenge to lead across boundaries of Us and Them, in search of the collective We. It's a persistent struggle to step outside the cultural, organizational, religious, political, or national worldviews that form your being, and to remain open to the clash of ideas around you.

Nevertheless, we know it can be done. From rural towns in the southeastern United States to luminous skyscrapers in Hong Kong, and from the rise of a modern Singapore to the chaotic streets of Jordan, we have had the privilege to examine how boundary spanning leaders are transforming borders that divide into boundless possibilities and alternative futures.

We hope this book will provide you with new insights and practices to navigate boundaries in a flat world and to help others adapt and thrive in complex and uncertain times. You can become part of that conversation if you visit the book's companion Web site at www.spanboundaries.com. The site contains tools and diagnostics for download, articles to read and share with your team, additional information about the authors and their organizations, and a place to share your insights and experiences with other boundary spanning leaders around the world. With a healthy balance of grounded humility and steadfast determination, we encourage you to translate the ideas in this book into action to create a more collaborative future. We invite you to join us as we share both the promise and the peril of the stories that leaders have told us in our work across the globe. We hope their stories inspire you as much as they inspired us.

ACKNOWLEDGMENTS

This book is a testament to the power of boundary spanning in action. It would not have been possible if it were not for the considerable talent, dedication, and creativity of a long list of colleagues and collaborators who worked with us over the past 10 years. The Leadership Across Differences (LAD) project, a multiyear research initiative based at the Center for Creative Leadership (CCL), involved colleagues working in collaboration across continents, functions, areas of expertise, levels, and perspectives. The LAD team not only studied leading across boundaries, we lived it. As such, we learned how challenging and also how rewarding boundary spanning work can be. For your years of dedication to the study of this topic, for helping to stretch our minds to think about leadership in new and innovative ways, and for your skill, expertise, and commitment to the research, LAD team, we thank you one and all.

A core group of LAD team members who were most influential in our thinking deserve extra thanks. We are indebted to Marian

Ruderman for her leadership, both formally and informally, her conceptual, analytical, and writing talents, and her encouragement and friendship that was given so freely to both of us. Thank you, Maxine Dalton, for your forward thinking in bringing this project to life and thanks to Kelly Hannum, who (along with Chris) served as project leaders for a number of years. And thank you to Jeffrey Yip, whose endless curiosity and creative mind served as a major sparkplug for the creation of this book. Here we thank with gratitude all the team members who significantly shaped the LAD project—Kathryn Cartner, Maxine Dalton, Jennifer Deal, Rachael Foy, Bill Gentry, Sarah Glover, Michael Hoppe, Ancella Livers, Belinda McFeeters, Vijayan Munusamy, Patty Ohlott, Marian Ruderman, Robbie Soloman, Joan Tavares, Todd Weber, Jeffrey Yip, and external colleagues around the world including Lize Booysen, David Dinwoodie, Claude Levy-Leboyer, Jonna Louvrier, Muhsen Makhamreh Sigmar Malvezzi, Stella Nkomo, Tammy Rubel, Lilach Sagiv, Shalom Schwartz, and Peter Smith.

We are grateful to CCL for providing a variety of resources that enabled the writing and production of this book. We especially want to thank David Altman for believing in our work and supporting the project. Thanks CCL for being a place that values putting ideas into action.

In addition to the financial support provided by CCL, we thank the Singapore Economic Development Board, the Z. Smith Reynolds Foundation, and the Marrow Fund, established in honor of Dr. Alfred J. Marrow, for generous grant funding. Though thanks are due to many organizations that participated in our research around the world, we give special recognition to the following for their support: Merrill Lynch, Blue Cross-Blue Shield, Bristol-Myers Squibb,

CARE, Chubb, ConocoPhillips, CRY, GlaxoSmithKline, the Greensboro Fire Department, Lenovo, Lutheran Family Services, Mercy Corps, Swiss Re, Syngenta, and Verizon.

Thank you to our editorial team, who worked with us every step of the way to shape the book and keep us focused. We thank Peter Scisco for reading and providing feedback, guidance, and probably most importantly encouragement, on multiple drafts. Thank you to Mary Glenn, Knox Huston, and the entire McGraw-Hill Professional publishing team, who liked our ideas in the early stages and then worked with us to turn them into reality. Thank you, Chris Arney, Traci Carter, Felecia Corbett, and Karen Lewis for your support in the production of this book, and to Rebecca Garau for helping us to say what we needed to say, only better. Thank you also to the many colleagues and family members who also reviewed our work and provided valuable insights and suggestions—John Alexander, Dick Ernst, Winifred Ernst, Dave Mason, Marian Ruderman, and Jeff Yip.

Finally, we want to thank the many leaders who shared their stories with us. We are grateful for your time and insights, and for sharing examples of both the peril and the promise that occur when group boundaries intersect and collide. We are especially grateful to Mark Gerzon for inspiring us as global citizens, and to John Herrera for sharing his story of the Latino Community Credit Union and the long and winding journey he took to create it.

Donna Acknowledges

I want to thank my CCL colleagues and friends. It has been my greatest privilege to work with you—the brightest, most capable, and caring people I have ever come across. You have inspired me to want to make the world a better place. Thank you for making my world better by knowing and working with you.

Thank you to my colleagues and friends at the University of Cincinnati, especially Joseph Gallo, Stacie Furst, Ted Dass, and Hal McCullough, for encouraging me to keep moving forward.

Thank you to the women in my life who have modeled boundary spanning leadership for me in so many ways. Thanks to Marian Ruderman, Belle Rose Ragins, Gail Fairhurst, and Suzanne Masterson, for your mentoring support throughout my academic career and for showing me how to let your passion, values, and quest for justice guide your work. For being a constant source of support and renewal, I wish to thank Nags Heart and the leadership collaborative in particular—Stacy Blake-Beard, Faye Crosby, Peggy Stockdale, Kecia Thomas, and Margie Krest. And to my life-long friends, Richelle Southwick, Maggie Daniels, Julie Holliday-Wayne, Aimee Manis, and Katherine Miller, I thank you for giving me the gift of friendship and "girl power" to accomplish my dreams.

Thank you to my family for giving me practical and spiritual support throughout this project and all my life projects. Thank you to my children for inspiring me to focus on future possibilities while slowing me down enough to enjoy the present. To Emmarie, for being my sunshine on the cloudiest of days and Alex, for teaching me so much about happiness and love. To my husband, Dave, for hanging in there with me as we grow older and hopefully wiser, and for all you did to help so I had time to work on the book. To my parents, who have supported me in every way possible. Mom, thank you for chicken salad, oatmeal chocolate chip cookies, warm hugs, cleaning my house, and, most importantly, for being my biggest fan. Dad, thank you for being the world's greatest grandpa and for helping me grow in faith and understanding of myself, others, and God. I also want to thank the many babysitters and neighbors who took such great care of my children while I worked on the book, and my great, big, supportive, loving Polish family—for letting me be a part of the fun and for letting Chris and me spend a memorable week at Long Lake working to improve the book and our slalom skiing too.

And finally, thanks to Chris, my coauthor and partner in crime, for asking me to join him on this wonderful adventure. I've enjoyed (almost) every minute of it!

Chris Acknowledges

The Center for Creative Leadership has been a constantly supportive and enriching environment for me to span boundaries, which in turn propels me to develop these capabilities in others. No two people better exemplify how this collaborative dynamic works more than Chuck Palus and Jeffrey Yip. Chuck and Jeff make me and everyone around them better—more creative, integrative, thoughtful, and fun. Thanks, Chuck, for being an invaluable thought partner toward the later stages of writing this book, and likewise thanks to Jeff, for our collaborations at the onset. Many of the primary terms in these pages, including boundary spanning leadership and the nexus effect, were hatched with Jeff over ambling conversations and bountiful meals in the streets of Singapore.

There are many more like Chuck and Jeff at CCL, but here I only get to thank those who uniquely inspired and supported me to write this book—Bill Drath, Lynn Fick-Cooper, David Horth,

Renee Hultin, Jennifer Martineau, Cindy McCauley, John McGuire, Bill Pasmore, Lyndon Rego, Diane Reinhold, and, last but not least, my sidekick for three years in Asia, Meena Wilson. As I write, new collaborations with new colleagues are in the works, so this list only grows.

Thank you, friends around the world and those that live within a two-block radius. The comings and goings of Devereux Street are a daily reminder of what it means to live and be in a community.

For the roots and wings to imagine this book, and for your support, love, and patience to bring it to fruition, I thank my family. The Ernsts and the Watkins provided a "home away from home" so the kids could continue to thrive even when Mom was knee-deep in dissertation writing while Dad was swimming in interview transcripts. Madeleine and Wilson, I love you dearly. And to you, Winifred, well, the two of us together, we can do anything.

And likewise, thanks to you, Donna. To loosely paraphrase T. S. Eliot, it's been wonderful to arrive where we started together and to know the place for the first time.

INTRODUCTION

On the seventy-ninth floor of International Financial Group's (IFG) global headquarters in New York City, *Paul Andrews* sits alone in a teleconference room. He has just wrapped up a meeting concerning one of IFG's most ambitious projects in years: to develop and deliver within six months a new financial service solution simultaneously across the Americas, Europe, and Asia. Minutes ago, faces and voices representing five functions, three levels of management, 11 countries, four suppliers, a customer panel, and seemingly every type of human diversity imaginable were rendered in nearly face-to-face precision across a wall-length screen.

Ambitious, talented, and experienced, IFG has identified the team members and partners as the right people to develop and deliver its innovative service, but at the moment, Paul wonders if his dream team can overcome the rifts and divides he observed during the meeting and how his leadership might enable better collaboration. He jots down some thoughts about how the disparate groups are working together, both the positives and the negatives, and notes the root causes of his concern:

Negatives	Positives
Rift—lack of trust between upper and middle management.	*Partnership*—Asia senior and middle management well coordinated. Shared vision.
Silos—R&D and operations not on same page. No respect.	*Collaboration*—marketing and sales well-linked. Lots of innovation potential.
Turf battle—jockeying suppliers. They feel like outsiders. No common purpose.	*Common ground*—excellent feedback from customer panel. Clear on the type of solution they want us to deliver.
Generation gap—young team members love the cutting edge technology, but old timers feel threatened by it. Need safety to overcome threat.	*Engagement*—willingness to share wide-ranging perspectives. Diversity seen as a strength.
Culture clash—Europe lacks buy-in. They think it's just another US HQ project of the month. Ownership lacking.	*Global mindset*—high energy to develop global solution. Commitment toward cross-regional thinking.

As Paul assesses the team, he realizes that even in a world of vast collaborative potential, powerful and limiting boundaries surround us. At IFG and in organizations and communities like yours, boundaries separate people into groups of Us and Them. These boundaries—some temporary, some deeply rooted—are built around both vertical and horizontal structures as well as diverse stakeholder, demographic, and geographic groups. Ideally, our organizations and communities can harness the collaboration and innovation that come from wide-ranging expertise, diverse experiences, and varied identities. All too often, however, the boundaries are borders— barriers that limit, confine, and lead to wasteful conflicts and counterproductive divides.

The word *boundary* has two very different meanings.

bound-a-ry
1. something that indicates bounds or limits; a *border* or
   bounding line
2. Also called *frontier*. The location of the most advanced or
   newest activity in an area
   —Random House Dictionary, 2009

In this book, we explore the notion that boundaries can be experienced in organizations and broader communities as two very different things. Boundaries may be borders that limit human potential, restrict creativity and innovation, and stifle necessary business and societal change. But boundaries also may represent frontiers: the location where the most advanced thinking and breakthrough possibilities reside. What explains the difference between limiting borders and limitless frontiers? In a word, leadership.

In navigating today's unfamiliar terrain, we are all challenged to think and act beyond the current borders that confine us, our teams, and our organizations as a whole. Developing innovative solutions requires reaching beyond present boundaries and seeking new frontiers at the nexus where groups collide, intersect, and link.

Like Paul at IFG, many of us—senior executives, directors, plant managers, community organizers—are at a loss about how to think and act in today's shifting leadership landscape. The challenges of boundaries call forth a need for new ways to bring groups together and, yes, new ways to practice leadership.

Boundary spanning leadership is composed of six practices for leading at the nexus between groups: buffering, reflecting, connecting, mobilizing, weaving, and transforming. Through these practices you will be able to transform borders into new frontiers to solve problems, create innovative solutions, and evolve and transform your organization to thrive in a flat world.

In so doing, you will be rewarded with new possibilities and inspiring results, including the following:

- Increased organizational agility to respond to a dynamic marketplace
- Advanced cross-organizational innovation processes
- Achievement of mission-critical bottom-line results
- An engaged and empowered workplace at all levels
- Flexible, cross-functional learning capabilities to solve problems and adapt to change
- A welcoming, diverse, and inclusive organization that brings out everybody's best
- New abilities to work in deeper, more open relationships with customers
- Better-managed risks and rewards through enduring cross-sector partnerships
- Well-integrated merged or acquired organizations
- A more socially responsible organization
- Higher-performing virtual teams
- Global mindsets and cross-regional collaboration
- Improved capacity to create shared direction, alignment, and commitment throughout the organization

Realizing these and other inspiring results is not just an ideal but an essential business reality. A new approach to leading across vertical, horizontal, stakeholder, demographic, and geographic boundaries is needed. We call this new approach boundary spanning leadership.

An Introduction to Boundary Spanning Leadership

Boundary spanning leadership is the ability to create direction, alignment, and commitment across boundaries in service of a higher vision or goal.[1,2] By employing the six leadership practices, you create direction, alignment, and commitment between groups to achieve critical organizational outcomes. These practices reside within the interactions across groups, teams, functions, units, organizations, and broader communities. As a boundary spanning leader, your job is to build a bridge and your role within that job is to provide the space for these practices to occur. Figure I.1 shows an example.

Figure I.1 Boundary spanning leadership.

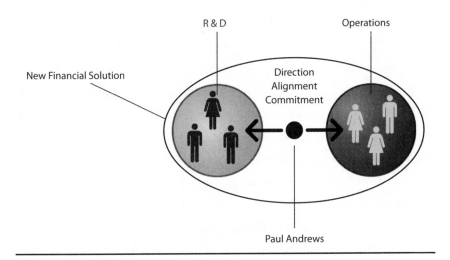

At IFG, Paul Andrews's task is to bring together multiple functional, regional, and stakeholder groups to develop a new financial service solution. A simplification of these relationships is illustrated in the figure. First, the diagram illustrates two groups, R&D and Operations (we left out all the other groups to keep things simple). Second, these groups need to collaborate to achieve a higher vision or goal: the creation of a new financial service. However, this won't be easy. These two functions operate as silos, with little respect or trust between them. To achieve the goal, Paul needs to span boundaries to create effective leadership across groups. In our research and practice at the Center for Creative Leadership (CCL), we define leadership in terms of accomplishing three outcomes:

- *Direction*: a shared understanding of common goals and strategy
- *Alignment*: the joint coordination of resources and activities
- *Commitment*: a commitment to collective success that is equal to or above the commitment to the unique success of any single group[3]

We hope you can appreciate the complexities of boundary spanning leadership in this simple example. In this case, generating increased direction, alignment, and commitment across two divergent functions—R&D and Operations—is challenging enough. Achieving that goal becomes even more daunting when you find yourself stuck in the middle of multiple groups and boundaries simultaneously. To put it bluntly, when you are leading in the middle between groups, the days of "I lead and you follow" are over. Gone are the days when leaders work *within* an intact group in which leaders and followers share a culture, values, and interests.

Instead, today you must lead *across* groups, at the juncture where wide-ranging experience, diverse expertise, and varied identities intersect. It is here at the intersection where two powerful human forces—differentiation and integration—collide that you can enact the six boundary spanning practices to catalyze collaboration, drive innovation, and transform your organization. Shortly, we describe more fully the six leadership practices you need to make that happen.

But first a few words about the organization of this book, a preview of what you'll find in these pages, and a model of boundary spanning leadership that pulls the main ideas together.

Book Overview

Part 1: The Forces That Pull Us Apart and Bring Us Together

The landscape beneath your feet is shifting dramatically. Advancing technology, changing global demographics, and expanding globalization are dismantling boundaries in organizations around the world rapidly. In Chapter 1, we explore how you will need to think and act differently across five types of boundaries: vertical, horizontal, stakeholder, demographic, and geographic. We'll also walk you through an activity to identify your own unique Nexus Challenge and return to it at points throughout the book as a means for you to apply the book's concepts to your own organization.

After providing an orientation to the five types of boundaries found in today's landscape, we focus on you and your unique identity as a leader in Chapter 2. You'll have a chance to "map" your identity: the unique attributes, characteristics, skills, and interests that make you *you*. You'll come to see how identities are formed out of the interplay between two fundamental, universal, and powerful human forces: the need for differentiation, divergence, and uniqueness and the need for integration, convergence, and belonging. This most basic of human needs to establish a positive identity—to simultaneously belong and to be unique—provides the science on which the ideas in this book are based.[4]

In Chapter 3, we apply what you learned about identity to demonstrate the unfortunate but all too real potential for destructive Great Divides—*the limited and counterproductive outcomes that occur when groups divide into Us and Them.* As technical and structural boundaries are dismantled in an "ever-flattening" world, the boundaries that remain in human relationships paradoxically become sharper and more jagged. The boundaries that matter most today are psychological and emotional rather than organizational and structural. Great Divides between Us and Them are about identity: our core values, how we define ourselves, and our beliefs concerning how we fit within our social world. Paul Andrews didn't attribute the root cause of the rifts and divides he observed in his team to systems, structures, or technology. He attributed them to the deeper dynamics found in human relationships: lack of trust, no respect, no common purpose, the need for safety to overcome threat, lack of ownership. There's no quick fix or technical solution for any of these problems: They address not *what* people do or *how* they do it but *who* they are.

To bridge, span, and reach across such complex boundaries in human relationships, you must learn to do three things: manage boundaries, forge common ground, and discover new frontiers. This is the core of the book and our focus in Parts 2, 3, and 4.

Part 2: Managing Boundaries

A boundary demarcates where one thing stops and another starts. To manage boundaries is to define and understand what differentiates groups. Ultimately, this book is about how you can bring groups together to achieve inspiring results. The first step to spanning boundaries is, ironically, to create or strengthen them. You must be able to see group boundaries clearly before you can bridge them. In Part 2, we describe the two practices—buffering and reflecting—that enable you to manage the boundaries between groups.

The practice of *buffering* involves defining boundaries to create safety between groups. Buffers monitor and protect the flow of information and resources across boundaries. To see buffering in action, we will visit South Africa in Chapter 4 and learn how Joe Pettit and Zanele Moyo worked together to manage the boundary that still exists between blacks and whites in a postapartheid organization.

Once groups have achieved a state of safety between them, the next practice, *reflecting*, involves understanding boundaries to foster intergroup respect. Reflectors represent distinct perspectives and facilitate knowledge exchange across groups. In Chapter 5, we'll go to Chatham County, North Carolina, to witness the incredible transformation that occurred within Rick Givens and ultimately within the community he led. Through his own inner journey, Givens used the practice of reflecting to become a boundary spanning leader.

What if your organization and your broader community were places of unconditional positive regard, psychological safety, and mutual respect across vertical, horizontal, stakeholder, demographic, and geographic boundaries? What new opportunities would arise? With this foundation in place, you are ready to move forward and upward, to go beyond managing boundaries and toward forging common ground.

Part 3: Forging Common Ground

Common ground represents what is universal and shared. To forge common ground is to bring groups together to achieve a larger purpose. Recall that the human need for uniqueness is balanced by an equally powerful need for belonging. In Part 3, we describe two practices—connecting and mobilizing—that enable you to tap into the human need to be part of something larger than yourself.

The practice of *connecting* involves suspending boundaries to build trust between groups. Connectors link people and bridge divided groups across boundaries. To witness connecting in action, we'll go to Europe in Chapter 6 and see how Daniel Sutton successfully led a cross-sector task force by building trust across three divergent groups—energy executives, environmentalists, and government leaders—to develop a new, more sustainable plan for their city.

Once the boundaries between groups fade into the background, the next practice, *mobilizing*, involves reframing boundaries to develop intergroup community. Mobilizers craft common purpose and shared identity across boundaries. History was made in 2005 when the Chinese computer company Lenovo announced that it had purchased IBM's global personal computer operation. In Chapter 7, we'll learn how leaders at Lenovo are bridging boundaries between East and West by building community in their quest to create the world's most innovative PCs.

What if your organization and broader community were places of mutual trust, community, and collective action where groups collaborated skillfully across vertical and horizontal structures, along with disparate stakeholder, demographic, and geographic groups? What new avenues for creativity and innovation would come into view? Connecting and mobilizing are the next practices in boundary spanning leadership. You are now ready to go further yet, moving beyond forging common ground to discovering new frontiers.

Part 4: Discovering New Frontiers

A frontier is a place of emergent possibility. It represents the outer limits, the location where the most advanced and breakthrough thinking resides. The frontier is where both of the powerful human forces—differentiation and integration—intersect in transformative new ways. In Part 4, we explore the final two practices—weaving and transforming—that enable you to discover new frontiers where similarities and differences meet.

Weaving occurs when boundaries are interlaced in new ways to advance intergroup interdependence. Weavers draw out and integrate group differences within a larger whole. In Chapter 8, we'll travel to India to observe how the CEO of the nonprofit organization Child Relief and You (CRY) used the practice of weaving to lead a wildly successful strategic change in support of the organization's mission.

Once groups have achieved a state of interdependence, the final practice, *transforming*, involves cross-cutting boundaries to enable intergroup reinvention. Transformers bring multiple groups together in new directions to realize emergent possibilities. The issue of energy sustainability represents perhaps the most critical boundary spanning dilemma of our time. In Chapter 9, we'll see how Mark Gerzon, one of the world's foremost authorities on intergroup leadership, is cross-cutting boundaries to create an alternative future that is distinctly different from the present.

What if your organization and broader community were places of interdependent collaboration, collective learning, and positively transformative change? What alternative futures could be created to thrive and adapt in an ever-changing world?

Part 5: The Nexus Effect

In the final section of the book, we bring all the pieces together. In Chapter 10, we encourage you to put the ideas in this book into action. We'll do this by sharing the remarkable story of John Herrera and by illustrating the Nexus Effect: *the limitless possibilities and inspiring results that groups can realize together above and beyond what they can achieve on their own.* You'll see how John was able to tap into the power of the Nexus Effect by using the six boundary spanning leadership practices to create the Latino Community Credit Union, the fastest-growing credit union in the country. It has far exceeded anyone's expectations, but it took a collective vision and the collaborative effort of many community leaders working across boundaries to make it happen.

Finally, in the Epilogue we take a look ahead. Through tremendous advances in communication and transportation technologies, the scale of human interaction now encompasses the globe. Yet it is also true that our potential for collaboration remains largely unrealized. The real-world stories throughout this book are regrettably the exception rather than the rule; they are about ordinary leaders achieving extraordinary things at the nexus between groups. In the Epilogue, we return to their stories one final time to consider the possibilities for a more interdependent, collaborative future.

We welcome you to the book and the exciting places we'll go. To navigate today's shifting leadership landscape, there's never been a more urgent need for boundary spanning leadership.

Boundary Spanning Leadership Model

By using six boundary spanning practices, leaders can transform the limited and counterproductive outcomes of a Great Divide into the limitless possibilities and inspiring results of the Nexus Effect. The boundary spanning model shown in Figure I.2 illustrates the upward

---

Figure I.2 The six practices of boundary spanning leadership.

NEXUS EFFECT

DISCOVER NEW FRONTIERS

Transforming - Enable Reinvention

Weaving - Advance Interdependence

FORGE COMMON GROUND

Mobilizing - Develop Community

Connecting - Build Trust

MANAGE BOUNDARIES

Reflecting - Foster Respect

Buffering - Create Safety

GREAT DIVIDE

---

spiral leaders must travel to increase intergroup collaboration. This spiral depicts how leaders progress from managing boundaries, to forging common ground, to discovering new frontiers at the nexus between groups. Through the six boundary spanning practices, leaders create a Nexus Effect to solve problems, create innovative solutions, and transform their organizations.

P ART 1

THE FORCES THAT PULL US APART AND BRING US TOGETHER

A dvancing technology, changing global demographics, and expanding globalization are rapidly dismantling structural boundaries in organizations around the world. Yet boundaries in human relationships persist and limit our potential to work effectively together. In Part 1, we describe today's shifting leadership landscape. The new landscape is a vast but rugged expanse in which the possibilities for collaboration and breakthrough thinking seem endless yet conflict, division, and isolation often prevail. Boundaries create borders that pull groups apart even as leaders strive to facilitate collaborative work and bring groups together. Leaders often find themselves "caught in the middle" between groups with widely differing values, beliefs, and perspectives. To bring groups together to achieve a higher goal or vision, it is necessary to understand the forces that pull groups apart.

In Chapter 1, we'll orient you to today's shifting leadership landscape by outlining the types of boundaries you need to lead across. In Chapter 2, we'll describe how these boundaries are manifested in identity and the interplay between two fundamental and universal human forces: the need for differentiation and uniqueness and the need for integration and belonging. In Chapter 3, we'll apply what you've learned about identity to demonstrate the unfortunate but all too real potential for Great Divides. Great Divides represent the worst-case scenario—when groups divide into Us and Them so that all the energy between groups is spent on conflict and counterproductive behaviors. In these situations, collaborative and innovative possibilities are limited and the Nexus Effect is out of reach.

CHAPTER 1

THE SHIFTING LEADERSHIP LANDSCAPE

Today's most pressing challenges span boundaries, and so too must leadership. A recent Center for Creative Leadership (CCL) survey paints a compelling picture of the many boundaries leaders must navigate in today's environment. We see a shifting leadership landscape that is rocky and jagged, filled with many turns and sharp curves, and constantly in flux. It is a landscape that is cause for concern and action. Among the 128 senior-level executives who participated in the CCL survey, 86 percent told us that it is "extremely important" that they collaborate effectively across boundaries in their current leadership roles. However, just 7 percent of those executives believed they were "very effective" at doing so.[1] That's a 79 percent "critical gap," the largest anyone can ever recall in our decades of collecting senior executive participant data at the Center for Creative Leadership (see Figure 1.1). These leaders are the CEOs, presidents, senior vice presidents, and directors

Figure 1.1 The critical gap.

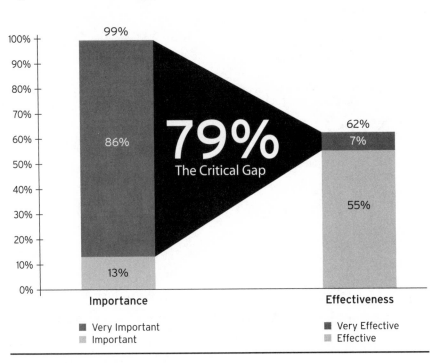

of the world's best companies. Their candor serves as a call to action for us all.

In the CCL research, we also asked the 128 senior executives to describe the types of boundaries they needed to work across. The boundaries they described were multifaceted and distinct, but there was considerable overlap. They included spanning vertical boundaries between hierarchical levels of the organization, horizontal boundaries between functions, stakeholder boundaries with customers and suppliers, demographic boundaries in working with people from diverse groups, and geographic boundaries of distance and region (see Figure 1.2).[2]

Figure 1.2 Five types of boundaries.

| Vertical | Horizontal | Stakeholder | Demographic | Geographic |

Our research at CCL, along with the work of others in the field, allows us to state confidently that these five types of boundaries are universal, transcending cultures, contexts, and time.[3] They've been an integral aspect of organizational life in the past, they're with us today, and they'll be here tomorrow. But as the senior executives made clear, today's shifting leadership landscape requires thinking and acting beyond limiting borders and embracing new frontiers where wide-ranging expertise, diverse experiences, and varied identities collide. When we asked the executives *why* it was important for them to work across the five types of boundaries, they spoke about human relationships. The boundaries that keep leaders up at night are not those which can be solved by simply restructuring the organizational chart or reconfiguring distribution channels. The boundaries that are the most challenging to leaders today are more psychological in nature. They involve relationships and thus are associated with strong emotions such as loyalty, pride, respect, and trust. relational competence

Here's a snapshot of various executives' responses in their own words:

> "Positive relationships are necessary for the integration of tasks."

"We must find a way to create paths of communication across silos."

"In order to implement any large-scale initiative, I need support and commitment from all levels in the company."

"Collaboration and integrating diverse viewpoints are the keys to improving performance."

"Building coalitions with stakeholders is essential to get the work done."

"You must work across boundaries to see the full picture."

"You need to bring people together and create buy-in. Collaboration makes the difference between average and great results."

"Trying to find synergy and areas of mutual interest is a constant challenge."

"As a leader, you need to cross over boundaries all day, every day."

The Five Boundaries of Leadership

Below, we describe the five boundary dimensions associated with boundary spanning leadership. Although we conceptually separate the five dimensions for ease of discussion, they are closely linked. For each boundary type, we provide a definition and examples, an explanation of the management origins of the boundary, and a discussion of how boundary spanning leaders are going beyond current borders to lead across new frontiers at the nexus between groups.

Vertical Boundaries
Leading across levels, rank, seniority, authority, power

"We have a boundary that runs up and down the organizational chart," laments the senior vice president of a retail company. "We have work to do to create better interaction between senior executives and middle to entry management." Today's shifting leadership landscape requires the establishment of direction, alignment, and commitment between groups from different levels and ranks in the organizational hierarchy. Vertical boundaries are the floors and ceilings that separate groups by title, rank, power, and privilege. Common terms within your organization that convey vertical boundaries may include *span of control, hierarchy chart, seniority, top-down/bottom-up, superior/subordinate, exempt/nonexempt,* and *cascade through the ranks.* The separation of groups into layers of top, middle, and entry level, each with corresponding levels of authority, is a ubiquitous feature in nearly all organizations. "I've grown up in an environment where perfection and information were subtle power tools—the old adage of information is power," explains a commander working in a division of the U.S. military. "There is a reluctance to change to an inclusive environment as you move up the hierarchy."

Span of control—the dividing of lower-level subordinates under a higher-level supervisor—is the traditional approach for managing the boundaries between levels. Strategy flows down, with production flowing up. "Within the big banks, the hierarchies are still very rigid and bureaucratic," explained the general manager of a state-owned bank in China. "Senior managers will go to great effort to maintain their boundaries." Yes, hierarchy endures.

Yet without question, today's shifting leadership landscape is transforming vertical boundaries, enabling new levels of interaction up and down the organizational chart. For example, the drive for innovation requires engaging the heads, hearts, and minds of people across levels. Expanding globally necessitates ongoing dialogue between senior executives at headquarters and country managers in the field. Rapid change in information and communication technologies has sped up the pace, increased the reach, reduced the cost, and dramatically leveled the playing field in organizations today. This much is clear: The shifting leadership landscape is redefining the "control" long associated with span of control.

Leading beyond borders, boundary spanning leadership seeks to create shared direction, alignment, and commitment across the lines of power and authority. In the CCL research, we found that executives are calling for a clear shift from hierarchy to partnership and from a culture of leadership at the top to a culture of leadership as shared responsibility. Less concerned with traditional issues of rank, power, and status, boundary spanners hunt for ideas and skills wherever they may be located in the organization. The practice of leadership is no longer tethered to the belief that authority is *unidirectional*, flowing from top to bottom. Rather, the authority to think and act is *multidirectional* in that talented people must be empowered to collaborate and make an impact at all levels. The result is that boundary spanning leadership leads to faster and better decisions being made by more engaged and involved people up and down the organizational chart.

 # Horizontal Boundaries
Leading across functions,
units, peers, expertise

"My organization consists of eight functional units and seven laboratories in which more and more of our problems require interdisciplinary solutions," explains the top executive of a government research and development (R&D) agency. "Unfortunately, each lab has its own management culture, and this causes real challenges in partnering. I have a mandate to attack this challenge." Today's shifting leadership landscape requires the facilitation of collaboration and common purpose across horizontal boundaries that mark functions, units, and disciplines. Horizontal boundaries also are found when two organizations merge or one organization acquires another. They are the walls that separate groups by areas of experience and expertise. Terms within your organization that commonly convey horizontal boundaries may include *division of labor, task differentiation, silos, stovepipes, turf battles, navigating the matrix, front office/back office, revenue center/cost center, legacy organizations, functions, units,* and *peers.* As these words convey, the negative costs of horizontal boundaries are manifest when one function is favored over another, when the work of one unit or product line threatens the viability of another, or when departments work at cross-purposes. Intergroup conflict, rather than collaboration, rules the day. "Functional groups within my division are siloed and just want to get things done within their own department," explains an executive in marketing and sales in a retail company. "They need to think and care about the whole."

Managing the boundaries between functional groups originates in the need for the division of labor. Today's organizations contain many functional groups, from marketing, to operations, to sales, and beyond. As organizations continue to grow, expand, and become more complex and global, the challenges associated with integrating horizontal boundaries are compounded. "With rapid growth over the past three years, clear roles and responsibilities have not been outlined ... and therefore there is considerable jockeying for control," explains the chief scientific officer of an educational institution.

Advocates of matrix structures argue that multiple reporting relationships facilitate integration by encouraging collaboration and information sharing across boundaries. Yet critics argue that these benefits are outweighed by the confusion created when employees have to navigate conflicting loyalties. Regardless of one's point of view, matrix structures undeniably add new challenges in leading across horizontal boundaries. "We need to deliver results with matrixed resources," explain the CEO of an American pharmaceutical company. "Setting priorities and aligning resources is complex when leaders find themselves operating without direct lines of authority. It requires strong influencing and collaboration skills."

A related challenge is the need to bring groups together after an organizational merger or acquisition. Explains a manager at an insurance company in China, "Our biggest challenge is how to create a coherent new organizational culture after the merger. We need to find a way to integrate our distinct values and habits." A remarkable aspect of mergers is the way competitors are transformed into collaborators overnight. "We merged with another retail organization," explains a pharmaceutical executive. "Whereas in the past we competed ... now we are working together to develop and deliver new products to the market." Consider how the iconic American company Anheuser-Busch was recently bought by InBev, a conglomerate in Belgium, or how the quintessential British luxury automobile Jaguar is now owned by India's Tata Motors. In mergers such as these, any number of challenges may arise regarding the integration of technical and operational systems. Yet when the production line employees who make Budweiser beer now work for a company based in Leuven, Belgium, and when Jaguar executives now travel to Mumbai to meet with their parent company, the greatest challenges involve aspects of identity and managing relationships. Indeed, the need for the *division* of labor is fast being replaced by an even more pressing need: the *integration* of labor.

Boundary spanning leadership strives for direction, alignment, and commitment across the frontier of varied expertise and experience. In the executive sample, we found that these leaders are pushing new ways of thinking and acting in the transition from functional leadership to cross-functional leadership and from walled-off units to open networks. Boundary spanners work best at the margin where functions, units, and disciplines intersect. They see limited value in bringing *one-dimensional* expertise to the table to generate new organizational solutions. Instead, they seek to harness *multidimensional* expertise at the juncture between groups. Differences in knowledge and experience are seen as wellsprings for fresh ideas to emerge, not as potential sources of conflict to avoid. The result is that boundary spanning leadership is creating the necessary linkages to harness cross-organizational collaboration and move ideas, information, people, and resources where they are needed most.

Stakeholder Boundaries

Leading at the interchange of an organization and its external partners, such as alliances, networks, value chains, customers, shareholders, advocacy groups, governments, communities

"We struggle in creating effective customer-vendor relationships," explains an American CEO. "There is a great need for creating common goals, but our objectives are often conflicting." The shifting leadership landscape requires the creation of fundamentally different approaches to collaboration at the interchange between an organization and its external environment. Stakeholder boundaries are the doors and windows of your organization. Are they open or closed to your customers, suppliers, and broader communities? Organizations increasingly are tied up with a dizzying array of stakeholder groups, including but not limited to shareholders, boards of directors, partners, alliances, suppliers, vendors, customers, advocacy groups, governments, nongovernmental agencies, and local and global communities. Recognizable terms within your organization that illustrate stakeholder boundaries may include *constituents, networks, walled-off, iron curtain, closed doors, corporate-centric, not our business, insider/outsider, cross-sector,* and *corporate social responsibility.* Stakeholder boundaries have the potential to create divides when organizations seek to maximize their individual interests through the exclusion or at the expense of the interests of their external partners.

Value chains—the processes that determine how organizations receive raw materials as inputs, add internal value to those inputs, and then sell finished products or services to customers—are a primary mechanism for managing the boundary between an organization and its stakeholders. The traditional view of the value chain is that each organization defines its own value chain independently, with little thought given to interdependence with partners along the chain. To clarify mission and strategy, it is important that organizations understand how they create unique value. Yet when carried to an extreme, an "every-organization-for-itself" mentality has the potential to lead to zero-sum gains, inefficiently used resources, wasteful conflict, and lost opportunities for creative and innovative solutions.

The shifting leadership landscape requires organizations to rethink how "value" is created in today's collaborative value chains. As boundaries blur across an ever-widening network of stakeholders, it becomes increasingly difficult to locate the edges between organizations, the employees within them, and the broader communities they serve. For example, consider how at Tata Motors in India, the most inexpensive car in the world—the Nano—has been unveiled. Among the Nano's many innovations, perhaps the most remarkable is the car's modular design. The Nano is sold in kits that are distributed, assembled, and serviced by local entrepreneurs and rural garages throughout the country. By knitting together a vast network of human capital inside and outside the company, Tata Motors is able to put the keys of a new car within the reach of millions of rising Indian consumers. With a $2,500 price tag, the Nano is half the price of its nearest rival, roughly equivalent to the cost of having an optional DVD player installed in a Western luxury car. These competitive realities will only intensify in the future. The convergence of groups inside and outside formal organizational boundaries ignites tremendous new growth opportunities. It also brings new risks and challenges. The bottom line is this: In good times and bad, we're all in it together now.

Boundary spanning leadership seeks to create direction, alignment, and commitment between diverse stakeholder interests. To tap new sources of value, leaders must learn to embrace contemporary models of collaboration that include cross-sector partnerships, customer-centric business practices, open source innovation, and corporate social responsibility (CSR) practices. Boundary spanners thrive by operating at the outer edges of their organizations, seeking new ideas and innovative opportunities. Not constrained by traditional myopic thinking, they seek to maximize collaborative value across the entire value chain. They realize that organizations today must go beyond *unilateral interests* that are characterized by an "each to his or her own" mindset. Instead, boundary spanning leaders are expanding new frontiers by engaging *multilateral interests* in ways that are increasingly systemic and sustainable. The result is that boundary spanning leadership generates a confluence of stakeholder interests in which organizations partner with customers, suppliers, vendors, shareholders, and communities to produce new sources of value jointly.

Demographic Boundaries
Leading between diverse groups, including the full range of human diversity from gender and race to education and ideology

Demographic boundaries are found in the space between diverse groups, including the entire range of human diversity from gender and race to education and ideology. If vertical boundaries are the floors and ceilings, horizontal boundaries are the walls, and stakeholder boundaries are the doors and windows, then demographic boundaries are represented by the diverse groups that work within the workplace. They are the people inside the building. Today's shifting leadership landscape requires the leveraging of different knowledge bases and diverse backgrounds as a potent force for value-creating innovation.

However, CCL research as well as extensive management research on this topic demonstrates that demographic diversity is a double-edged sword. Under certain conditions, diverse teams and organizations are capable of realizing distinct advantages in creativity and innovation processes.[4] Yet when these conditions aren't met, diversity can lead to a net neutral or negative effect. An executive in pharmaceuticals captures these realities: "We are incorporating more and more diversity into our organization from what used to be a very monolithic culture. It brings enormous advantages but also management challenges." Terms that highlight the presence of demographic boundaries within an organization may include *heterogeneity, multicultural, mosaic, glass ceilings, generation gaps, intolerance, diversity divides, ideological battles, personality differences,* and *culture clashes.*

Organizational values and beliefs play an important role in the way demographic boundaries are erected in organizations. In past CCL research, we identified three types of cultural values or beliefs for managing diversity: the "hands off" belief, in which the organization is inactive in managing demographic boundaries; the "direct and control" belief, in which the organization actively monitors and reinforces demographic boundaries; and the "cultivate and encourage" belief, in which the organization establishes the conditions and environment for healthy, creative, and collaborative intergroup relationships to develop.[5] Although all three types of cultural beliefs are prevalent today, organizations that adopt the cultivate and encourage belief have a distinct advantage in capitalizing on global changes in employment patterns.

In recent years, the demographics of the global labor force have been transformed. As a case in point, consider that in 2007, 3 billion people age 15 years and older were working. This represents a 17 percent increase from the prior decade. Of the 45 million jobs created between 2006 and 2007, 57 percent were created in Asia, 21 percent in Africa, and another 10 percent in Latin America and the Caribbean. In sharp contrast, only 4 percent of the worldwide creation of jobs in 2007 occurred in the combined developed economies.[6] These global growth trends will only intensify. The world's population is forecast to hit 7 billion in 2011. Of today's 1.2 billion youth, nearly 90 percent live in developing economies, with 8 of 10 hailing from Africa or Asia.[7] This is the global workforce of the very near future.

Embracing these changes, boundary spanning leadership creates direction, alignment, and commitment in the space between diverse groups. Boundary spanners value human differences as a source for sustainable growth. To improve organizational performance, the executives in the CCL research study seek to harness changing demographics by minimizing diversity divides, glass ceilings, and generational gaps and by maximizing the creative tension that accompanies diverse perspectives, opinions, and ideas. Rather than establish homogenous teams with *monocultural views*, they attempt to create heterogeneous teams powered *by multicultural differences.* The result is that boundary spanning leadership ignites the potential for creativity and innovation at the intersection where diverse experiences, backgrounds, and perspectives collide.

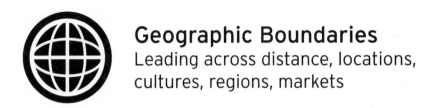

Geographic Boundaries
Leading across distance, locations, cultures, regions, markets

"We must learn to collaborate not only across our vast country but with people from around the globe," states the general manager of a telecommunications company in China. Today's shifting leadership landscape requires the advancement of direction, alignment, and commitment across wide-ranging locations, regions, and markets. Geographic boundaries are represented by your physical office location as well as the phones, fax machines, and Internet connections you use to bridge time and distance. Terms that demarcate geographic boundaries within your organization may include *regions, markets, East/West, native/foreigner, global/local, HQ/field, mothership/satellite, language differences, virtual teams,* and *geographically dispersed.* Boundaries of geography create constraints when there is a need for collaboration across different locations. "Our firm is divided by office location, with 15 offices across seven states," remarks the CEO of an American business. "These different locations create boundaries that I need to work effectively across."

Managing boundaries between geographic locations is grounded in the fundamental tension between the integration and differentiation of processes, systems, and structures. In the past, organizations were both the product of and created products for their local markets. Today, consumer markets, organizational operations, and labor pools are global.[8] An American sports apparel company, for instance, may obtain its fabric from China, design and market its clothing in the United States, have the clothing manufactured in

Bangladesh, and sell the products through a chain of stores with worldwide locations. The dismantling of geographic boundaries creates sourcing and scale efficiencies as well as new markets and sources for capital. Yet determining what processes to integrate across geographies and what to customize for local needs remains a real challenge. "Optimizing global processes while driving growth and profitability is a key factor for our success," states the president of a pharmaceutical company. "I must contend with geographic, market, and cultural differences which impact our ability to deliver the same level and quality of service in all parts of the world." These tensions and trade-offs will only increase as the effects of globalization spread to every last corner of the globe.

Forty years ago 60 percent of the world's top global companies were U.S.-based. Today that proportion has dropped to less than a third.[9] The BRIC countries (Brazil, Russia, India, and China) and many others are stepping onto the global stage and competing successfully. Consider this eye-opening statistic: While U.S. GDP (gross domestic product) fell by 6.1 percent during the first quarter of 2009, China posted a mirror-image GDP rise of 6.1 percent.[10] The implication of expanding globalization is that people, goods, values, and information are crossing national borders faster and more freely than ever. As barriers are removed, borders are crossed and people from diverse groups are brought into new types of contact, creating complex webs of relationships.

Boundary spanning leadership seeks to create collaborative direction, alignment, and commitment at the frontier between locations, countries, and markets. To capture new sources of value, the executives in the CCL study are seeking greater cross-regional collaboration and the development of managers with global mindsets and worldviews.[11] Boundary spanners see physical distance and market differences not just as problems to solve but as new opportunities to realize. Leadership thought and action no longer are constrained by a *monoregional*, one-size-fits-all approach. Instead, *multiregional* approaches prevail in which regional differences are viewed as a source of organizational learning and new growth markets. The result is that boundary spanning leadership is building webs of connected virtual groups across the world to solve problems faster, design more creative products, and serve customers better.

Navigating Unchartered Terrain

The historical challenge for leadership has involved finding ways to operate effectively within the boxes and lines of organizational charts—within the boundaries we discussed above. The challenge today is finding ways to realize new ideas and opportunities that lie beyond those traditional boundaries. Specifically, the leaders who participated in the CCL research described challenges related to working across the five types of boundaries, yet they didn't talk about each type of boundary with the same frequency. Across the 128 executives, a total of 181 examples of boundaries were identified. On average, the executives were able to cite a least one type of boundary, and some described up to four types. Below, we describe the results of the CCL analysis and draw three conclusions for leading in today's unchartered terrain:

- Horizontal boundaries (71 percent) were cited nearly three to one over the other four dimensions. We bet this finding doesn't surprise you. Facilitating lateral, cross-functional collaboration is one of the most common presenting issues that clients bring to us at CCL. The unintended consequence of today's matrixed and regional structures is that walls have been erected between groups that need to be collaborating. As a result, "silo busting" has become one of the leading pastimes for managers and executives today.

- Vertical boundaries (7 percent), in contrast, were the least frequently cited dimension. We believe that in the past, this percentage was significantly higher. To this day, fingers remain pointed at hierarchy as the root cause of any number of organizational ills. However, perhaps as a result of decades of delayering and improved communication systems, these executives perceive vertical boundaries as less relevant than the other four types.

- Geographic (26 percent), demographic (17 percent), and stakeholder (17 percent) boundaries were identified with relatively similar frequency. In contrast to vertical boundaries, our expectation is that these percentages will rise dramatically in the years ahead. As organizations expand their global footprint, employ an increasingly diverse talent pool, and seek new competitive advantage through complex interorganizational alliances, joint ventures, and partnerships, leadership increasingly will be practiced at the juncture where geographic, demographic, and stakeholder boundaries intersect.[12]

For ease of discussion, we described each of the five boundary dimensions in this chapter separately. Yet as you know from your own experience, they are all intertwined. The great challenge of boundary spanning leadership is to understand and span the multiple and interacting boundaries that define, divide, and connect us. In navigating this unchartered territory, the potential for destructive rifts and divides looms large. Rarely do you have the luxury of simply trying to bring together groups X and Y. Rather, on any given day, you are dealing with competing and often conflicting agendas between groups A, B, C, and D simultaneously. Your reality is probably similar to that of *Tom Lambert*. Tom describes his challenge like this:

> As the head of production for a large life sciences company, I need to work closely with the marketing and sales teams on demand forecasts in order to provide the customer service desired. Working closely with research and development is critical to provide a stream of new products that can be manufactured on cost and on quality. Also, I need to collaborate with my peers in top management to ensure that my team gets the resources required to be successful. Finally, as a unit of a large multinational company, all of these collaboration points are complicated by the requirement to work through regions worldwide. This is how I strive to advance our more significant objectives.

In looking beyond Tom's immediate challenges, however, we see tremendous new opportunities. In his efforts to span each of these "collaboration points," Tom is able to tap into a range of options, new ideas, and advanced thinking far greater than what would be available if he remained confined by today's borders. For Tom, yourself, and leaders worldwide, tomorrow's opportunities reside at the juncture between wide-ranging expertise, diverse experiences, and varied identities.

Wherever boundaries collide, the promise of new possibilities and inspiring results awaits. But so does the peril of limiting and counterproductive outcomes that occur when groups divide into Us and Them. The difference, in large part, is you and the leaders throughout your organization. Given your critical role in creating a nexus between groups, we close this chapter by providing an activity that enables you to identify your unique Nexus Challenge, one that you can solve only by leading effectively across boundaries.

Your Nexus Challenge

What is a pressing challenge you currently face that can be solved only by leading across boundaries? If your reality is like that of the executives who participated in the CCL research, you have no shortage of answers to this question. We assume that you are looking for actionable ideas and approaches to navigate and ultimately solve the challenges you and your organization face. This activity is designed to help you do just that. By spending a few minutes reflecting on the questions below, you'll be able to name a specific "Nexus Challenge" you'd like to focus on while reading this book, a challenge that can be solved only by leading across boundaries. Then, at a number of points, we'll return to your specific challenge and help you apply the book's key ideas to your situation. As a result, when you finish the book, you'll have identified several concrete action steps—both short-term and long-term—you can apply within your team, function, region, or organization as a whole. The activity has five steps (also available at www.spanboundaries.com):

Step 1: What are the most pressing leadership challenges you currently face? Think big—the things that *really* matter for driving individual and organizational success. Things like solving a critical organizational problem; developing an innovative new process, product, or solution; or leading an important organizational change. Write down the three to five challenges that come to mind.

Step 2: In this list, which are challenges that can be solved only by leading effectively across boundaries? They cannot be solved by leading within your team, function, region alone. Identify the one or two challenges that best fit the following criteria. This challenge requires:

- Reaching across boundaries by creating greater direction, alignment, and commitment between various groups
- Change not just in operational systems and structures but more deeply in issues of human relationships and identity: not just "what we do" but also "who we are"
- New approaches to leadership; what's worked in the past isn't fully sufficient for dealing with the present; new techniques, tactics, and tools are needed

Step 3: Now it's time to decide. Which challenge is best suited to applying the ideas and concepts of boundary spanning leadership? This is your Nexus Challenge. The guidelines below will help you describe your challenge by giving it an effective "headline." You can write down your headline in the inner circle in Figure 1.3.

- Describe your challenge with a short 4- to 10-word headline.
- Start with "How to."
- Be sure to include an action verb.

For example, let's say your Nexus Challenge revolves around fostering greater collaboration across functions to develop and deliver more customer-focused products or solutions. In this case, good headlines might include "How to Break Down Silos" and "How to Increase Cross-Functional Collaboration to Serve Customers."

Step 4: Take a moment to describe your challenge in terms of the four questions in the outer circle: the what, why, how, and what if of your challenge. You can write your responses in the circle (in Figure 1.3 or on a copy of the circle downloaded from www.spanboundaries.com).

Step 5: Finally, keep your Nexus Challenge in mind as you read ahead. Your challenge is unique, just as the challenges faced by leaders in the stories in this book are unique. Yet the lessons from these stories often transcend contexts and cultures, whether you work in a global corporation or a local government agency. That's the power of a good story. Specifically, we will ask additional questions in the six boundary spanning practice chapters

(Chapters 4 through 9) to enable you to connect the stories in the chapter to your Nexus Challenge. In Chapter 10 we'll come back to your challenge one last time so that you can capture your insights and consolidate your potential actions steps.

Figure 1.3 Your nexus challenge.

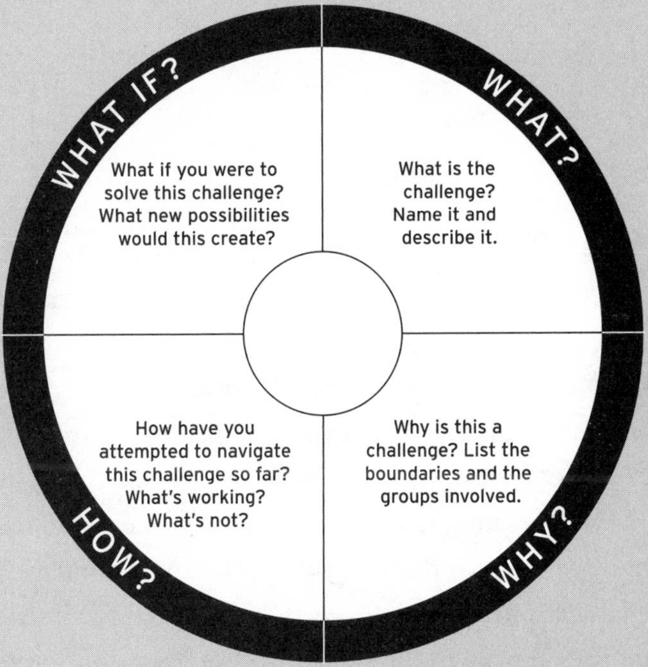

WHAT IF?
What if you were to solve this challenge? What new possibilities would this create?

WHAT?
What is the challenge? Name it and describe it.

HOW?
How have you attempted to navigate this challenge so far? What's working? What's not?

WHY?
Why is this a challenge? List the boundaries and the groups involved.

CHAPTER 2

US AND THEM: WHY IDENTITY MATTERS

W ho am I? That is the question we will explore in this chapter. However, you may be wondering what this has to do with leading across boundaries. The answer is that identity is at the heart of leadership across boundaries. Identity (your own identity as well as the identity of the groups you lead) is formed from the interplay between two basic fundamental human needs: the need for differentiation or uniqueness and the need for integration or belonging.[1] We believe that the reason the five boundaries identified as challenges in our executive survey are so difficult to manage is not that they represent physical or technological differences that divide and separate groups but that they represent differences in who we are and how we define ourselves.

As the world becomes flat and we remove many of the boundaries that kept groups from working together in the past (physical boundaries such as geographic distance and limited technology), we are left with stronger and more pernicious boundaries that involve human relationships—boundaries that separate Us and Them. Identity, the delicate balance between unity and separation, is at the core of what separates Us from Them[2] and what we believe is the real challenge of boundary spanning leadership. Walk into a corporate boardroom, join a global teleconference, or hold a meeting with key stakeholder groups, and one thing is certain: Boundaries exist between Us and Them. Identity matters. In this chapter, our goal is to give you new insights into the concept of identity—what it is, how it influences our interactions with others, and why it creates boundaries between Us and Them that present significant challenges for you as a leader. To understand identity and why it matters in the workplace, we begin with the question asked above: Who am I?

In working out an answer, take a blank sheet of paper and draw a large circle on it. (You can download a copy of this activity at www. spanboundaries.com.) Think of the circle as a representation of your whole self: all the aspects that make you who you are today. Inside the circle, fill in the various aspects of your identity. To represent the relative importance of the various aspects of identity in your life at this time, write the words in large and small letters; the larger words represent more important aspects of your identity, and the smaller words represent less important aspects. For example, in our circle, we would include things such as *leadership expert, organizational psychologist, parent, male/female,* and *outdoor enthusiast. Parent* and *leadership expert* would be the largest words in our circle. Now take a moment to complete your identity circle.[3]

Our guess is that most of you included a combination of family and community roles, hobbies, professional affiliations, interests, and demographic groups in your identity circle. Most likely, your identities varied in size; some were larger than others, representing a more significant proportion of time or greater importance. This illustrates several important things about identity. First, our identities are composed of a complex combination of multiple identities that represent (1) the roles we play in relation to others, (2) the interests, hobbies, and activities that make us unique, and (3) demographic groups to which we belong and that others would ascribe to us.

This complex combination that forms our identity serves an important purpose for each one of us because it allows us to meet two fundamental needs: integration and differentiation. It contributes to our self-concept and self-esteem by defining who we are in relation to others and provides us with a sense of belonging. At the same time, it helps us define how we are unique and different from others. The roles, interests, hobbies, and activities that make us unique represent our personal identity, whereas the demographic groups we belong to represent our social identity. Although this may sound somewhat paradoxical, both components (belonging and differentiation) are important to developing a healthy sense of who we are and how we fit into the world in which we live.

Ironically, we rely on others to help us define who we are as individuals. Imagine that you lived your entire life on a desert island. What type of person would you be? Although answers to this question may have popped into your mind (e.g., I would be self-sufficient, a hunter, peaceful, lonely), the reality is that you have no idea. Much of our identity is defined through our social comparisons with others, largely based on our relationships with others— both how we belong and connect and the ways we are unique or distinct. Consider the fact that at times we all want to both "fit in" and be seen as "unique." In fact, the same aspect of our identity may serve dual purposes, depending on the situation.

For example, consider a scenario in which you attend a professional conference or workshop. It is a weeklong training session that concludes with certification as an expert in Six Sigma. Since the training budget is tight this year, you are the only person in your work team selected to travel across the country to attend the training workshop and will be expected to share your knowledge of Six Sigma with others when you return. You're feeling a bit alone and out of place, since you are far from home and it seems that most of the workshop attendees have come with colleagues. Imagine that you are pleasantly surprised to see someone across the room you vaguely recognize as working for your company, but in a different department. You both laugh as you recognize the corporate pins you are wearing on your suit lapels and immediately strike up a conversation. Although you have had very limited interaction with this person within your company, you feel an instant connection. You begin a friendly conversation that quickly turns to people you both know and experiences you have in common within the company.

What happens is that someone we may never see or spend time with back in the office suddenly becomes "like me"—one of Us. We feel an instant sense of connection and belonging. However, what probably will follow is that when you return to your home office, you no longer feel a strong sense of connection to this colleague. Instead of connecting with this person or others in your work team on the basis of your identification with the company, you instead distinguish yourself by wearing the pin you received from the workshop that identifies you as an expert in Six Sigma. You are now motivated to do things that help you stand out among others within the company and distinguish yourself as unique. Wearing the pin that identifies you as a Six Sigma expert helps you accomplish this goal.

Identity—the way we define ourselves, our core values and beliefs, and our connection to others—comes into play in our interactions with people at work each and every day.[4] The various aspects of our identities guide our behavior in a variety of situations, and most, if not all, help us define ourselves in a positive light relative to others and contribute positively to our self-concept. Yet not all aspects of a person's identity are equally important. Returning to your identity circle, take a look at the size of various aspects of your identity. Just as some aspects are drawn larger and others smaller, some components of a person's identity are larger or more important than others, and this varies over time and situations.[5] Caring for an elderly parent can be a psychologically demanding and time-consuming component of one's identity for a period of time but disappears when the parent passes away. A manager's identity as a member of the sales department may not feel particularly central to his identity during the annual sales team retreat because everyone else is also on the sales team. However, it becomes highly central to his self-concept when he joins a cross-functional project task force in which he is the only member of the sales team and therefore is expected to provide that unique perspective.

In addition to level of importance (less or more), the other crucial aspect of identity we need to consider is dominance—whether you are a member of the dominant group (in-group) or a member of the nondominant group (out-group). Take a look at the different aspects of your identity and circle those which tend to place you in the dominant group in your organization. For example, if you work in a male-dominated environment such as an engineering firm, being female may mean you are part of the nondominant group at work. However, if you are a female executive working in a hospital, your gender may place you in the dominant group as the majority of employees in that industry are female.[6] Look at the circle you created and consider this question: What impact does identity dominance versus nondominance (being a member of the in-group versus the out-group) have on your ability to lead effectively in your organization?

The issue of dominance or in-group versus out-group status is important to consider in reflecting on identity issues and the way identity dynamics affect people in the workplace. Unfortunately, very few of us (if any) escape life without feeling like a minority or an outsider, at least sometimes. This is a very human experience. Each of us has been in the position of being in the dominant group and the nondominant group at times. However, it's easy to forget what it feels like to be an outsider and quite difficult to take the perspective of someone in the out-group because when we are in the in-group, we generally take this for granted.[7] We don't think about this aspect of our identity much because we don't have to—it doesn't create any barriers for us, and it's not unusual. By definition, it is the majority or dominant identity and therefore the identity group with the most power and voice.

Although the groups we belong to and identify with help us develop a positive self-concept and contribute to our sense of belonging and uniqueness, there are also negative consequences of identity groups. Unfortunately, identity creates significant borders between groups of people, making it very difficult for group members to get along and work together. Aspects of our identity can separate us, fuel suspicion and distrust, and create what seem to be insurmountable barriers to understanding other groups' perspectives. In short, identity sometimes causes "Great Divides" both in society and in the workplace—*the limited and counterproductive outcomes that occur when groups divide into Us and Them*. A famous "experiment" with grade school children illustrates how easily groups can break apart and how destructive identity differences can be.

Consequences of Identity: We versus Them

In the late 1960s, a grade school teacher from Riceville, Iowa, named Jane Elliott decided to create a Great Divide within her third grade classroom. She had been watching news of Martin Luther King, Jr.'s assassination. She says she was troubled watching the news reports as she heard racist remarks from a variety of leaders and commentary about the poor state of black-white relations in the United States. She remembered the part of the Sioux Indian prayer that says, "Oh, Great Spirit, keep me from ever judging a man until I have walked in his moccasins." It was then that she decided that her third grade students were going to learn what it was like to walk in another person's moccasins.

Riceville, Iowa, was almost exclusively white, so Jane knew that simply telling her students about the consequences of racism and prejudice would have little impact; she had to find a way for them to experience this for themselves. She did that by creating an in-group–out-group situation right in her classroom.[8] On April 5, 1968, the day after King's assassination, Jane announced to her students that blue-eyed people were better than brown-eyed people. They were smarter, cleaner, and better behaved and would get special privileges such as second helpings at lunch and extra time at recess. The brown-eyed children had to wear felt collars around their necks, were not allowed to drink out of the same water fountain as the blue-eyed children, could not play on the equipment during recess, and had to wait until blue-eyed children had used the rest room to take their turn.

A Great Divide split open immediately. Blue-eyed children became bossy and arrogant, and "brownies" became either timid and depressed or angry and belligerent about their situation. One of the brown-eyed boys actually punched his blue-eyed friend in the stomach because he called him a "brownie." A brown-eyed girl cried on the playground as she huddled in a corner all by herself because her blue-eyed friends were using the playground equipment. A blue-eyed boy gave the teacher a pointer and suggested that she use it if the brown-eyed children got out of hand. The next day, Jane turned the table on her students and announced that she had been wrong the day before; the truth was that brown-eyed children were more intelligent and well behaved and would therefore get special privileges. The brown-eyed children were more than happy to take their collars off and give them to the blue-eyed children who had taunted them the day before. They too reveled in their "superior" role and dramatically improved their performance on academic tasks they had done very poorly on the day before. At the end of the second day, Jane ended her experiment and told the children what she had done and why. She told them to think about this exercise any time they saw someone with different colored skin and to remember what it felt like to be treated badly because of their eye color.

What started as a simple two-day activity in a classroom of third grade students has become an iconic example of how quickly and easily we form groups and favor members of our own group. Jane Elliott's experiment garnered national attention as the public was shocked to learn how easily she could manipulate the third graders' perceptions of one another and how quickly discrimination and conflict flowed as a result. Her actions were simple yet profound. She highlighted a difference between the children and elevated the status of one group relative to the other. This seemed to be all that was necessary to influence their treatment of one another and even their performance on academic tasks.

The students and their teacher were forever changed by this exercise, as they describe in a PBS documentary in which the teacher and her students are reunited 17 years later. At the reunion, many of Jane Elliot's students shared how lucky they felt to have been a part of her unusual classroom experiment. They believe it influenced them later in life as they were more tolerant of other races and how as parents they were passing this tolerance down to the next generation. Many participants had the same reaction. They were surprised at how quickly and easily they treated out-group members poorly. Students who had been their best friends quickly became their enemies in the span of a single day. Jane did not tell her students to treat others badly; she simply split them into a superior group and an inferior group, and they responded on the basis of the labels they were given. Jane Elliot's third grade classroom activity shows just how quickly categorization can occur and borders are created to distinguish between Us and Them.

We said earlier that our personal and social identities contribute to our self-esteem, help us differentiate ourselves from others, and provide us with a sense of connection and belonging. Although this is quite positive, it is important to understand that there is also a negative consequence associated with the identity process. We naturally compare ourselves with others and distinguish between Us and Them. People who share aspects of our identity are seen as one of Us, or members of the in-group, whereas people belonging to different identity groups are often viewed as Them, or members of the out-group. As much as we may like to think that we are more inclusive than this statement suggests, psychologists have demonstrated that human beings very naturally and unconsciously categorize themselves and others into in-groups and out-groups.[9]

Much like computers, we naturally categorize all the information we receive from both internal and external stimuli into categories or "folders." It is simply the brain's way of organizing and making sense of the millions of sensory inputs it receives each minute. We instantly process the information that is before us and try to identify what it is we are experiencing. This happens with all our senses.

If we smell a unique scent blowing in the wind, we immediately try to identify it as something we know and are familiar with—a flower or fruit tree. We look at an unusual animal at the zoo and categorize it as a feline or amphibian. We look at another person walking toward us on the sidewalk and instantaneously make judgments about that person that places him or her into categories that are either similar to or different from us. When the person looks like us with respect to skin color, gender, ethnicity, clothing, language, and so on, we probably will view that person as one of Us.

Unfortunately, what this means is that we make instantaneous "snap" judgments about others all the time—and many of those judgments are wrong. This comes naturally, in fact instinctually, and is the natural consequence of the way our brains process information. We make these distinctions quickly and sometimes over meaningless aspects of our identity. Jane Elliott created a strong Us and Them divide that was based solely on differences in eye color. The fact that group categorization occurs quickly and easily and that people are more likely to view in-group members more positively than out-group members is one of the most consistent findings in social psychological research.[10]

It seems that we attach a halo of sorts to in-group members and see these individuals as having many positive qualities and attributes. This halo distorts our perceptions of others and leads to a strong positive bias toward people who are like us. Results from numerous studies have shown that managers tend to trust, support, spend time with, hire, and promote people they perceive to be like them, resulting in biased leadership decisions. As adults, we are no more immune to these forces than were the kids in Jane Elliott's classroom.[11]

Leading on Unstable Ground

Identity dynamics that split groups into Us and Them are at the heart of the challenge you will face when managing across the five types of boundaries. Identity is the reason working with different groups requires a delicate balance between meeting the two fundamental needs of differentiation and integration. Identity plays out at work each and every day as we all strive to experience a sense of belonging and connection while distinguishing ourselves as unique from others. Identity dynamics create problems at work when we must find a way to work with other groups despite significant differences in our most defining values, perspectives, and beliefs. Consider the five types of boundaries and the way identity dynamics may create challenges for you when groups define themselves on the basis of their differences and split into Us and Them.

A *vertical boundary* can become a border when identity plays out in the different perspectives or vantage points of the top management team versus first-line supervisors. The identity of senior leaders is based largely on their vantage point within the company—the big picture and looking out for its long-term viability. First-line supervisors of course have a very different vantage point, and their role and identity are based on a view of the company from the trenches in which day-to-day operational demands take priority. Bringing any two groups whose identities within the company lead them to see company interests from very different vantage points can create significant challenges. A *horizontal boundary* may highlight identity differences between the sales and engineering teams. The members of the sales team define their group as the growth engine of the company because they drive revenue and profits more than any other and see themselves as the "face of the business." Yet the members of the engineering team would also define their group as the growth engine because they generate new ideas and products responsible for future market share. Thus, horizontal boundaries can present a challenge as you attempt to span lines of expertise and identity differences become a barrier. Identity dynamics come into play when you must find a way for different *stakeholder* groups to collaborate when, by definition, they each have different and at times competing interests. Managing across *demographic boundaries* means crossing generational lines of difference when baby boomers' identification is tied to loyalty, a strong work ethic, and dogged determination, whereas Gen Xers pride themselves on enjoying life rather than "working themselves into the grave." In this case, the different generational groups view organizational commitment in radically different ways that can create problems for their leader, who must find a way to evaluate and reward both groups fairly. Finally, *geographic boundaries* can result in the separation of groups on the basis of distance when, for example, Westerners define themselves by and take pride in their entrepreneurial spirit, whereas Easterners pride themselves on tradition and conformity. Such identity differences pose challenges for a leader managing a multinational team.

Navigating the complex identity dynamics of Us and Them requires that you achieve a delicate balance between knowing when to define and strengthen boundaries to meet the fundamental need your organizational members have for differentiation and uniqueness and knowing when to span boundaries and foster unity to meet the fundamental need for integration and belonging. Although this challenge is daunting, your task of leading across boundaries is made even more difficult by the fact that your own identity as a leader plays a crucial role. You are not exempt from identity dynamics or the divisions that occur between Us and Them. In fact, your own identity will contribute to the problem at times.

Because leaders are often members of the in-group, it is common for them to lack awareness of identity group dynamics. Recall our earlier discussion in which we said that you probably will not think much about the dominant aspects of your identity. You don't have to. You can take these aspects of your identity for granted, and you don't have to expend valuable cognitive resources worrying about whether your identity affects your ability to get promoted, land a key client, or obtain a high-profile assignment. It is for this reason that many leaders lack the critical awareness necessary to recognize the identity issues that are at the core of boundaries. Leaders often find themselves caught completely off guard when identity differences impede efforts to create direction, alignment, and commitment or feel pulled in many different directions and attempt to tread lightly as they feel caught in the middle when identity differences result in competing values, viewpoints, beliefs, and approaches to work and boundaries become borders.

Leadership scholars have shown that we all have predetermined ideas about what an effective leader will do, what a leader looks like, and how a leader will interact with others.[12, 13, 14] In other words, the groups you lead expect you to look, act, and respond in a certain way. When you behave consistently with their expectations, they'll be motivated to follow you. But when you don't fit their expectations of what a leader should be and they do not perceive you as "one of us," you probably will have great difficulty motivating and influencing those groups. This creates a significant dilemma that you should be aware of when you are in a leadership role.[15] Shared identity can create cohesiveness in a group. If you are perceived as being a good representative of the values and vision of the larger group, you are likely to have greater success in creating direction, alignment, and commitment within the group. However, the trade-off is that in-group cohesiveness comes with a price because it also fosters competition between groups. The more you are perceived to be "one of us" by one group, the more you will be perceived as "one of them" by another. Attempting to bridge those two groups when you clearly belong to one and not the other becomes difficult, if not impossible. If you attempt to create a bridge to span the identity groups, you may make matters worse rather than better.

Take, for example, the story of *Virginia Sheffield*, vice president of operations for a multinational financial management and advisory firm in Hong Kong, China. She is British and is considered to be a member of the "Westerner" minority group; the majority of her colleagues and subordinates are Chinese. We spoke with one of her Chinese colleagues, *Zhou Ying*, who told us about Virginia—her leadership style, her interactions with colleagues and subordinates, and the way her identity and her approach to others have created a significant rift within the team. Virginia has been with the firm for a long time, and although she has been living in Hong Kong for 10 years, she speaks very little Cantonese. Zhou Ying tells us that Virginia spends time socializing and interacting with other Westerners—her peers and direct reports from Australia and the United Kingdom—but very rarely takes time to talk with the local Chinese and ask how they are doing. Apparently, this had been going on for about two years and was fairly obvious to those around her since she seemed to give special attention to the 10 Westerners out of a work group of 120. There is a shared perception on the part of Chinese members of the team that she "takes care of the Westerners."

At one point, Zhou Ying even approached Virginia during an informal gathering and told her that he thought it would be nice if she spent some time talking to her employees more often. Although she responded positively and agreed that she should spend more time getting to know them, the perception is that she still makes very little effort to do so. Unfortunately, the result has been a definite split between Westerners and Chinese within the operations unit and a negative perception of the unit within the company as a bad place to work, at least for the local Chinese. Zhou Ying and his Chinese colleagues feel that they are left out of many important business decisions and that their director has no idea that people are unhappy, feel excluded, and are experiencing low morale because she doesn't interact enough with Chinese employees to know how they feel about coming to work each day. Many are considering leaving the unit and the firm altogether.

Clearly, the perception of in-group favoritism is causing significant harm within this team. It may be that Virginia is truly unaware of the rift she has caused and would be very surprised to hear from others that she is perceived as favoring her in-group. She may give very little thought to whether she interacts with Westerners or local Chinese more often and may instinctually and unconsciously interact more with people with whom she shares a language and culture. Or perhaps she is self-conscious about being a Westerner and feels that she doesn't quite fit in with a predominantly Chinese workforce and unconsciously finds comfort and acceptance by interacting more with Westerners. In our experience working with hundreds of leaders, it seems safe to assume that Virginia, like many other leaders we have talked with, did not consciously set out to create an Us and Them division. Instead, our experience and work in this area tell us that it is much more likely that she is simply unaware of how her identity affects her perceptions of and interactions with others.

Our hope is that by reading this book you will be able to avoid the many challenges Virginia faces in trying to create direction, alignment, and commitment across a Great Divide. We present the case of Virginia simply to illustrate the importance of understanding your own identity and being aware of the potential you have to create divisions between Us and Them and how identity dynamics can turn a boundary into a border that limits and constrains collaboration across groups.

CHAPTER 3

INTERGROUP BOUNDARIES: THE GREAT DIVIDE

At the peak of the heat and humidity during the summer of 1954, 22 eleven-year-old boys were dropped off by their parents at Robbers Cave State Park in a densely wooded area in the Sans Bois Mountains in Oklahoma. Their parents would have no contact with them for three weeks, but the boys were too excited to care. They couldn't wait to pitch their tents, search for snakes, and get dirty. What they didn't know was that a group of researchers were almost as excited as they were to come to camp, but for very different reasons. Unknown to the boys, they were to become participants in one of the most famous psychological experiments of all time.

Half the group arrived on June 19 and immediately was assigned to the same bunkhouse. The other half arrived on June 20 and was assigned to a different bunkhouse, far enough away from the first group so that neither knew the other existed. For the first week, the members of each group spent time getting to know their bunkmates.

They ate meals together; went swimming, canoeing, and hiking; and especially enjoyed playing baseball. Friendships quickly formed, and within just a few days the boys began to act and make decisions not as separate individuals but as a group. This happened for both groups of boys, and they even came up with names for their bunkhouses: the Eagles and the Rattlers.

During the second week of their stay, the boys finally became aware that another bunkhouse existed at camp.[1] Counselors brought the Eagles and the Rattlers within earshot of each other.[2] Almost instinctively, the Eagles and Rattlers began to make comments that favored their own group. They each boasted how their bunkhouse was better at baseball and challenged the other group to a game to prove it. Distinctions between "Us" and "Them" became clear, and the boys grew protective of their things and their space. And so the competitions began. The groups competed with each other in everything from baseball to tent pitching and from tug-of-war to cabin inspection. The competitions brought out their worst: namecalling, refusal to eat in the same cafeteria, cabin raids, and fistfights. The Eagles went so far as to steal and burn the Rattlers' flag. Within a few weeks, two groups of boys alike in almost every way possible (race, education, socioeconomic status, region) acted as if they had nothing in common. They splintered into Us and Them and were caught in the middle of a Great Divide.

What appeared to be a scene of escalating chaos and conflict was actually a tightly controlled scientific experiment. The Robbers Cave study was a test of a well-known theory known as the contact hypothesis.[3] This theory suggests that an effective approach to reducing conflict between groups is to allow them to have contact with each other. The basic premise is that if groups have an opportunity to interact and spend time together, they will begin to develop more positive attitudes toward one another.[4] The researchers had correctly predicted virtually everything that happened up to this point. Identity groups formed quickly among the boys simply as a result of staying in the same bunkhouse. The boys developed strong positive feelings toward their own group and even stronger negative feelings toward the other group, especially once they were allowed to compete with each other.[5] The next part of the experiment involved trying to mend the Great Divide.

During the next several days, the Eagles and the Rattlers had several opportunities to interact with each other. But rather than reduce conflict as the contact hypothesis would predict, more opportunities to interact only added fuel to the fire. In one telling example, the groups were given a chance to "make peace" while having a meal together, yet an argument spiraled out of control and a massive food fight ensued. Why didn't contact work in this situation? Why did the Eagles and Rattlers end up throwing mashed potatoes at one another rather than discovering what they had in common as they spent more time together? Were they doomed to spend the rest of the summer "at war"?

We'll get back to the Eagles and the Rattlers later in the chapter. For now, suffice it to say that decades of research have taught us that things are often not quite this simple. In most cases, it takes more than "bringing groups together" to realize the benefits of effective collaboration. This is just as true in your organization as it is in a boys' summer camp in Oklahoma.

What we know from the Leadership Across Differences (LAD) research project and our work with organizations around the world is that simply bringing groups together when there is a history of competition or conflict is likely to lead to ineffective outcomes associated with a Great Divide: stifled creativity and innovation, failed partnerships and alliances, diminished problem-solving capability, turf battles between functions and units, cultures of disengagement and distrust, and severely decreased organizational productivity. As we've mentioned, our purpose in writing this book is to enable you to develop the capabilities of boundary spanning leadership. With this new approach, you will be able to transform destructive and constraining borders into constructive and positively transformative new frontiers. But first it is critical that you understand the challenges that probably will get in your way.

There is tremendous potential at the juncture where groups collide, intersect, and link—potential for destructive conflict or for creative collaboration between groups. In this chapter, we explore the destructive side of colliding intergroup boundaries—the Great Divide. When groups feel threatened and are so focused on their differences that they fail to see common ground, schisms of Us and Them become more entrenched with each interaction. The creation of shared direction, alignment, and commitment becomes more and more out of reach, resulting in limiting, constraining, and counterproductive outcomes at work. Whereas the Nexus Effect may be the most positive outcome that occurs when group boundaries collide and new frontiers are created, the Great Divide can be considered the most negative outcome. It constitutes the worst-case scenario: Identity differences become so divisive that groups exert considerable energy on counterproductive behaviors. Valuable resources are expended on the conflict itself rather than on productive work. In this case, groups would be better off working in isolation. In the pages that follow, we will equip you with the knowledge you need to identify potential Great Divides. You then will be able to take steps to close the divides between groups or steer clear of them altogether.

Distrust across the Great Divide

Distrust can get in the way of effective group collaboration, especially when groups have a history of negative interactions.[6] Unlike the Robbers Cave experiment, in which the boys did not know one another before meeting at camp, groups in the workplace often come with negative preconceived ideas of one another. For example, when a new joint venture is created that requires two previously competitive groups to now work collaboratively, it is likely that you will be able to "feel" the tension in the room when those groups meet for the first time. Distrust toward Them will be particularly strong if there is a widely held perception that the groups are very different in important ways (i.e., different values and beliefs) and if there is a history of negative interactions between the groups. In that case, group members on both sides are likely to anticipate negative consequences. This of course becomes a self-fulfilling prophecy as both groups approach the interaction with distrust of the other.

Bridging boundaries is not for the faint of heart. Divides often run deep. Distrust between groups may stem from events far beyond your direct sphere of influence. Yet we argue that it is better to deal with this distrust as early as possible to prevent intergroup boundaries from breaking wide open. Consider the events that occurred in the fall of 2008 at a meatpacking plant in Greeley, Colorado. The story of JBS Swift & Company made headlines when 150 Muslim employees protested their treatment by not showing up for work one day. The story is told from the perspective of a supervisor in the plant, Bart Hunter.[7]

Hunter arrived at the plant late on Friday because he had an off-site supervisors meeting. The meeting had gone well. Despite the fact that the company endured a raid by Immigration and Customs two years earlier, resulting in the detainment of 270 Hispanic employees, the company was performing well. JBS hired Somali refugees to replace the Hispanic employees, and productivity was up. Bart had been the evening shift lead supervisor for the last five years and liked going to work on Fridays. Everyone was usually in a good mood and ready for the weekend. But he knew something was wrong as soon as he rounded the corner into the parking lot and saw hundreds of his employees outside yelling and raising their fists in protest.

He ran up to the human resources director, who was standing a good distance from the protesting crowd, and asked what was going on. She seemed to be in shock, not knowing what to do. She explained to Bart that over 200 Muslim employees had walked out to protest the fact that they were not allowed to take prayer breaks at sunset. They argued that this prayer cannot be changed and must coincide with sunset because during the holy month of Ramadan, Muslims cannot eat or drink until they have conducted sunset prayers.

Bart knew that tensions between Somali workers and plant officials (overwhelmingly white Christian men) had increased in recent weeks. This was a conservative part of the country, and distrust toward Muslims had grown since the September 11 terrorist attacks in New York City. The distrust between Muslims and Christians that had become an issue in communities across the United States was playing out in the plant. When a group of employees approached him to request a change in the break time, Bart shrugged it off, figuring it would be forgotten with time. To be honest, he didn't want to ask for special favors for any group and increase the tension that already existed between the Somali Muslims and Hispanic Christians. He hoped that everyone would continue to get along and that plant operations would run smoothly. But rather than being forgotten, the issue gained momentum. The initially small group of employees who complained encouraged others to join in, and he found more people flooding his office with requests for change. Bart felt enough pressure to take their request to his boss, who responded by writing a memo to employees stating that the company break time would be changed from 9 p.m. to 8 p.m. That should have been the end of it, or so Bart and his boss thought.

With this latest turn of events, however, the Muslim population only got angrier and more vocal. The Somalis complained that the break time was still too late and that management was not being sensitive to their need for prayer. Bart could sense the growing frustration but explained that with over 300 Muslim workers out of 1,300 working the shift in Greeley, a large prayer break would put too much stress on the remaining workers. In the memo, Bart's boss told employees that a lunch break earlier than 8 p.m. meant employees would be required to work nearly four hours without a break, a dangerous situation on a production line where nearly 400 head of cattle are slaughtered each hour. Bart overheard employees talking with one another in their native languages and assumed they were mad about this issue. Yet he still thought it would blow over in time and figured there wasn't much else he could do.

But now Bart had no idea how he was going to be able to run the evening shift with so many missing employees. The plant closed early that day. Over the weekend, Bart and the other supervisors held an emergency meeting and decided to inform the employees that if they didn't return to work by Monday, they would be fired. They felt they had no choice but to force the employees to go back to work. This resulted in the termination of 150 employees who decided to stay home.

What Causes Boundaries to Crack Wide Open?

In the story of Bart Hunter and JBS Swift & Company, we see first-hand the destructive outcomes that are possible when leaders fail to span boundaries and find common ground. Bart's organization could not operate as a whole because it had a dividing line running through it. What causes these boundaries to crack wide open and become borders that limit and constrain an organization?

Dividing lines that run through organizations and sometimes crack open under pressure are similar to the boundaries between tectonic plates in the earth's crust. Researchers Dora Lau at the Chinese University of Hong Kong and J. Keith Murnighan at Northwestern University have introduced the concept of *faultlines* to explain how dividing lines occur in intergroup interactions. Faultlines are "hypothetical dividing lines that may split a group into subgroups based on one or more attributes."[8] Similar to geological faults in the earth's crust, faultlines are always present but may go unnoticed until an external force triggers them. Like geological faults, they create friction or energy as boundaries rub together, pull apart, grind, and collide. In organizations, faultlines can be found vertically in hierarchical structures, horizontally in functional units or division structures, geographically in regional differences, demographically in diversity, and between stakeholder groups involving customers and suppliers.

These faultlines are always present yet often remain dormant. At JBS Swift & Company, the boundaries between Christian and Muslim workers were already there but inactive. When Muslim workers requested a change in the lunch break time, however, the divisions between the two groups were activated. Distrust and anxiety emerged, and what was once a manageable crack became a destructive chasm. In our research with colleagues at the Center for Creative Leadership, we have sought to understand the types of events that activate faultlines between groups.[9] We refer to these actions as triggers: events that split groups into Us and Them. We have found that preceding virtually every Great Divide was some type of a trigger that activated the faultline. Faultlines that distinguish groups shift from dormant and invisible to active and visible. The tension between groups that once lay beneath the surface rises to the top in the same way that the underlying pressure beneath geologic faults in the earth's crust surfaces when faults collide. Although triggers can be an opportunity for learning and growth, our focus here is on presenting four types of triggers that stood out in the LAD research project and to illustrate how each can lead to a Great Divide.

As part of the LAD research project, we analyzed 187 interviews conducted in a variety of organizations across 16 different countries to identify triggers. (For more information, see Appendix A.) We asked a series of questions to uncover the underlying events that activated faultlines between groups. In analyzing the data, we identified four major categories of triggering events: *breach, side-swipe, submersion,* and *clash.*[10]

Breach

In geology, tectonic plates sometimes pull apart from each other, creating chasms or gaps in the earth's crust. A breach occurs when the members of one group feel they are treated differently than members of another group are treated. Identity and intergroup differences become highlighted, and the groups pull farther and farther apart with each interaction. This was the most common type of trigger we found in our data. It often happened when there was a perception that rewards, punishments, promotions, or resources were given to one group but not the other. In other words, one group was valued by the organization and the other was not.

We discovered that in-group and out-group members interpreted these types of events differently. Members of the out-group interpreted this as favoritism and bias, whereas members of the in-group often perceived the events as an expression of loyalty to their group. This of course sets the stage for further divisions and distrust. Take, for example, a situation in which Bank A acquires Bank Z. The chief financial officer (CFO) from Bank A announces that he is filling his senior leadership team with mostly long-term employees of Bank A. His announcement may be viewed positively by Bank A employees; after all, he is taking care of the employees who helped make it the successful company that it is today through decades of hard work and commitment. However, Bank Z employees view this act as proof that they are undervalued in the new organization.

Returning to the JBS Swift & Company example, a boundary between Muslims and Hispanics existed in the organization, and a breach occurred when the Muslim employees asked for the opportunity to practice sunset prayers during Ramadan. When that request was denied, the Somali employees viewed it as evidence that they were not valued within the organization. However, the Hispanic employees at the plant felt very strongly that the Somalis' request should be denied because granting them "special" treatment meant more work for other plant employees and would send the signal to Hispanic employees that they were not valued. Bart and other leaders at the plant faced a serious dilemma: No matter how they handled this situation, their actions probably would be perceived as a breach by one group or the other. We'll return to this dilemma in which leaders find themselves "stuck in the middle" and faced with a trade-off in Chapter 4.

Side-Swipe

Picture two geologic plates slowly grinding past each other as they move in opposite directions, as is the case with the San Andreas fault in southern California. Similarly, groups often brush past one another and cause serious damage along the way. A side-swipe occurs when one group offends, insults, or humiliates another group. In some cases, the offense is a mistake or misunderstanding, but in other cases, comments or actions are blatant attempts to put down or demean another group. Side-swipes, even if they initially involve only two people, can quickly escalate to become a Great Divide, resulting in shaky ground for anyone in the vicinity.

In our research we came across many examples of a side-swipe trigger. One involved a situation in Mozambique between a white expatriate male manager and a black receptionist. The interviewee told us the following story:

> There was a policy that denied employees [the right] to receive visits during general work hours. ... And one day the wife of

one of the white directors came to see him. ... The receptionist said, "I'm sorry, but I can't call your husband here. If you
would prefer, I will send him a message, and he will ring you."
And she said, "No, I have to go to my husband now." And the
receptionist said, "Look, I'm sorry. You have to understand
that I'm simply complying with the policy of the organization." ... And the lady got angry; she eventually reached for
her cell phone and called her husband. ... He went downstairs
to the receptionist, he yelled at her, calling her all kinds of
names, including names like you stupid, ordinary black—
things like that."

The interviewee went on to tell us that the situation escalated
quickly as black employees met with the white director to express
their belief that he had been wrong and the white director involved
other white senior leaders. The Great Divide became even deeper
once a black cleaner defied the organizational hierarchy and took
the story to the media and labor authorities. The white director
eventually was asked to leave not just the company but the country
as well.

Submersion

In geology, plates sometimes move toward each other. One plate
then may be forced underneath the other. This also can be the case
with groups in the workplace. It most commonly happens when one
group is expected to act just like another. One group expects another
group to blend in to the organization, fit in with others, or assimi-
late. The members of the group that are expected to blend in feel

that their identity or sense of self is threatened; they are expected to change who they are, along with their values, beliefs, and practices. As you might imagine after reading about identity in Chapter 2, the group that feels threatened often reacts strongly to this expectation. They tend to fight back in an attempt to hold on to their group identity.

As an example, consider a geographically dispersed team with members in the United States and Spain. The team schedules a conference call at 10 a.m. The American members expect to start the meeting promptly at that time and proceed with the first agenda item. The Spanish members, however, join the call 5 to 10 minutes later. The team leader, an American, sees nothing wrong with starting the meeting exactly on time and jumping right into the agenda. The Spanish team members feel rushed and uncomfortable without having talked about nonbusiness issues for a few minutes first. This difference in meeting styles causes group boundaries to emerge and creates problems for work group functioning since one group is expected to act like the other and change its behavior accordingly. This team later experiences another example of submersion when meeting for the annual retreat. The meeting is held in Spain, and U.S. members are offended when Spanish members begin speaking to one another in their native language of Catalan during dinner. Although this was normal everyday behavior for the Spanish team members and was not meant to be insulting to anyone, the U.S. team members felt excluded as a result. Both of these are examples of submersion in which one group is expected to alter its behavior to be more like the other.

The trigger often is viewed differently, depending on the vantage point of group members. In the examples above, the Spanish team members probably felt threatened by the expectation that they give up their cultural preferences and language to blend in with the Americans. In contrast, the U.S. team members perceive their Spanish colleagues as not wanting to be a part of the team and purposely trying to exclude them from the conversation. Thus, although a particular event may be experienced differently, both sides may view it as a reason for conflict.

Clash

In geology, when plates move toward each other, one plate may be pushed under the other. However, another outcome is that the plates continue to push against each other, neither giving way, until the force between the two pushes both plates upward. This type of geologic action has been the cause of some of the highest peaks on the earth, such as the Alps and Himalaya mountain ranges. Similarly, when group boundaries in the workplace collide, a clash occurs when neither group will budge. We see this type of trigger occurring when groups hold diametrically opposed beliefs or values. What is seen as "right" by one group is seen as "wrong" by another. The values or beliefs may involve religion, morality, politics, or something else.

For example, in collecting our data we spoke with an employee from a social service organization in which a worker was asked to accompany a client to an abortion. The worker refused, saying it violated his religious beliefs. Some sided with the worker, and others in the organization felt it was part of his job. In another example, we heard from a worker that the personnel manager was shocked to find that someone in the organization was a bigamist from Africa and said, "This can't be possible. We can't accept people like this working here." Yet another example is how different people perceive the practice of exchanging money for a promotion. Some groups regard this as unethical behavior; other groups (often from a different culture) view the offering of a monetary gift as a common and expected practice that demonstrates respect.

A final example comes from the Episcopal Church (TEC), which recently had to try to reconcile a widening boundary between stakeholder groups.[11] TEC is headquartered in the United States but affiliated globally with the 77 million-member Anglican Communion headed by the Archbishop of Canterbury in the United Kingdom. A Great Divide was created in TEC when in 2003, the leadership elected the Reverend V. Gene Robinson, the church's first openly gay bishop, at its general convention. As a result of that decision, church leaders were faced with dioceses threatening to defect. Ultimately, some dioceses and local congregations in the United States defected, and many of the defectors bonded together to create their own more conservative Anglican church.

The election of Reverend Robinson prompted equally strong reactions around the globe. The Anglican Church in Zambia cut all ties with the Episcopal Church, and in 2004 eighteen Anglican archbishops, most of them from Africa and Asia, representing more than 55 million Anglicans, called on the Episcopal Church to "repent" its prohomosexual policies within three months or face expulsion from the Anglican Communion. Today, some leaders still hold firm beliefs that homosexual behavior is contrary to Scripture and that blessing same-sex relationships is not acceptable; however, the majority support an inclusive identity. Even though many dissenters have left the church, the leaders continue to struggle with the Great Divide that was created by this clash of beliefs.

Why Leaders Fail to Act

Triggers activate a powerful source of energy that can create a destructive Great Divide between groups when mismanaged or not managed at all. When a trigger leads to a Great Divide, this can set off a ripple effect such that each negative interaction results in groups pulling even farther apart. In some cases, what starts as a simple misunderstanding can quickly escalate to the point where the whole organization is forced to shut down.

Recall the situation faced by Bart Hunter, the evening shift lead supervisor, who found himself in the unenviable position of firing 150 Somali employees who failed to report to work to protest their inability to practice sunset prayers. Unfortunately for Bart, filling the vacant slots to get production back up to speed was just one of several things keeping him up at night. The situation turned from bad to worse when the local media got wind of the situation and quickly began to report on the problems of JBS. In fact, Bart read in the newspaper the next day that those who still had jobs at the plant were helping fired employees pay for food and rent. Suddenly, Bart had a public relations nightmare on his hands. He learned that the union had filed grievances for discrimination and wrongful termination against the company. Now the national news media were swarming the plant and the town of Greeley. Dozens of national media outlets were reporting on the troubles of JBS, none of them casting the company in a good light. Bart and the other leaders in the plant now faced the challenge of trying to quickly repair relationships with its remaining Somali workers to recover from a tainted company image and find a way to get the plant up and running again.[12]

Almost daily, it seems, headlines emerge that illustrate how triggering events caused by a breach, side-swipe, submersion, or values clash wreak havoc on organizational performance, not to mention the negative psychological implications for the groups involved. Why, then, do leaders often fail to act when fault lines crack open, potentially dividing their team, unit, or organization? Though the reasons are multifaceted and complex, several possible reasons emerged from the LAD research project.

First, leaders may deny or fail to acknowledge that a problem exists because they fear that drawing attention to and naming the problem will intensify the fracture or make matters worse. It's as if the leader sees a neon sign flashing that says, "Danger: Do not go near a fault line." A second reason leaders may fail to act is the belief that time heals all wounds. With the passage of time, once tempers cool, the situation will resolve itself or fade into the background. A third reason is that divides often start as small cracks before transforming into deep chasms. When there is a history of competition and conflict between groups, seemingly trivial events or the slightest provocation can lead to a Great Divide so large that it cannot be bridged. For example, in the next chapter you'll read about an incident in South Africa that at first seemed to erupt over a petty feud between blacks and whites over who used all the milk in the break room. Seemingly trivial events can lead to a Great Divide when groups have a history of distrust or when a small event takes on large proportions because it is one in a long line of minor offenses. Some call these minor offenses "micro-inequities."[13] Micro-inequities are like drops of water in a bathtub: Single drops do not cause much harm, but over time they begin to erode the enamel from the tub. In the workplace, triggers can be like little drops of water that over time erode trust, respect, and safety. A final reason, and the one we believe is the primary driver behind inaction, is that leaders simply don't know what to do. As we have been saying throughout this book, leading at the intersection where groups collide and intersect is challenging work.

Similar to Bart Hunter at JBS Swift & Company, we found that all too often leaders hope conflict between different identity groups will fade away if left alone. Unfortunately, in many instances, what appears as petty conflict between groups at work quickly intensifies, involves many people, and escalates to the point where productivity and performance are diminished and direction, alignment, and commitment are nearly impossible to achieve. Once a fault line becomes activated and a Great Divide emerges in the organization, in-group members begin to discount the ideas and opinions of out-group members, and any opportunity to generate creative and innovative ideas gets lost in the conflict.[14] Thus, our hope is that after reading this book you will be more likely to spot Great Divides and better equipped to deal with them quickly so that you don't miss out on the opportunity to capitalize on the Nexus Effect or, worse, sit helplessly by as tensions rise to the point they reached when workers at the JBS Swift & Company meatpacking plant walked off the job in protest.[15]

Identifying Potential Triggers

In this section, we offer a tool that may be helpful as you attempt to evaluate the amount of heat, energy, or tension between groups in your workplace. We call it a Heat Index (see Table 3.1) because we believe it is important that leaders continually evaluate the degree of heat between identity groups.[16] It is important that you take the temperature, so to speak, of groups in your organization to determine how likely it is that negative energy will erupt when groups collide or that positive energy is bubbling up, waiting for a force (you) that will harness this energy and use it effectively. In this chapter we have focused our attention on triggers and the counterproductive outcomes of the Great Divide. However, in our work we have found that even when a trigger is negative and interactions between groups result in conflict, positive outcomes may still emerge. But unfortunately, it is common for triggers to result only in negative outcomes and for leaders, who are typically members of the in-group and thus unaware of out-group concerns, to miss important cues that predict conflict across groups. Thus, we've provided in Table 3.1 a series of diagnostic questions you can use to determine how likely it is that a Great Divide will occur, resulting in counterproductive outcomes and failure to achieve direction, alignment, and commitment.

Working from left to right, what you will see in the columns are (1) the four types of triggers we identified in our work on this topic, (2) beliefs, feelings, and behaviors that indicate this type of trigger in your organization (e.g., what you are likely to see and hear from others), and (3) questions that indicate the temperature, heat, or intensity of distrust and disrespect between groups. If you answer yes to any of the questions in the right-hand column, this indicates that there is very likely a split between groups. And the more you answer yes to these questions, the more likely it is that the underlying tension between these groups will result in a Great Divide. In some cases, you may decide that the potential for a Great Divide is so strong that groups should not work together at all but instead should

be managed so that work is done independently. This is probably a
wise decision if one or more of the following are present:

- There is a history of tension and conflict between groups within
  the organization.
- There are fundamental differences in values and beliefs between
  groups that cannot be resolved or bridged.
- The nature of the work to be accomplished can be achieved
  independently or with limited interaction among group
  members.
- There are significant differences in power, status, or availability
  of resources between groups such that one group feels devalued
  compared to the other.

However, you may be able to create a nexus between groups if the
following is true:

- Each group has critical information or knowledge.
- Each group has critical skills that complement each other.
- Each group has distinct or unique access to resources.

Table 3.1 Heat Index

Definition	Indicators (beliefs, feelings, behaviors)	Trigger potential
Breach When two groups are pulled apart because they are treated differently	• "They were treated better than us." ("She prefers that group.") • Injustice/favoritism; loyalty • Unequal treatment or opportunities	Does one group feel that they were treated badly compared to another group? Does one group see a behavior as favoritism while the other sees the behavior as loyalty?

Table 3.1 (continued)

Definition	Indicators (beliefs, feelings, behaviors)	Trigger potential
		Does one group hold the perception that they do not have access to the same opportunities that other groups have? Is there a power struggle between groups over access to resources? Does one group feel it faces barriers to advancement in the organization because of its identity/status? Is there a perception of or real bias against a group? Is there an unequal allocation of rewards, punishments, benefits, opportunities? Does one group feel it lacks a "seat at the table" or feel locked out (lacks voice or input)?
Side-swipe When one group rubs the other the wrong way (says or does something to insult or devalue the other)	• "They think we are not as good as them." ("You people…") • "Less than," devalued, insulted, or left out • Offensive comment, slur, insult, or humiliation of someone from another group	Does one group feel insulted, left out, hurt, offended by the other group? Does one group attempt to put the other "in its place" by demeaning members of the other group or the group itself?
Submersion When two groups collide and one group is expected to be subsumed or become part of the other	• "They should act like us or they should let us be ourselves." ("Be like us.") • Identity threat • Intolerance of other groups	Is an outgroup feeling that it must give up its identity to be a part of the organization? Is the ingroup feeling that out-group members do not want to be part of the team/ organization?
		Does one group expect the other to act like them? Does one group try to do things or have diffuclty doing things differently than the other group?

(continued)

Table 3.1 *(continued)*

Definition	Indicators (beliefs, feelings, behaviors)	Trigger potential
		Does one group feel threatened by the other? Is one group afraid of losing its status? Is one group not able to practice or express its values and beliefs?
Clash When the values or beliefs of two groups smash into each other and there is no give and take	• "They are wrong and we are right." ("We are right.") • Sense of violation of deeply held beliefs • Intractable—we won't budge, draw a line in the sand, rigidity	Do groups have diametrically opposed values or beliefs? Does one group view the other as abnormal? Is one worldview in conflict with another worldview? Is one group rigid/inflexible or unwilling to compromise because of its beliefs or values? Does one group view the values, beliefs, or behavior of another as unequivocally wrong?

Looking Ahead: The Work of Boundary Spanning Leadership

In this chapter we focused on the negative side of what can happen at the intersection of group boundaries when identity is threatened and differences create a border that limits and constrains collaboration. Thus, you may be feeling that Great Divides are inevitable and that all you can do is brace for the chaos and attempt to minimize the damage. Fortunately, that's not the case. The good news is that you have the power to create the conditions for the Nexus Effect—the positive side of what can happen at the intersection of group boundaries.

Let's go back to the story at the beginning of the chapter about the Eagles and the Rattlers at summer camp. Fortunately, the boys' summer camp experience did not end with mashed potatoes on their foreheads. But it did take more than just spending time together to close the Great Divide. The experimenters created a series of events in which the boys had little choice but to work together. For example, the experimenters secretly sabotaged the camp's water supply but told the boys that some vandals had tampered with the pipes and there was no longer water flowing through the camp. Upon hearing this, both groups of boys volunteered to help find the problem and fix it. Working together, they narrowed the source of the problem to a broken faucet and then worked together side by side to fix it. Although the boys worked well together on this task, dinner was again interrupted that evening by another food fight.

It was only after the boys had a chance to work together on several tasks to achieve a common goal that things began to turn around. For example, the boys were told that the truck delivering their food for the week had broken down. As one might imagine, the idea of lacking food was enough to motivate 22 eleven-year-old boys to work together to get the truck running again. After a few days of working together to accomplish tasks like this that benefited both groups, the boys began to interact with one another very differently. The name-calling stopped, and the boys were now taking turns singing songs at the evening campfire.[17] By the time the boys boarded the bus headed for home, they had all become friends. In fact, the Rattlers used their remaining prize money to buy milk shakes for all the boys on the bus!

The Robbers Cave Study in Oklahoma illustrates many of the messages we have been trying to convey in these first few chapters. The study demonstrates that group identity forms quickly, resulting in positive bias toward the in-group, and that groups in competition often develop negative attitudes toward one another. The experiment also shows that simply bringing groups together is often not enough to reduce distrust and disrespect. The researchers found that it was only when the boys had to work together to solve a problem or reach a common goal that the Great Divide began to disappear and cooperation across boundaries occurred.

The lessons learned from the Robbers Cave experiment, the other examples in this chapter, and the Leadership Across Differences (LAD) research involving hundreds of leaders from around the world is clear: As a leader, you play a key role in spanning boundaries and transforming divides into new frontiers.

PART 2

MANAGING BOUNDARIES

In Part 1 of this book, we hope we convinced you of two things: Effective leadership in today's world transcends boundaries, and spanning boundaries across groups is hard work. Despite leaders' best efforts to bring groups together, identity differences can splinter groups into Us and Them, resulting in potentially destructive Great Divides.

In the remainder of this book, we shift the discussion from illustrating the problem to focusing on solutions. Parts 2, 3, and 4 are organized around three sets of interrelated strategies: managing boundaries, forging common ground, and discovering new frontiers. Out of these three approaches come the six practices of boundary spanning leadership that lead to the Nexus Effect. With each practice, you move farther up the spiral from boundaries as borders that limit and constrain to boundaries as new frontiers for tackling tough problems, developing innovative solutions, and transforming an organization.

In Part 2, we introduce the first two leadership practices—buffering and reflecting—that make it possible for you to manage boundaries between groups (see Figure P2.1). Although this may seem contradictory, the first thing you must do to span group boundaries is to create or strengthen them. As you learned in Part 1, identity is created out of the interplay between two fundamental forces: the need for integration and belonging and the need for differentiation and uniqueness. The practices of buffering and

---

Figure P2.1 Managing boundaries.

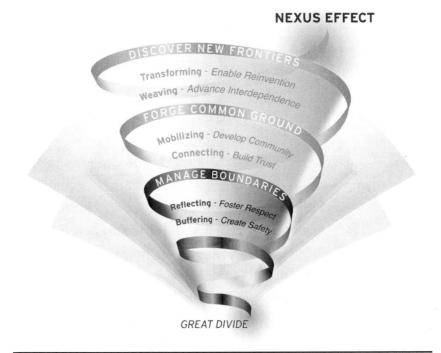

---

reflecting tap into the second force: our need to be members of groups that are unique and different from other groups. Until boundaries are clearly defined and effectively managed, groups will find it nearly impossible to work collaboratively and you will find that boundary spanning leadership is an insurmountable goal. You must be able to see group boundaries clearly before you can bridge them.

The practice of *buffering* involves defining boundaries to create safety between groups. Buffers monitor and protect the flow of information and resources across boundaries. To see buffering in action, we will visit South Africa in Chapter 4 and learn how Joe Pettit and Zanele Moyo worked together to manage the boundary that still exists between blacks and whites in a postapartheid organization.

Once groups have achieved a state of intergroup safety, the next practice, *reflecting*, involves understanding boundaries to foster intergroup respect. Reflectors represent distinct group perspectives and share knowledge and experiences across groups. In Chapter 5, we'll go to Chatham County, North Carolina, to witness the incredible transformation that occurred within Rick Givens and ultimately within the community he led. Through his own inner journey, Givens used the practice of reflecting to become a boundary spanning leader.

CHAPTER 4

BUFFERING: CREATING SAFETY

I n 2004, Joe Pettit, a white male senior manager at Insurance Incorporated, found himself in the middle of a Great Divide in postapartheid South Africa.[1] Ten years earlier, that country had experienced one of the most dramatic shifts in political power the world has ever known. Literally overnight, government rule shifted from the numerical minority (whites) to the numerical majority (blacks) when Nelson Mandela became the nation's first democratically elected president. Although a number of legal reforms to redress past discrimination quickly followed, attitudes and beliefs were much slower to change. At Insurance Incorporated, blacks often felt they were treated as inferior and whites felt their jobs were threatened by employment equity targets. This was complicated by the fact that white managers were now expected to train and mentor their replacements and black candidates often were perceived as unqualified for the jobs into which they were being promoted.

Despite those daunting challenges, Insurance Incorporated had made considerable progress since apartheid. Focused efforts had been made to shift the organizational culture from a white-dominated, hierarchical, autocratic culture toward greater transparency, inclusion, participation, and accountability. However, those efforts, as well as the leadership of Joe Pettit, were put to the test over what appeared on the surface to be an office squabble over milk and sugar.

At the standing senior management meeting, a white male manager accused a group of black female administrators of using all the milk and sugar in the break room. The manager was upset because there was no milk or sugar for his customers' tea. He assumed that the supplies were depleted by the group of black administrators who ate breakfast at work in the morning. As was common for blacks who worked at Insurance Inc., this group of women lived far from work and had to get up at the crack of dawn to take public transportation to the office each day. That meant that they often ate breakfast together as a group in the break room. Therefore, the manager assumed that they had used all the milk and sugar.

Not knowing exactly how to handle the situation or who was at fault, the leader of the management team decided to institute a rule in which no one was allowed to eat breakfast at work. The black female administrators were told about this during a staff meeting. Naturally, they were upset. No one had discussed the issue with them, and they felt they were being punished for something they had not done. The new rule meant that they would have to skip breakfast or eat so early that they would be hungry again by the time they arrived for work. Most of the black women ate vetkoeks (a salty doughnut) for breakfast and did not even use milk and sugar.

Also, they knew that some white women ate their morning cereal at work and did use milk and sugar with their breakfast. But only the black women were accused.

Initially, Joe Pettit had the same view as other senior managers, that the situation was trivial and not worthy of management's time. In fact, when human resources was made aware of the situation, the HR manager found it "ridiculous" that employees were divided over milk and sugar and made it clear that he and his staff were not going to waste their time by getting involved. But Joe changed his mind after Zanele Moyo, a black female assistant accountant at the middle management level came to see him. Zanele had a very frank discussion with Joe, explaining that she thought it was important that someone hear the black women's side of the story. Joe listened intently to what Zanele had to say, asked questions, and came to realize that the incident was causing a divide in the organization and that eventually this would affect organizational productivity if nothing was done. As Joe explained it, "To be quite honest, I didn't have the full understanding at the time ... We had an open, frank, and robust discussion about this ... and how it had developed into an issue where people were taking sides based on culture and racial grounds."

Zanele told Joe that the black female administrators had shared with her how mistreated they felt. Not knowing what to do, they responded by withdrawing as much as possible. They were now buying their own milk and sugar and keeping their supply separate. They no longer took tea breaks with their white colleagues and refused to attend any social events organized by the company. Zanele knew that many white managers viewed this as simply being uncooperative, but she told Joe that she thought what the black women really wanted was acknowledgment from management that they had been wrongly accused. She thought they actually did want to be part of the larger team.

Joe respected Zanele for being brave enough to bring the issue to his attention. After talking with her, he tried to get other senior managers involved, but none were particularly interested. He eventually took it upon himself to send an e-mail acknowledging that a mistake had been made and apologizing for that mistake. He knew that this would not make up for the past, since the senior manager who declared that eating breakfast was no longer allowed during office hours did not apologize for the incident. Yet he hoped that his e-mail would help bridge the divide between blacks and whites so that they would again feel comfortable working together as a team.

The Practice of Buffering

In essence, the debate over milk and sugar at Insurance Incorporated is a story about threat: workers feeling as if their unique identity and sense of self were under attack. Navigating complex dynamics associated with postapartheid South Africa may feel like a far cry from your own reality, but issues of threat probably are not. At Insurance Incorporated, Joe and Zanele addressed this threat head-on by engaging in the boundary spanning practice of buffering. They took action to help the black female administrators gain back a sense of *safety and security*, and they worked to initiate a dialogue that would set the stage for repairing hurt feelings so that the black women once again would feel they were valued in the organization. Other leaders in the organization saw the conflict as a trivial waste of their time that would quickly blow over. Zanele and eventually

Joe, however, recognized that underneath the surface issue lay a Great Divide between blacks and whites caused by apartheid.

Fortunately, they did not do what leaders in a situation like this often do: try to erase the boundaries between groups and get everyone to work together as one big happy family. Although something like this sometimes may be the right strategy (we'll discuss this in Chapter 6), it will not work in situations in which groups feel that their identity is threatened. When groups feel threatened, they instinctually try to pull away as a means of coping with the situation. This is exactly what the black female administrators at Insurance Incorporated did. They naturally turned inward, toward their own group members, for support and security by withdrawing from the organization and refusing to attend social events. They strengthened the boundary not to cause trouble but instinctually as a way of trying to protect themselves and their group identity amid the messages they were getting from management that they were to blame for anything that went wrong in their team. Joe and Zanele recognized that before they could span the boundary between blacks and whites in their work team, they had to work on creating an environment where groups felt safe.

Luckily, few of us are faced with the situation of trying to build a safe environment in a postapartheid country where tensions and distrust between blacks and whites run many generations deep. Yet in project meetings, virtual teleconferences, annual retreats, shareholder events, and elsewhere, leaders constantly navigate potential divides, splits, and coalitions between groups. Boundaries are a fact of organizational life, and it is difficult to know when to call out and protect them and when to break them down. It took a great deal of courage for both Zanele and Joe to confront and discuss a very difficult boundary such as race. Most people shy away from dealing with such sensitive topics. It must have been difficult, particularly for Zanele as a black female, to act as an advocate for the group of black women administrators. It takes courage, strong listening skills, and a great deal of sensitivity to focus on what differentiates and separates groups in a world that tells us to look past or ignore our differences. Setting and defining boundaries is challenging work.

Your Nexus Challenge may be more about managing boundaries than about tearing them down. You may need to fortify the boundaries between the sales and marketing departments to mitigate conflict. You may need to create or strengthen a boundary between your team and headquarters when competing agendas detract from productivity. You may need to manage the exchange of resources carefully when two organizations merge into one. In a flat world where information travels at the speed of light, monitoring and protecting the flow of information and resources across groups is a critical aspect of leadership. Defining boundaries to create intergroup safety is the first step toward the Nexus Effect.

Defining Boundaries

Boundaries help people feel safe. They can keep unwanted things or people out and provide us with a defined space where we feel welcome by being around others who are like us. Take the boundaries that define nations. Every nation has policies about who does and does not belong within its borders. People around the globe often define themselves in part by their nation and feel a strong sense of community with their fellow citizens. When boundaries between nations are threatened, people react strongly and defend their borders at all costs. In organizations, people also react strongly when boundaries across hierarchy, function, demographics, region, and stakeholder groups are threatened. That occurs because these boundaries serve an important function in the workplace. As we discussed in Chapter 1, boundaries will always exist in organizations. Even as they disappear because technology and a global market allow us to work with others anywhere in the world, the psychological boundaries between people caused by identity differences remain and in some cases become even deeper and more entrenched. Although boundaries sometimes become borders that limit or constrain collaboration, they are also necessary for groups to have a defined purpose and role within the larger organization.

Figure 4.1 illustrates the practice of buffering. Buffering is about defining group identities and involves shielding or protecting groups from outside influences or threats to identity. In the figure you see two circles (groups). The line drawn between the two circles represents a boundary that must be clearly defined to protect and differentiate each group. Once the boundary is clearly marked,

Figure 4.1 Buffering.

information, people, and resources can be filtered through it as appropriate. Buffering allows groups to develop and maintain a strong sense of identity and define their reason for being. The result is that buffering builds intergroup safety: *the state of psychological security that develops when intergroup boundaries are defined and maintained.* Creating intergroup safety through the practice of buffering is the first step toward the Nexus Effect.

Defining boundaries within groups and teams is called boundary work. Effective teams work hard to establish and maintain boundaries and manage interactions across those boundaries. According to the researchers Samer Faraj and Aimin Yan, boundary work is tricky because it requires creating boundaries that are porous enough that resources and information can get in but resistant enough to keep uncertainty and competing demands out.[2] As a boundary spanning leader, your job is challenging. You must help groups work across, around, and through boundaries to engage in productive work with other groups inside and outside the organization. At the same time, you must serve as a buffer between group boundaries to protect groups and keep them whole. If boundaries become too weak or disappear altogether, the group you are leading may become uncertain about its identity—who are we, and what are we supposed to do?

Take, for example, a cross-functional team established to roll out a new smart phone product line. Lisa,[3] the team's leader, is initially excited about leading this team because she believes she has put together the ideal team to roll out a new product line. From start to finish, she'll be required to get input from multiple functions to make the product a success in the market: R&D, sales, finance, marketing, and customer service. Her enthusiasm quickly fades, however, as she realizes the team isn't making much progress. Even though the team was created to get input from all the key internal stakeholders, it has met as a whole only once during the last month. Inevitably, members are called away to handle emergencies and crises in their own functional groups and are pulled in too many directions by competing priorities and demands. Lisa knows that unless she can help the group carve out a clear identity and find ways to protect its members' time and energy, the product will never get off the ground. As Lisa has experienced, groups without clear boundaries are unable to buffer themselves effectively from the disruptive demands of the external environment.

Boundaries help us define who we are and, just as important, who we are not. Groups will not be able to collaborate effectively across boundaries until they feel protected and safe within their own areas. Being part of a clearly defined group with people who are similar provides us a sense of safety and security and also fulfills the fundamental need for differentiation or uniqueness. When boundaries are unclear or too permeable, it is far too easy for others to trespass across those boundaries and create counterproductive interactions across groups.

Buffering in Action

Buffering is a way to monitor and manage the boundaries between groups. There are any number of buffering tactics you can use in your organization. Below are five tactics we observed in our research and practice with organizations around the world. See also Appendix B for a table describing additional actions you can take to enact buffering as well as other boundary spanning practices.

Buffering Tactic 1: Separate Groups

One tactic that may be necessary in certain situations to help groups accomplish a specific task is to separate the groups. The goal is to eliminate interactions across boundaries altogether. When group boundaries are violated and conflict frequently erupts, physically separating the groups may be the only solution that helps them focus on the task at hand. If, for example, you answered yes to many of the questions we posed in the Heat Index, this means you may be forced to separate groups to achieve direction, alignment, and commitment. For example, in a clothing manufacturing facility in Jordan, leaders told us that they addressed the problem of a Great Divide between Jordanians and foreign workers by assigning each group to different shifts. Members of one group worked the day shift, and members of the other group worked the night shift. This way, both groups had minimal contact with each other, boundary demarcations were clear in multiple ways, and the groups could function effectively by avoiding each other completely.

In some faith-based organizations, we found that one way to avoid conflict with groups that held different values was to select only employees who espoused the same religious values and beliefs as the organization's founder or leadership team. Group boundaries were clearly controlled on the basis of who was selected into and out of the organization. Separation can be an effective tactic in certain situations to protect group boundaries. However, separation of groups is often not a reasonable solution to intergroup conflict when collaboration across boundaries is critical to the organization's success or the nature of the work requires interdependence.

Buffering Tactic 2: Reduce Threat from External Influences

Recall our opening story about Joe Pettit and the black women who were wrongly accused of using all the milk and sugar in the break room in South Africa. Although Joe probably did not recognize this at the time, his e-mailed apology to the women most likely went a long way toward reducing threat in this situation. The integrity and value of the group of black women were threatened by the fact that they had been accused of something they did not do and were promptly punished by management, which forbade them to have breakfast at work—without once consulting with the group to hear their side of the story. Joe's apology at least acknowledged management's wrongdoing. This simple act probably helped reduce the intensity of the negative feelings of the women and their instinctual need to withdraw and protect themselves from others.

Many times, identity threat is caused not by an aggressive attack pitting one group against another but by the inevitable changes occurring regularly in organizations that prompt feelings of insecurity. Threat to group identity may be experienced in many ways, but often this involves feelings of loss. Groups at work may feel threatened by the loss of resources, the loss of status or power, or the loss of the status quo. Whenever there is organizational change, perceptions of threat are probably not far behind. Steps must be taken to temper the perception of loss to reduce threat and resistance. During times of change, it is important that you help employees see "what's in it for them" to prevent groups from digging in their heels or isolating themselves from other groups in self-defense. Reducing the negative impact of external influences may involve protecting or shielding the group from threat or loss. Helping groups see how their identities and roles evolve as the organization changes can help those groups feel safe and secure despite the turbulence around them.

Buffering Tactic 3: Make Boundaries Visible for Others

There are times when you must make boundaries clear and visible for others because a boundary is being disregarded or violated in some way. The black women in our South Africa story had no voice. No one made an effort to understand their side of the story until Zanele intervened on their behalf. As a black woman with access to management, Zanele was able to speak for the group and help others see that a boundary had been violated. By approaching Joe Pettit and then convincing him that the heart of the conflict ran deeper than simply who used the milk and sugar, she acted as the voice of those women and shared their perspective, concerns, perceptions, values, and needs with Joe.

As fallout from the global economic recession, businesses are divesting, acquiring, and being acquired. During an acquisition, it is easy for the members of the acquired group to feel that their identity is lost and no longer valued. Or they may feel torn between the security of the old organization and wanting to belong and become successful contributors to the new one. Regardless, to feel that they belong to the new organization, members of the group that has been acquired will need to feel that they have a voice and that their needs and values are not being overlooked or ignored. Their identity will have to be protected until a new unified identity emerges between the two organizations. If those boundaries are erased too quickly, the acquisition will feel like a hostile takeover as members of the old organization feel that their identity, voice, and sense of safety and security are lost.[4] There are any number of tools available, such as team contracting, establishing rules of engagement, using team governance models, and creating operating agreements to make boundaries more visible. They add the specification and clarity needed to manage complex interactions across boundaries by addressing issues such as who does what, when, where, why, and how.

Buffering Tactic 4: Create a Unifying Team Identity

Another buffering tactic is to create or strengthen a group's identity by clarifying its mission and vision and making roles and tasks clear for its members. You must know where your group boundaries lie before you can take steps to prevent those boundaries from being violated. Recall the plight of Lisa, who struggled to pull together a cross-functional team to roll out a new smart phone product line. Although she had put together a team that could ideally make the product a success because its members were able to approach it from every necessary angle, the team was unable to make progress because its members were pulled in too many different directions. In addition to creating the right team composition, Lisa needed to take the time to create a unified team identity.

What she must do at this point is clarify with her own team its mission and determine who will be responsible for what. They must define who they are and who they are not. In other words, each member must determine what he or she is required to do as a result of membership on the new team and what he or she no longer should be doing as a result of the new role. Thus, Lisa's role in buffering is to clarify each member's contribution to the overall team. This will enable each member to negotiate with the functional leaders in the organization; this is a fundamental strategy for recognizing the boundary of this particular team so that it can accomplish its mission.

Buffering Tactic 5: Build Team Cohesion

Another tactic Lisa will need to use once she has defined the team's mission and each member's role in accomplishing that mission is to develop cohesion among the team members. It is important to focus first on the task: what the task is and how to accomplish it. But once the team moves toward execution of the task, conflict is more likely to emerge. This is when the leader should turn her attention to creating team cohesion.[5] As is the case in many teams that come together to work across boundaries, a new boundary must emerge in the process of creating a cross-functional team and team members must feel a part of the new group. In addition to defining the team's mission and tasks, the team members must feel that they belong to the new team, that it is an important and valued part of their identity. To accomplish this, Lisa will need to spend time and resources building team cohesion by engaging in team-building activities and events so that the team members can develop their own unique identity. She may plan a "field trip" for the team to visit a customer base that represents its market, or she may hold off-site meetings with time built in for socializing to allow team members to get to know one another. It is important that this newly formed group feel good about membership in the team and come to understand how it is unique and different from other groups within the organization. Once boundaries are defined and team members are emotionally engaged members of the group, commitment and success will follow.

The Leader's Role in Buffering

To accomplish buffering, you need to monitor and manage the flow of resources, information, people, practices, and perceptions across boundaries. You can be the buffer that protects and shields your group from external threats, competing demands, and adverse pressures. Although you cannot eliminate all the negative influences that may flow across the boundary and adversely affect your group, you can buffer or lessen the impact those influences have on the group members and help them maintain a sense of safety and identity in the face of such pressures. Both Joe Pettit and Zanele Moyo played the role of buffers at Insurance Incorporated in South Africa.

During our interview with Joe, he told us how Zanele handled the situation, with his admiration for her approach shining through: "She said there is an issue here, let's deal with it, which took a lot of strength and a lot of responsibility. . . . She took a hell of a lot of responsibility on her shoulders." When Zanele describes the situation, she doesn't seem to view her role as unique or heroic, just a matter of someone telling it like it is: "Insurance Incorporated has historically been a white organization. When I first joined the company, I was not allowed to speak to the clients, who were mostly white. So that is how many of our managers who have been here for 15 years were brought up. They can't just change overnight just because South Africa now has a black president. Change in the culture of Insurance Incorporated can only happen when it happens in the same way the people here do things—more slowly."

Acting as a buffer, Zanele accomplished two very important things. First, she convinced Joe that a boundary had been violated and that this was a significant issue worthy of his attention. Second, she monitored and managed the flow of information from the group of black women to management. Because their boundary had been violated, the black women withdrew to the point where they were almost ostracized from other groups in the organization. Nothing was getting in or out. Zanele became a buffer and managed the flow of information so that the women's perspective was able to flow outward to management and they finally had an opportunity to voice their concerns and needs.

Similarly, Joe served the role of buffer and managed the flow of information from the group of predominantly white male managers to the group of black female administrators. Given legitimate concerns regarding job security in a changing South Africa, he recognized that the members of his team were forced to confront deep feelings of threat. He asked them to try to see "the other side of the issue" but was unable to gain any traction. So he took it upon himself to try to correct the wrong that had been done. By listening to the women's concerns through his conversations with Zanele and sending the e-mail apologizing on behalf of management, he helped reduce the tension and threat experienced by the black women. It took Joe and Zanele working together, both as buffers, to monitor and manage the boundaries and interactions between their respective racial groups. They monitored and managed the flow of information across groups, reduced the negative impact of external influences, and effectively buffered the tensions between blacks and whites and between administration and management. This work was essential for helping to rebuild intergroup safety: the state of psychological security that develops when intergroup boundaries are defined and maintained.

Caution: The Pitfall of Buffering

A potential blind spot that may emerge when one is engaged in the practice of buffering involves the leadership trade-off.[6] The trade-off is that the actions you take to reinforce or support one group probably will cause greater tension and conflict within other groups. Because buffering involves defining and clarifying group boundaries, any steps you take to clarify boundaries and buffer what gets in and out of a particular group will often be at the expense of other groups. So, for example, the e-mail apology Joe sent to the group of black female administrators in an attempt to acknowledge the violation of their group's boundary probably was not viewed as a favorable course of action among his white male manager counterparts. As a buffer, you take on a role in which you consider the needs, values, perspectives, and identity of one group. This creates a potential pitfall when other groups feel that their perspective, which is in conflict with that of the group you are attempting to buffer, is not being considered.

Lisa, the leader of the smart phone design team, will have to change her leadership role and act more as a buffer if her group is going to be successful in the future. She will have to learn to protect group members from being pulled in so many directions that the cross-functional team she has put together is never able to meet as a whole. She will have to work with the functional leaders in the organization to redefine roles and make it crystal clear what her group members are and are not responsible for. And she will have to create a new cohesive team identity to strengthen her team's boundary and help members see and value what is unique about this team and what its primary mission will be.

Similarly, you will have to find ways to protect your group from outside influences and filter what comes into and out of it. You will have to learn to monitor, protect, and reinforce the information, resources, and people that flow across boundaries. At times you will find that you must act as a buffer and shield your group members from anything that threatens the group's identity or mission. At the same time you must allow relevant information and resources to flow into the group when needed. When you are able to act successfully as a buffer at the intersection of groups, you will find that you have created a safe environment that allows collaboration to take root and eventually flourish.

Buffering and Your Nexus Challenge

Defining boundaries by monitoring and protecting the flow of information and resources across groups helps create intergroup safety (see Table 4.1). The questions listed in column 1 of the table will guide you in applying the practice of buffering to your unique Nexus Challenge as well as other challenges you face when attempting to manage boundaries between groups.

Table 4.1 Buffering Summary

Definition What is buffering?	Monitor and protect the flow of information and resources across groups to *define boundaries and create intergroup safety.*
Rationale Why does buffering work?	*Buffering* occurs when group identities and boundaries are clearly defined. Different roles, responsibilities, values, goals, and perspectives are clarified. The flow of information and resources across the boundary is carefully monitored and filtered. When group identity is protected from outside influence or threat, group members feel safe and secure within their group and their need for differentiation or uniqueness is met.
Tactics How is the practice to be accomplished?	1. Separate groups. Eliminate interaction across groups. 2. Reduce threat from external influences. Protect and shield your group from outside threats or loss. 3. Make boundaries visible for others. Develop clear agreements and understandings across groups. 4. Create a unifying team identity. Within your team, clarify who will be responsible for what. 5. Build team cohesion. Increase feelings of belonging by engaging in team building activities and events.
Outcome What is the result?	*Intergroup safety*—the state of psychological security that develops when intergroup boundaries are defined and maintained.

Discern: Assessing the Current State

Buffering defines boundaries to create intergroup safety. On a scale of 1 to 10 (where 10 is the highest), how would you rate your team or organization on intergroup safety?

Intergroup safety increases the more the following is true:

- Group members feel a strong connection to the group and identify with its mission and goals.
- There is a clear distinction between the identity of each group; each knows what it stands for and what it is responsible for accomplishing.
- Groups are protected and shielded from external threats.

Reflect: Exploring New Approaches

How can you become a more effective buffer for your group, monitoring and managing what goes out and what comes in?

How can you ensure that your team has a clear sense of identity so that group members understand their mission, roles and responsibilities, and unique contribution within the larger organization?

How can you encourage other groups to respect the boundary that surrounds your team?

Apply: Taking Action

What is one idea, tactic, or new insight you've learned about buffering that you could apply to your Nexus Challenge?

CHAPTER 5

REFLECTING: FOSTERING RESPECT

In 1999, Rick Givens, chairman of the Chatham County Board of Commissioners in North Carolina, was fed up. His hometown seemed to be flooded with illegal immigrants, with more coming each month. He believed this was acting as a drain on the county's resources and weakening health care and social services. Taking the problem into his own hands, he wrote a letter to the U.S. Immigration and Naturalization Service, asking for agents' help "in getting these folks properly documented or routed back to their homes."[1] The letter was like pouring gasoline on a fire. Some members of the Latino community were outraged. Others were frightened. Yet many leaders in the rural southern conservative community strongly supported his position. County meetings turned into screaming matches. But what happened next changed Rick's view of illegal immigration forever.

He accepted an invitation to be one of the first participants in a program called the Latino Initiative, designed to provide a unique opportunity for educators and community leaders to learn firsthand about Mexican culture and family structure.[2] The highlight of the program was a one-week visit to Mexico that included three days in Mexico City, three days in rural schools, and a visit to the home of a Mexican family that has a son, a daughter, or a husband living in the United States. One of the goals of the Latino Initiative is to help leaders recognize the needs of Latinos and identify the agencies that can address those needs to help immigrants become better integrated into life in North Carolina. Members of the Latino community were invited on the trip to Mexico, including John Herrera, senior vice president of Self-Help. You'll learn more about John Herrera and his work in Chapter 10. Initially, Rick and John were like oil and water, clashing on virtually every point. However, once they spent more time together and got to know each other on a more personal level, they began to let their guard down, listen to each other, and ultimately come to understand the other's perspective. This seemed to open the door for Rick to learn about and begin to appreciate Mexican culture and the people he met during his visit.

During Rick and John's stay with a family, they had dinner with one of the three sons living illegally in the United States.[3, 4] The son was home visiting for the weekend but told Rick that getting back to his job in Los Angeles on Tuesday was as simple as paying a smuggler to tell him where no one would be watching the border. It was then that Rick realized his county's problems with illegal immigration would not be solved by simply rounding immigrants up and sending them home. He came to understand the complexity of the problem and the role both countries played in exacerbating or failing to deal with it. Rick also came to see that this son, like so many other illegal immigrants, had come to the United States because he felt it was his only option to provide a better life for his family. Rick began to understand why so many Mexicans felt they had no choice but to come to the United States; wanting to provide the best life possible for one's family was a value Rick shared with the illegal immigrants. For the first time, he was able to see the perspectives of those on both sides of the issue. He concluded that the right course of action was to help integrate the workers who were already part of Chatham County: "I'm man enough to admit when I'm wrong. … Given what I know now, we would be much better off trying to help these people to accomplish their goals so we don't live in two separate communities."[5]

A pivotal moment for Rick occurred just a week after he returned from his trip. His letter to federal immigration officials continued to receive a lot of attention that only grew while he was in Mexico, especially among white supremacist groups. An anti-immigration rally was planned at city hall where David Duke, a white nationalist who was the founder of the Louisiana-based Knights of the Ku Klux Klan and a perennial candidate in U.S. presidential elections, was to be the headline speaker. Rally organizers wanted to use the event as a forum to push their national agenda and use Chatham County as a poster child, including the person they now labeled "traitor Rick," for the negative effects illegal immigration has on a community.

Along with the police chief and the sheriff (who also participated in the Latino Initiative program), Rick did what he could to encourage others to boycott the rally. They frantically called county residents, trying to convince them that Duke's approach was not going to solve the county's problems with immigration and would only make matters worse. Rick also partnered with John Herrera, who made calls to members of the Latino community, encouraging them to turn the David Duke rally into a nonevent by boycotting rather than protesting it. Their efforts paid off: Duke spoke that day before an unexpectedly small, albeit spirited, group. Afterward, Rick felt a strong commitment and personal responsibility for helping others see what he came to see as a result of his participation in the Latino Initiative and his relationship with John Herrera. He began to advocate for the fair treatment of immigrants in his community and argued that the county would save money by informing qualified immigrants how to use their tax IDs to get insurance. He met with his congressman to urge him to secure a larger portion of federal English as a Second Language (ESL) funds for the state, met with 28 United Way organizations to learn what services each one provided to the Latino community, and worked with Latino leaders on an initiative to put a soccer field in the community park.

Rick's transformation has had a lasting impact on Chatham County. A decade later, in 2009, county officials took a strong public stand against a federal program that would allow local law enforcement officers to enforce federal immigration laws and flag any illegal immigrants who were arrested for deportation.[6] Chatham officials expressed concern that the program would lead to distrust of law enforcement, separation of family members, and racial profiling. George Lucier, the chair of the Chatham County commissioners at the time, released a statement that acknowledged the vital role of diversity and immigration in the county. "Our county has been blessed with a diverse population for much of its existence," he said in the statement. "This has included people of color and immigrants, who were not always American citizens or documented residents. All of these residents have enriched our economy, our character and our culture as well." Chatham County's leaders went from seeing illegal immigrants as a drain on their county to viewing them as an asset. By nearly all accounts, Chatham County now serves as a model for successfully integrating immigrants into the community. People continue to move to Chatham County, and there is a steady influx of whites, African Americans, and Hispanics. Unemployment remains comparatively low. Home values are up, and new schools are being built. The future is bright for this rural community.

The Practice of Reflecting

Whether you work in business, education, or government, the story of Rick Givens and Chatham County offers powerful insights into leading in a flat world. It speaks to the opportunity that may be found where boundaries collide and groups on either side of a divide can learn to respect one another. Rick's experience in Mexico helped him understand the differences and similarities between white U.S.-born residents and illegal immigrants from Mexico living in Chatham County. This experience, seeing both sides of a boundary and enabling other groups to do the same, can be facilitated through a leadership practice we call reflecting.

To reflect is to cast back or show an image of something. In the same way that a mirror, a photograph, or a still body of water casts a reflection of an image for others to see, the practice of reflecting involves showing an image of each group to the other. It involves sensitizing each group to the other's needs, values, beliefs, and preferences; illuminating the differences and similarities between groups; and helping each group understand the identity of the other.

As a result, groups are able to see a boundary from both sides, come to accept that boundary, and ultimately respect the differences between them.

Rick Givens and John Herrera both spoke of the transformative nature of their trip to Mexico, in particular the time they spent with a poor but proud mother who invited the two men into her home. John recounts the story like this:

> To get to this family's home, we drove down a dirt and mud road. Then we walked a long distance—we saw no one working, there were no jobs, nothing. A woman greeted us at the door. She took us in and showed us a picture of her two sons living in what she described as "the most beautiful city"—it was not Chicago or New York, but Siler City in Chatham County! As she's telling us about her sons, she walks around, grabs her only chicken, breaks its neck, and puts it in hot boiling water to defeather and cook it. She was so honored that people from her son's town had come to visit. Rick looked over to me and said, "She's not going to feed us that thing? That's the only animal she's got left." But that's exactly what she did. And you know what, it was delicious.

Both John and Rick said they were deeply moved by that act of generosity, and Rick realized that he might also choose to cross the border into the United States if he were in the shoes of an impoverished Mexican man wanting to provide better for his family.

Like John and Rick, you practice reflecting when you enable groups to learn about one another and develop respect for their differences as well as commonalities. The word *respect* comes from the Latin *respectus*, meaning "to look back at" or "to look again." When divided or opposing groups are able "to look again" at one another, they begin to see beyond the biases and misunderstandings that separate them. The result is intergroup respect: *the state of intergroup awareness and positive regard that develops when groups understand their similarities and differences.* Helping groups learn about one another and respect the boundary between them is a foundational step that must be taken before you can forge common ground between groups (as we'll discuss in Part 3 of this book). Although Rick's transformation after his visit to Mexico was dramatic, you can practice reflecting on a daily basis in small but meaningful ways. Whenever you take time to learn about the experiences, needs, values, and challenges of another group, that is reflecting. And whenever you enable others to understand differences in the experiences, needs, values, and challenges that another group faces, that too is reflecting.

As a leader, you often are called on to represent the position or needs of one group to another. Your Nexus Challenge may involve requiring members of your team to understand the needs of various stakeholder groups, such as your customers or suppliers. It may involve helping senior male leaders better understand the unique challenges faced by women who confront a glass ceiling as they move up the organization's corporate ladder. Or it may involve steps you take to develop a global mindset within your groups to be successful in a global market. There are probably many times when you are faced with the challenge of helping two groups learn to respect each other despite the boundary that separates them. Fostering intergroup respect through the practice of reflecting is the second step toward the Nexus Effect.

Understanding Boundaries

The practice of reflecting involves representing distinct perspectives and facilitating knowledge exchange across groups. Before groups can span boundaries, they must be able to see the boundary from both sides. As shown in Figure 5.1, reflecting involves the mutual sharing of identity differences (i.e., perspectives, goals, needs, values) while keeping group identity fully intact. Boundaries are clarified and further defined through a deeper understanding of the similarities and differences that exist across groups. The result is intergroup respect, which, as we said above, is the second step toward the Nexus Effect. With this step in place, groups can begin to see common ground in goals and objectives and pave the way for creating a collective vision.

Our work, along with the research of others, tells us that to lay the foundation for groups to work together toward a common goal or

---

Figure 5.1 Reflecting.

---

mission, people must feel secure in their own group and then be able to acknowledge the validity of the other group.[7] This is not easy because a sense of safety and security often comes from holding negative views of the other group. We feel more confident in our own group when we view the other group as less in some way: less able, less competent, less valuable, and so on. We often feel a stronger sense of connection to Us when we are working against Them.

Take, for example, a labor union in a manufacturing firm. The union's existence depends in part on maintaining a view in opposition to management, and vice versa. If over time the priorities, values, and needs of management and labor become highly similar, there is no need to continue to have a labor union. It could close up shop and no one would care because the differences between management and labor have disappeared. Thus, the identities of the union group and the management group depend in part on maintaining and focusing on their differences.

Those who do research on identity-based conflicts tell us that groups must break out of this cycle to move forward and work together. They must find a way to feel secure in their own group by focusing on the positive aspects of their group, not by invalidating the other. They must be able to let go of the assumption that They must lose for Us to win.[8] Jay Rothman, a renowned expert in resolving deep divisions between groups, says that one way to do this is to start by highlighting the differences between groups to understand what the reasons for conflict or misunderstanding may be.[9] The next step is to help groups talk to one another in an open and honest way so that each can share its hopes, its fears, and what it cares most deeply about.[10] He argues that it is only when both groups can accept their differences that they can begin to work on resolving their problems and find ways to collaborate. In both of these steps, active and appreciative listening across boundaries is absolutely essential.

Senior leaders at DriveTime[11] exemplify the practice of reflecting in a program they created that was designed to give their employees the opportunity to learn more about their customer community. DriveTime owns and operates the largest chain of used-car dealerships in the United States exclusively for subprime customers: people with modest incomes who have credit difficulties. In 2003, the company created SchoolTime, an employee-led charitable foundation in which local offices enter into long-term partnerships with elementary schools in their community with high percentages of "at-risk" students. Employee teams raise funds and volunteer their time to provide support to students, their parents, and their teachers. Leaders at DriveTime believe the program not only provides an opportunity to "do good" within their community but also provides a chance for its employees to gain a deeper understanding of the lower-income strata of the community it serves. Employees develop greater empathy for and awareness of their customers in ways that stand in stark contrast to common perceptions of the subprime used-car industry as one that preys on a vulnerable population.

Reflecting in Action

Reflecting involves representing distinct group perspectives and facilitating knowledge exchange across groups to understand boundaries and foster intergroup respect. Each group shares an image of its values, needs, hopes, fears, and priorities with the other. In the process of doing this, both groups begin to understand the boundary between them and accept both differences and similarities between the two groups. When competing or opposing groups develop greater positive regard for each other, greater direction, alignment, and commitment can develop between them. Below are several tactics that you can use to engage in the practice of reflecting. We recommend that groups begin by learning about one another, then uncover deep differences, and finally begin to identify commonalities.

Reflecting Tactic 1: Create Opportunities for Groups to Listen and Learn about One Another

Leaders at DriveTime created a program that allowed their employees to partner externally with elementary schools that service at-risk students to serve the community and better understand and empathize with its lower-income customers. Members of one group (DriveTime employees) were able to get out of the office and into the schools to learn about another group (their customer community). When such opportunities for learning about other groups are offered, intergroup respect can be enhanced and strengthened.

There are many ways you can enable groups within your organization to listen and learn across boundaries. Create opportunities for your team to learn about other functions, regions, and product lines by attending their communication sessions, reading postings on their intranet sites, and seeking to understand their strategic goals and priorities. Shadowing, job rotation, and site visits encourage people to experience life in the organization from a different vantage point. Enabling members of your team to stay an extra day during an international business trip creates opportunities to learn about the local customers and culture. Inviting leaders from other groups to talk with your team creates the space to explore potential synergies that allow both groups to be more successful. Each of these steps will foster greater awareness about other groups and the potential collaborative opportunities between them. These types of experiences can be applied systematically in ways that enable you, your teams, and your organization as a whole to develop capabilities for leading across boundaries.

Reflecting Tactic 2: Ask Powerful Questions to Uncover Deep Differences

Asking powerful questions can uncover the root of the challenges groups face when attempting to work together: the values, assumptions, perceptions, and emotions that often form a wedge that leads to conflict rather than collaboration. Recognizing visible surface-level differences between groups is relatively easy, but deep-level differences that are not always evident but still get in the way of collaboration must be uprooted carefully. By asking powerful questions and encouraging groups to ask questions of one another, you create space for groups to reveal their deep-level differences.

As CCL colleagues Chuck Palus and David Horth describe in their book *The Leader's Edge*, there are three characteristics that typically distinguish powerful questions: They invite exploration, resist easy answers, and invoke strong passions.[12] All three of these attributes are critical for fostering intergroup respect by understanding perspectives and sharing experiences across boundaries.

Here are some examples to get you started. If there are two groups in the room, try asking the members of each group one or more of the following questions:

- What values are guiding your thinking? What is one value you are unwilling to give up? What is a value that you believe both groups share?
- What is an assumption that you hold about the other group? What is the source of this assumption? How could you further test or explore this assumption?
- What does your group say about the other group? What do you believe they say about your group?
- What is something about your group that the other group does not know? What is something you'd like to know about them?
- What is a concern you have in working with one another? What is an aspiration?

Powerful questions such as these help bring out the "elephant in the room." They create an opening for groups to reveal and talk about the differences that create tension and prevent collaboration but are not being discussed. Powerful questions allow deep identity differences to surface. As a result, groups may develop a new awareness not only of the nature of their differences but also of their source—why these deep differences exist and why they matter so much to the groups involved. Or they may realize that certain assumptions they hold about one another are off base. Or they may learn something new about one another that builds positive regard between them. The next time you're in a meeting and sense there's an unspoken deep divide between groups, ask a powerful question. Profound new insights probably will emerge.

Reflecting Tactic 3: Let Commonalities Emerge from Differences

Differences between groups tend to stand out, but what about the commonalities? Rick Givens was able to find common values between himself and the illegal immigrants residing in Chatham County during his visit to Mexico. Rick discovered that like himself and like many of his friends, the Mexican immigrants were motivated by the desire to improve the lives of their families. They were doing what they thought they had to do to give their children a good life. Rick returned to North Carolina committed to helping others see what he saw in Mexico: Love for family was a guiding force for the Latinos coming to Chatham County, just as it is for families that have lived in the county for generations.

Rick was genuinely surprised by finding that he shared some deeply held values and beliefs with the illegal immigrants he previously felt were a threat to his family's well-being. By "looking again," he realized that at the heart of the issue, both sides were acting out of love for family. What often happens when groups begin to attempt to understand one another is that they realize they have much more in common than they originally thought. Digging into and understanding differences often uncovers the similarities that lie underneath. Thus, it is important to create opportunities for groups to learn about the ways in which they view and experience the world differently and to continue to dig deeper to uncover the values and perspectives they share.

In working with leaders in the classroom, both of us have used an exercise in which we employ some version of the identity circle you created in Chapter 2 that asked you to reflect on a single question: Who are you? After completing this activity, we ask people to find someone they believe is different from them and talk about their identity. This often helps participants uncover their similarities and realize that they have more in common than originally thought. In fact, we think it is important to start with a discussion of differences and then allow the conversation naturally to uncover similarities. If you jump into looking for commonalities too quickly, you may miss them. It is only through sharing differences that we realize they are actually smaller than the aspects of identity that we share.

Reflecting Tactic 4: Counteract the Tendency for Groups to Want to Make Them Like Us

Working together across boundaries requires accepting the differences that separate groups. However, energy and resources are wasted when a group tries to collaborate with another group by attempting to make Them more like Us. As you know after having read the chapters on identity and Great Divides, this almost always backfires. Groups just dig in their heels. Therefore, to accomplish reflecting, it is important to encourage groups to accept one another and focus on change from within.

Our story about Rick Givens and Chatham County is a great example of this. Rick initially focused all his energy on trying to change or deport the illegal immigrants. He later realized that this was futile and that the best use of his time and energy was to try to change Chatham County to make it a better place for the immigrants to live and be productive and contributing citizens. With John Herrera's help and insight, Rick was able to see how what he observed in Mexico played out at home in North Carolina. For example, they witnessed the common practice of a police officer being offered a bribe in Mexico. John was able to help Rick see that that was why the Latinos in Chatham County were distrustful of law enforcement officers. Through these experiences and John's interpretation of what they were seeing in Mexico, Rick was able to understand and then accept the differences between the two cultures. Once Rick focused his energy on accepting the other group rather than trying to change it, both groups were able to work together collaboratively to better the community for all.

Organizations spend a great deal of resources to persuade customers, clients, and organizational members to act in a certain way. Yet there is a line that gets crossed when one group attempts or hopes to change the core identity of another. Remember that identity is not about *what* we do or *how* we do it, but *who* we are. Asking groups to abandon important aspects of who they are will only create larger divides when groups feel threatened. When engaged in the practice of reflecting, counteract this tendency in yourself and others by encouraging groups to accept the values, needs, and viewpoints of one another.

Reflecting Tactic 5: Slow Groups Down to Speed Them Up

Though counterintuitive in an ever-faster world, slowing groups down for learning, perspective taking, and knowledge exchange is essential. Time-outs and routine breaks enable groups to make sense of the complexity of the tasks they face.

Consider an example from Abrasive Technology Inc. (ATI), a manufacturing organization you'll learn more about in Chapter 9. In changing from a functional to a process-centered organization, ATI identified "learning" as a critical organization-wide competency. Cross-functional teams were empowered to stop any manufacturing operation on the spot to gain a better understanding of the process and ask questions of one another. Time was provided for real-time learning across boundaries of functional experience and expertise. ATI discovered that even though time may have been lost on the front end as operations slowed to allow learning to occur, this translated into greater speed down the road. Slowing down helped the teams reduce missteps and rework by taking the time needed to understand differences in assumptions, beliefs, and even work styles across functional groups.

You can help groups engage in perspective taking and knowledge exchange by avoiding the temptation to move to problem solving or a shared mode of operation too quickly. Instead, build time into the process to engage in dialogue with the goal of understanding different points of view, perspectives, and ways of operating. Be a role model and encourage others to uncover facts, assumptions, and emotions. Ask groups to listen actively and accept the idea that underlying beliefs have merit and validity on all sides. By slowing down and enabling groups to take a more complete look at the situation, you'll uncover new alternatives and better ideas to speed up and solve a problem. In so doing, you'll foster greater awareness and positive regard between groups as they learn to appreciate their distinct knowledge and expertise.

The Leader's Role in Reflecting

In playing the role of a reflector, your job is to enable groups to see and understand the needs, goals, values, work styles, preferences, expertise, and experiences of other groups. By representing distinct perspectives and facilitating knowledge exchange across groups, you foster intergroup respect. Rick Givens and John Herrera both became dedicated to their role as reflectors in helping the Latino and Anglo Chatham County residents better understand one another. As a result, both men played an important role in forever changing the relationship between immigrants and nonimmigrants in Chatham County.

Rick returned from Mexico a changed man. He worked hard to help other community leaders see the challenges faced by the Latino community and understand how valuable it would be for the entire community to work together to integrate all its members. John told us that Rick's presence as a reflector was significant: "It takes someone who sounds, looks, and acts like one of them to change things for the better."

As we see in Rick and John, to play the role of reflector, you become the source that transmits or casts an image of one group to another. Like a mirror, you must reflect and represent the image or identity of one group to another. This means that you must clarify for yourself the similarities and differences between groups. You will have to start by capturing the image and identity of each group, free from judgment and bias. Only then can you accurately share the knowledge, perspectives, and experiences of each group.

Caution: The Pitfall of Reflecting

A pitfall in reflecting is that inevitably there will be times when you belong to or are perceived to belong to one of the groups you are attempting to help other groups understand. Thus, no matter how unbiased you are in your thoughts and behaviors, you will be seen as one of Them. Your own identity and membership in one of the groups prevent you from being perceived as an impartial outsider who can see each side of the boundary as equally valid and neither group as representing the "wrong" viewpoint. Because there is little you can do in these instances (particularly when it involves an identity you cannot change, such as your race or gender), your best option may be to engage another leader who is seen as an impartial outsider by all the groups involved.

Your role as a reflector isn't easy. Research tells us that people naturally tend to view different groups in rigid and oversimplified ways.[13] For example, it is easy for us to see that not everyone within our own group thinks or acts the same way. But we don't have this flexible view of other groups. We tend to think that They all act and think alike. We focus on how the other group is different and exaggerate those differences. This makes for a black-and-white view of the world.

To lead across boundaries, you will have to resist this urge to oversimplify and move beyond looking at the world as Us versus Them.[14] Rather than viewing one group as right and the other as wrong, you'll need to stretch to open your mind to other possibilities, many ways of accomplishing the same goal, and the reality that many viewpoints can be valid at the same time. This means seeing the world as filled with mostly shades of gray, with few instances in which things are black and white. Richard Webster, current sheriff of Chatham County, sums up this reality as follows:[15] "People tend to look at immigration as black or white. But it's about 1 percent black and 1 percent white, with 98 shades of gray in between." Rick Givens and John Herrera would agree. Reflecting requires that you make a concerted effort to remain flexible enough to understand and then appreciate the differences that surface when boundaries between groups collide. When groups understand the boundary that exists between them, they are able to build intergroup respect, the next step needed to forge common ground at the nexus between groups (see Table 5.1).

Reflecting and Your Nexus Challenge

Representing distinct perspectives and facilitating knowledge exchange across groups help foster intergroup respect. The questions below will help you apply the practice of reflecting to your unique Nexus Challenge as well as other challenges and opportunities you face in managing boundaries across groups.

Discern: Assessing the Current State

Reflecting creates understanding of boundaries to foster intergroup respect. On a scale of 1 to 10 (where 10 is the highest), how would you rate your team or organization on intergroup respect?

Intergroup respect increases the more the following is true:

- Group members understand the similarities and differences that exist between groups.
- Similarities and differences in values, perspectives, backgrounds, and beliefs are honored.
- Groups treat one another with positive regard.

Table 5.1 Reflecting Summary

Definition What is reflecting?	Represent distinct perspectives and facilitate knowledge exchange across groups to *understand boundaries and foster intergroup respect.*
Rationale Why does reflecting work?	In *reflecting*, boundaries are clarified and further defined through a deeper understanding of the other groups. It involves sensitizing each group to the others' needs, values, beliefs, and preferences. Once group members feel safe and secure with their own group identity, they can begin to identify both the similarities and differences that exist across groups. Reflecting uncovers the differences that separate groups, but also the similarities upon which common ground may be forged.
Tactics How is the practice to be accomplished?	1. Create opportunities for groups to listen and learn about one another. Role-model and encourage others to actively seek out ways to learn more about other groups. 2. Ask powerful questions to uncover deep differences. Seek answers to powerful questions to better understand why deep-rooted identity differences exist and why they matter so much to those involved. 3. Let commonalities emerge from differences. Once differences are revealed, also allow similarities to be uncovered so that common aspects of identity are revealed as well. 4. Counteract the tendency for groups to want to make Them like Us. Encourage groups to accept one another rather than expending wasted energy to change the other. 5. Slow groups down to speed them up. Encourage groups to slow down and examine all sides of an issue, and engage in perspective taking and knowledge exchange to bring facts, assumptions, and emotions to the surface.
Outcome What is the result?	*Intergroup respect*—the state of intergroup awareness and positive regard that develops when groups understand their similarities and differences.

Reflect: Exploring New Approaches

How can you create an environment where groups share their unique perspectives, knowledge, and expertise?

As a reflector, you become the source that transmits or casts an image of one group to another, just as a mirror reflects an image. How can you reflect and represent the image or identity of one group to another in your workplace?

Perspective taking is a critical skill required to be an effective reflector. How can you engage in experiences that would allow you to step outside your comfort zone and see the world from a very different perspective or better understand a group that is quite different from your own?

Apply: Taking Action

What is one idea, tactic, or new insight you've learned about reflecting that you could apply to your Nexus Challenge?

PART 3

FORGING COMMON GROUND

Human beings have survived and flourished throughout history by cooperating and collaborating. History tells us that at the heart of any effective organization, community, or society there are people and groups that come together to accomplish something larger or greater than what they could have accomplished alone. Today, advancing technology, changing global demographics, and expanding globalization have increased radically the potential of human collaboration in all corners of your organization and the world. Yet this shifting leadership landscape has dramatically increased the potential for peril. Groups previously separated now collide and intersect on a daily basis.

In Part 3, we introduce the next two leadership practices—connecting and mobilizing—that make it possible for you to forge common ground across vertical, horizontal, stakeholder, demographic, and geographic boundaries. Distinct from buffering and reflecting, these practices involve drawing attention away from intergroup differences and toward what groups have in common. Recall that the universal human need for differentiation and uniqueness is balanced by an equally powerful need for integration and belonging. Indeed, a central organizing principle of human relationships throughout history—in corporations and communities—is enabling groups to identify with a common We rather than a divided Us versus Them. What if your organization was a place of trust, mutual confidence, and belonging across organizational levels and functions, as well as between different demographic and stakeholder groups? Here we'll continue our journey up the spiral by describing two practices that will enable you to tap into the powerful human need to be part of something larger than oneself.

Specifically, Chapter 6 focuses on the practice of *connecting* to suspend boundaries between groups. Connectors link people and bridge divided groups to build intergroup trust. To see connecting in action, we'll go to Europe and describe how Daniel Sutton successfully led a cross-sector task force to develop a new, more sustainable plan for a city.

Chapter 7 looks at the practice of *mobilizing* to reframe boundaries between groups. Mobilizers craft common purpose and shared identity to develop intergroup community. We'll see how leaders at Lenovo are bridging boundaries between East and West to create an integrated and innovative global computer company. Together, connecting and mobilizing enable you to forge common ground that binds groups together to solve problems, drive innovation, and create positively transformative results (see Figure P3.1).

Figure P3.1 Forging common ground.

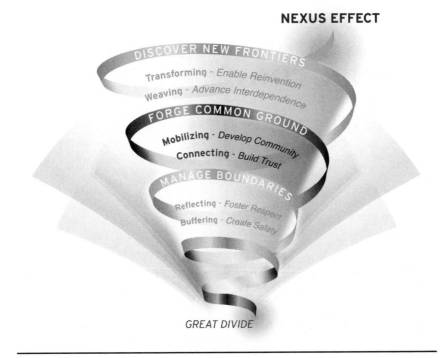

CHAPTER 6

CONNECTING: BUILDING TRUST

The opportunity that Daniel Sutton had been waiting for finally fell into his lap. As the European director of corporate social responsibility (CSR) for a global oil and energy company, Daniel, a sanguine yet pragmatic executive, had led a number of successful CSR initiatives in the past.[1] Yet there was always something that bothered him. The initiatives he led were often internally focused and involved primarily in-house participation. He felt that although those efforts had a positive impact, much more could be accomplished through an external partnership that engaged multiple stakeholder groups. This opportunity arrived the day he received an invitation from his city to lead a strategic cross-sector task force. The city's charter called for the creation of a plan that would reduce its greenhouse gas emissions 30 percent by 2020 and pave the way for achieving carbon-neutral status by 2050.

Upon accepting the role, Daniel's first order of business was to convene representatives from the three key stakeholder groups—energy executives, environmentalists, and civil/government leaders—for an introductory meeting at his corporate office. At the onset of the meeting, Daniel began by laying out the group charter: "We have been given a unique opportunity to bring together our broad-ranging expertise to create a new collective vision for our city." Upon opening things up for comments, however, Daniel quickly realized that a collective vision was nowhere in sight. He knew there were feelings of mistrust: Two years earlier the three groups had attempted to work on a shared initiative that failed miserably. Each side was not able to get beyond its individual interests. Yet Daniel was caught totally off guard by the openly hostile remarks that followed. One of the environmentalists remarked, "How could we even begin to think about what is needed down there on the streets when we're sitting up here in this wood-paneled, gilded executive conference room?" One of the energy executives retorted, "Actually, we are up here making decisions while the politicians among us sit around and just talk about making decisions." The government officials, who had been silent until then, now felt compelled to speak. One remarked, "Well, I'm proud of the fact that we create new policy and move our city forward instead of focusing solely on protesting initiatives like our environmentalist friends have been known to do."

Taking a walk that evening, Daniel realized that to bridge the long-standing divisions between the groups, he was going to have to try a different approach. Looking up at the rising moon, he realized that he needed to help build personal relationships to enable the task force members to get beyond the labels of "politician" and "oil executive." He decided that his next move would be to organize an invitational weekend retreat at a country lodge outside the city center.

A couple of weeks later, as Daniel boarded a bus to the countryside for a retreat with the three groups, he noted how the members of each group cloistered themselves in the back, middle, and front of the bus. Daniel knew he had his work cut out for him. Yet his goal was clear: to allow the task force members to get to know one another on an individual basis. Upon arriving at the destination, Daniel handed out a slip of paper with text on both sides. On one side there were room assignments in which he purposefully paired people from different stakeholder groups, such as an executive and an environmentalist, to share a room. On the other side there were three questions: "What is one your fondest childhood memories of being outside in nature? What is the source of your passion concerning environmental sustainability? What is something you have in common with each task force member?" As they all prepared to check in to their rooms, Daniel asked them to reconvene in ten minutes with their hiking shoes on. They were going to take a long walk.

Heading out into the midday sun, Daniel encouraged people to have conversations to share their responses to the three questions they had received in the hotel. Not surprisingly, three discussion groups formed: the environmentalists, executives, and politicians. Daniel just kept walking. Finally, Margaret, the president of a nonprofit environmental agency, "broke ranks" and struck up a conversation with Bob, a senior oil executive. They talked about their memorable experiences in nature. They discussed their passion for reimagining modern transportation. In the discussion, they discovered something they had in common. Margaret and Bob both had read an intriguing article about how a public-private partnership could be utilized to create a network of hydrogen fueling stations. As they walked farther, they began brainstorming about how such a partnership could be formed in their city. This was just the first of many cross-sector conversations that took place during that long walk as well as throughout the weekend. On the bus ride back to the city, Daniel felt confident his goal had been accomplished. Members from the three groups were scattered throughout the bus, with wallets and cell phones being passed about to share photos of the family members they were returning home to.

In the weeks that followed, Daniel built upon this experience to encourage cross-group relationships. He held weekly face-to-face meetings involving all the task force members. Rather than hold each meeting at his corporate office, they rotated locations throughout the city. An online virtual space was created to allow members easy access to one another for questions or suggestions. Informal evening get-togethers were held at local restaurants and coffee shops. One weekend, a group member organized an outdoor cookout, inviting family members to attend for a day of feasting, followed, of course, by a walk in the park. At each of those meetings and events, Daniel ensured that the conversations stayed focused on the task at hand yet included time for sharing personal experiences.

Differing intergroup perspectives and disagreements remained present throughout their tenure, yet a level of friendship and trust had been created to get the participants through the rough patches. As the task force prepared to present its plan to the city, the members reflected on how far they had come since the initial meeting in the executive conference room. Through Daniel's efforts to build trust by suspending boundaries, the environmentalist, energy executive, and government groups came to value the creative tensions between them. This led to some of the most innovative solutions in what they collectively agreed was a transformative plan for their city.

The Practice of Connecting

In leading the cross-sector task force, Daniel utilized the leadership practice of connecting. After their initial conflict-ridden meeting in the executive conference room, Daniel realized that just "bringing groups together" wasn't going to work, and so he took a different course. He created a neutral space that enabled the environmentalists, energy executives, and government officials to get to know one another as individuals. While walking out in the countryside, the various task force members began to have very different conversations. Their interactions were person-based rather than group-based. For the first time, they were able to see beyond their differences and focus on what they had in common. Over time, they developed mutual confidence and integrity in their words and actions. Daniel successfully suspended boundaries that were getting in the way.

Business, as well as any community undertaking, is about the creation of collaborative, trust-based relationships. Thus, you and the leaders throughout your organization are in the business of building relationships. Yet in today's shifting leadership landscape, there is a striking difference. In the past, leaders often had the luxury of building trust *within* an intact team or group in which the team members largely had a common purpose, background, and set of values—a common identity. Today, leaders like Daniel must find new ways to build networks of mutual trust *across* disparate groups and teams that often have competing or conflicting group interests.

What is your Nexus Challenge? Breaking down silos between functions? Working in more closely with suppliers or vendors? Flattening organizational hierarchy? Delivering results in a matrixed structure? Whatever your challenge, today you are required to do more than build trust with the individuals within your team. You also must build strong, trusting, and confidence-based relationships across the many groups and teams that constitute your organization.

Suspending Boundaries

The practice of connecting seeks to forge relationships by creating person-to-person linkages rather than group-to-group linkages. As illustrated in Figure 6.1, connecting occurs when groups "step outside" their group identities and "step inside" a neutral zone where

Figure 6.1 Connecting.

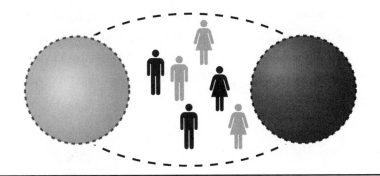

people can interact with one another as individuals. When people step outside their group boundaries, they suspend, or put on hold, their identity differences, even if only for a limited time. What happens is that over time and sustained interaction, the boundaries that created rigid borders between groups begin to fade into the background. People learn to set aside their group differences and make connections on the basis of their individual similarities. The result is intergroup trust: *a state of mutual confidence and integrity that develops when boundaries are suspended and new relationships are built.* Building intergroup trust through the practice of connecting is the third step toward the Nexus Effect. With this step in place, groups can create a shared direction, common expectations regarding the coordination of tasks, and mutual confidence that each group is committed to the interests and well-being of others.

Research conducted over the last several decades confirms that intergroup contact is one of the most powerful approaches to breaking down intergroup boundaries.[2] Recall the incredible findings of the Robbers Cave study conducted with 22 eleven-year-old boys. At first it appeared as though the Eagles and the Rattlers were destined to a summer as warring tribes. Yet when the boys were given opportunities to work together to achieve a shared goal, their distinction as members of competing groups fell into the background and their commonalities as 11-year-old boys rose to the foreground.

Intergroup contact provides an opportunity to learn about different people. In the process, we begin to deemphasize or "decategorize" group boundaries and instead emphasize individual relationships.[3] As we learn more about other groups, the level of distrust decreases and the level of trust increases. What happens is that we begin to see people outside our group as individuals with similar needs, values, hopes, and dreams and over time view them as more similar than different. Our view of what constitutes Us becomes larger to include people who once were considered Them. Mutual confidence expands as each group develops confidence that other groups will consider its interests. Integrity also develops as relationships are characterized by increasing levels of candor and sincerity. Your role as a connector is to create an environment in which people can interact as unique individuals rather than members of distinct groups. In light of the central role that identity plays in human relationships, this is often easier said than done.

Consider the case of *Mr. Yamada*, a savvy and gregarious Japanese project manager in Hong Kong whose job required him to work for short stints in countries throughout the Asia Pacific region.[4] His role required that he quickly build productive and task-oriented cross-national teams in order to launch new information technology (IT) initiatives. In sharing one of his success stories, Yamada spoke about how he built relationships while on assignment in Korea. When he organized regular after-work events for his team members from Australia, Indonesia, Japan, Korea, and New Zealand, the team members discovered that the cultural stereotypes they held did not apply to the other members of the team. In providing space for personal relationships to develop, Yamada was able to build the level of trust needed to launch IT projects in a timely fashion.

Yamada went on to share another story, one that almost had a very different outcome. In launching a new project out of Hong Kong, he again attempted to link people by organizing after-work activities. This time his efforts were met with resistance. He found that though his expatriate colleagues from Europe enjoyed going to an Irish pub, his local Chinese colleagues preferred a karaoke bar.

Those differences were reinforced in the workplace. Project delays, work-arounds, and behind-the-scenes within-group conversations were the norm. The actual technical work was not the problem. The problem, according to Yamada, was that the different national groups were never able to get along: "It was a clash of civilizations between East and West ... and I found myself stuck in the middle." Ultimately, Yamada found an elegant solution. Hong Kong is a city blessed with some of the finest cuisine from all corners of the globe. By organizing weekly "Dine around the World" events, Yamada used food as a medium to develop personal relationships across different cultures; this in turn created a more positive and trusting work environment back in the office.

Connecting in Action

The practice of connecting enables you to create a neutral zone where people can interact as unique individuals rather than members of distinct groups. As a boundary spanning leader, you can use a number of different connecting tactics to link people to build trust.

Connecting Tactic 1: Meet in a Neutral Zone

To suspend boundaries between groups, you need to take into account the physical environment. We use the concept of a neutral zone to represent a location, environment, or space that is welcoming to groups on all sides of a divide. When Daniel held the initial cross-sector task force meeting in the conference room of his corporate office, it immediately put the other two stakeholder groups on edge. The lavish furnishings and use of rare tropical woods made the environmentalists feel uneasy, and the high-rise view evoked feelings of envy from several of the politicians who generally were forced to endure dimly lit rooms and concrete walls. Clearly, the conference room was perceived as the "home turf" of the energy executives. As with an out-of-town team entering its competitor's home stadium, the meeting space served to accentuate differences rather than help them fade into the background.

Fortunately, the atmosphere altered dramatically when Daniel changed the location and organized the weekend retreat in the country. The off-site location served as a neutral zone, or "third space."[5] The outdoors served to remind the task force members visually and physically why they were called together: to create a more sustainable vision for their city. As such, it became a fertile place for cross-boundary collaboration to begin to take root.

Connecting Tactic 2: Create Attractor Spaces

Organizations are full of physical boundaries separating groups, functions, levels, and divisions. In most office buildings, floors divide employees by level, walls separate people by function, corridors serve to "funnel" groups into their designated locations, and complex security procedures keep unwanted people out. Of course, physical boundaries in the work environment serve a worthwhile purpose in placing groups of people with similar work responsibilities in close proximity. Yet they often get in the way of groups that need to be collaborating. To balance these inevitable tensions, you need to create "attractor" spaces that encourage serendipitous cross-boundary relationships to develop.

Take the Googleplex, Google's headquarters in Mountain View, California.[6] Everything from the entry-level "town square" to the "village library" beckons employees to leave their desks and mingle. Throughout the building, floors are organized into flexible "neighborhoods" arranged by recognizable "landmarks": the shared community spaces that make it easy for people to meet across neighborhoods. Employees eat for free in an open cafeteria with a giant white board to capture ideas from emergent conversations. Granted, few of us have the ability to create a Googleplex, but the lessons from Google are still relevant. If you want to break down borders and develop close, trusting relationships, you need to create spaces and nooks that invite spontaneous, boundary-spanning conversations.

How to Create Shared Community Spaces

To develop attractor spaces in which person-to-person relationships can be formed across boundaries, you can create the following:

- "Creativity labs" where people can go for brainstorming, dialogue, problem solving, and serious play
- Well-equipped "war rooms" for a task team to construct maps, track progress, and hold strategy meetings
- Centrally located cafés and dining spaces with various size tables and comfortable chairs that bring people together across the organization to talk about the latest news
- "Serendipity areas" such as reading rooms, outdoor patios, and lounges that invite people to leave their desks and mingle[7]

Connecting Tactic 3: Utilize Communication Technologies to Link People Together

In the span of a few short years, company intranet sites and virtual collaboration technologies have gone from being the exception to being the norm. Similarly, networking environments such as LinkedIn, Facebook, and Twitter have exploded on the scene. By themselves, these technologies may serve only to create borders as like-minded groups create their own virtual worlds. MIT Media Lab founder Nicholas Negroponte popularized the term "the Daily Me"[8] to capture the human tendency to visit Internet spaces that are "like us" and avoid sites that are "like them," which reinforce our way of looking at the world. You can counteract this tendency and use the same technologies to suspend boundaries and create new connections instead of fortifying borders.

In using workplace communication and networking tools, you can encourage team members to share *both* professional and personal information. For example, your company Yellow Pages or online team profiles provide an ideal place for sharing person-to-person information. Odds are that disparate team members will check out these profiles with predetermined images in their minds that are based on typical group categories such as "finance guy," "admin assistant," "old-timer," and "tech geek." Yet the odds also suggest that aspects of this image will fall apart when team members view the individual profiles, noting hobbies, interests, unique skills, favorite movies, books, food, and the like.

After the weekend retreat, Daniel asked the task force members to upload their personal and professional profiles to a shared networking space. Those pages became an important resource not only for team members to know who to tap for areas of expertise but also for members to learn more about one another as unique individuals.

Connecting Tactic 4: Build Leadership Networks

Both formal and informal events that take place during work hours are one of the easiest yet least effectively utilized tactics to link people and bridge divided groups proactively. On the positive side, most organizations have any number of work-based events to bring wide-ranging groups together: an annual corporate event, a celebration of an important organizational milestone, and internal brown-bag lunches or colloquiums, as well as informal meetings and get-togethers. On the negative side, these events often do little or no good in building trust-based relationships across boundaries.

We've all experienced the awkward feeling that arises when different groups share a collective space yet stand at opposite ends of the room or there is a company dinner at which the marketing group sits at one table, finance at another, and logistics at yet another. As the old saying goes, birds of a feather flock together. Just bringing groups together is not sufficient. To build trust and foster collaboration, you need to link people together thoughtfully and systematically to span relationships across boundaries. Daniel successfully accomplished this at the weekend retreat by pairing individuals from different stakeholder groups to share a room as well as by asking the task force members to find something they had in common with every other person while taking a walk in the country.

Alternatively, consider the high-tech approach used by a large bank that wanted to create a more collaborative horizontal network of leaders to service client needs. As a colleague explained to us, each banker was given an electronic name tag at a daylong conference that could communicate with every other tag in the room. The name tags stored key information about each person, such as areas of expertise and client listings. When a banker passed by someone he or she didn't know and that person happened to have a similar client contact, the tags would emit a signal and the contact name would appear on a small display screen on their tags. By proactively creating an environment for connections to develop, the firm was able to build relationships between bankers to service client needs.

Connecting Tactic 5: Mix It Up Outside the Office

Last but not least, building relationships outside the office is another timeless approach. The formality of established work protocols, status hierarchies, and process routines can be left behind, allowing more informal relationships to develop. As in the tactic immediately above, your role is to serve as the connector. A social services agency in Asia, for example, uses Friday afternoon soccer matches as a way for Chinese and Malay employees and volunteers to bond over a common passion. The agency's president and management team members are regular participants and actively encourage conversation and interaction between individuals in the two groups. Further, senior leaders rotate as "captains" for each match and take conscious but subtle steps to ensure that each team includes a mix of both ethnic groups. On occasion, the senior leaders get everyone together after the game for a discussion about how people worked together on the field and how that knowledge could be applied to the workplace. Rather than focus on ethnic or religious differences that might separate them, these soccer matches encouraged Chinese and Malay staff and volunteers to interact with one another as unique individuals.

The Leader's Role in Connecting

To enact the practice of connecting, your role is to link people and bridge divided groups. As humans, we are built from birth to create relationships with others. Yet we are also designed to quickly discern friend from foe and Us from Them. As a connector, your role is to take advantage of the natural human capacity to create positive and collaborative relationships while minimizing the potential for destructive divides. Connectors bridge otherwise disconnected groups of people, creating networks of trust-based relationships across boundaries within organizations.

You might assume that the more relationships you foster, the better the performance you can draw from teams and groups. Conventional wisdom says bigger networks are better. In fact, what researchers have found is that larger networks often lead to *decreased* rather than *increased* performance and productivity. What actually matters is not the size but the quality and attributes of the network. Rob Cross, a leading expert in the area of organizational network analysis, demonstrates that the highest-performing leaders tend to share three important characteristics: They forge ties that bridge groups both inside and outside their organization, invest in relationships that cross boundaries, and create trusting, high-quality relationships, not just big networks.[9] Below we describe how each of these three characteristics offers new insights in terms of how you can be a skillful connector.

First, connectors forge ties. The connector's role is to bridge disconnected or fragmented groups, including hierarchical levels, functional areas, external stakeholders, and groups divided by demographic differences or physical distance. In the story of Daniel Sutton, for example, Daniel realized that to have a large-scale impact, he needed to position himself within a network that extended beyond his organization's borders. Landing the assignment to lead the cross-functional task force gave him that opportunity. Connectors like Daniel seek projects, roles, and opportunities that enable them to bring groups together beyond the boxes and lines of the organizational chart.

Second, connectors actively and visibly develop relationships across boundaries. In doing this, you create an environment for continuous learning both for yourself and for the teams you lead. To create this environment, you need to fight off the natural tendency to spend a disproportionate amount of time at work—and outside work—with colleagues just like yourself. Instead, you should strive to create a balanced network with people of different backgrounds and sources of expertise who work in different parts of the organization. In the case of Mr. Yamada, for example, it would have been completely natural for him to spend his social time outside of work with the other Japanese nationals on the team. Yet Yamada made concerted efforts to invite his colleagues from any number of different countries to join him. In visibly taking the time and effort to reach across boundaries, Yamada created a space for his colleagues to follow suit.

Finally, connectors forge ties that are anchored in strong relationships. Rather than create large networks grounded in superficial behaviors, we encourage you to spend time growing authentic, trust-based relationships. Yamada and Daniel excelled at connecting people across divides not by force of personality, though both leaders had strong interpersonal skills. Instead, they invested time and effort to create neutral zones where people could get to know one another as unique individuals, not just members of unique groups. For Yamada and Daniel, nurturing and cultivating relationships was not seen as an aside but as a central aspect of leadership.

Caution: The Pitfall of Connecting

A pitfall of connecting that requires you to take caution is that the members of one group may feel a sense of threat or resistance when brought into contact with the members of another group. If there is a history of tension, conflict, or mistrust between groups, you could unwittingly spark a Great Divide rather than achieve your intended outcome of building relationships.

In the Yamada story, for example, the expatriate workers enjoyed going to the Irish pub because it reconnected them to their European identity, just as the Chinese locals valued their cultural singing tradition. Had Yamada required the Europeans to sing karaoke or the Chinese to cheer for the favored rugby team at the pub, it most likely would have been a recipe for disaster. Instead, he organized weekly "Dine around the World" events at various ethnic restaurants throughout Hong Kong. By thoughtfully creating a neutral zone and employing patience and persistence, Yamada created a space for productive boundary spanning relationships to develop.

You too can serve as a connector between groups in your organization or broader community. You too can find ways to link people, bridge divided groups, and build intergroup trust. As is the case in developing any type of human relationship, this is a practice that requires space, patience, and time. As we saw with Daniel and the task force, connecting is not a quick fix but a practice that must be nurtured and cultivated over time. With each new interaction, cross-boundary contact feels less foreign and more familiar. Boundaries slowly but surely begin to be erased and fade into the background. You will certainly experience setbacks along the way, but you also will make systematic progress. You need to remember that the boundaries that have kept groups apart in your organization have been intact for years, sometimes decades. Yet with patience and persistence, you can play a crucial role in breaking down those boundaries and building strong, trusting relationships (see Table 6.1).

Connecting and Your Nexus Challenge

Linking people and forging relationships across boundaries is essential for building intergroup trust. The questions below will help you apply the practice of connecting to your unique Nexus Challenge as well as other challenges and opportunities you face in forging common ground between groups.

Discern: Assessing the Current State

Connecting suspends boundaries to build intergroup trust. On a scale of 1 to 10 (where 10 is the highest), how would you rate your team or organization on intergroup trust?

Intergroup trust increases the more the following is true:

- Strong person-to-person relationships exist across groups.
- There is mutual confidence between groups; each group is confident that the other will consider its needs, values, and interests.
- There is integrity between groups; interaction across groups is characterized by candor and sincerity.

Table 6.1 Connecting Summary

Definition What is connecting?	Link people and bridge divided groups to *suspend boundaries and build intergroup trust.*
Rationale Why does connecting work?	With *connecting,* groups "step outside" their group boundaries, creating a neutral zone for group members to interact as individuals. People begin to realize they are not as different as they once thought. As they learn more about one another, negative beliefs, feelings, and behaviors about group distinctions are replaced by positive beliefs, feelings, and behaviors about what group members share in common.
Tactics How is the practice to be accomplished?	1. Meet in a neutral zone—a location, environment or space that is welcoming to all groups. 2. Create attractor spaces—informal conversation nooks, serendipity areas, cafes, or creativity labs that invite boundary-spanning conversations. 3. Utilize communication technologies to link people together. Create online environments that foster person-to-person relationship building across boundaries. 4. Build leadership networks. Use organizational events (i.e., colloquiums, brown-bags, office celebration, annual events) to bridge disconnected people that need to be working together. 5. Mix it up informally outside the office. Get groups away from formal office protocols, status hierarchies, and process routines and mix it up outside the office.
Outcome What is the result?	*Intergroup trust*—the state of mutual confidence and intergroup integrity that develops when boundaries are *suspended* and new relationships are built.

Reflect: Exploring New Approaches

How can you more actively serve as a "bridge" to connect people or divided groups in your organization?

As the expression goes, birds of a feather tend to flock together. How can you balance this natural tendency by taking steps to develop more trusting relationships with people from widely different backgrounds, expertise, and roles?

Who is someone you need to better reach across a boundary and connect with? How can you take steps to develop a deeper, more trusting relationship with this individual?

Apply: Taking Action

What is one idea, tactic, or new insight you've learned about connecting that you could apply to your Nexus Challenge?

CHAPTER 7

MOBILIZING: DEVELOPING COMMUNITY

The global business news wires buzzed: "Mainland Chinese Company Acquires American Icon." History was made in 2005 when the Chinese computer company Lenovo announced that it had purchased IBM's global personal computer operation.[1, 2] It was the first mainland Chinese acquisition of a major American brand, and the news rippled around the world. Senior executives in the new merged company were keenly aware of the disruption at Hewlett-Packard after it purchased Compaq several years earlier. Total sales dropped as the two brands siphoned each other's sales, and there was incessant fighting between the two divisions. In the early days after the IBM deal, similar clashes began bubbling up in the newly merged company. Tense conference calls between Chinese and American executives were frequent. Tough decisions regarding market strategy alienated certain groups. Salary differentials became a point of contention, and a major backlash occurred when several popular executives were let go.

Beyond attempting to merge and streamline product lines, Lenovo leaders had an even more challenging question to address: How were they going to lead at the crossroads of two distinct organizational and national cultures? The new company consisted of more than 1,500 Americans joining the firm's 9,000 primarily Chinese employees, with major hubs in China, France, India, Japan, and the United States. "We had two different company cultures, with different processes, systems, and methodologies," explained Yolanda Conyers, vice president for global integration and diversity. "Layered on top of this we had different societal cultures, with different approaches to decision making, communicating, and relating to one another."

Senior leaders moved quickly to reframe the new Lenovo not as a Chinese or a U.S. company but as one with a vision to create a unified global personal computer (PC) maker with leading market positions in developed and emerging economies alike. Leaders used symbols and events to convey the emergence of a new shared Lenovo global identity. Lenovo-only branding was implemented across a number of products, and the company celebrated the change at a party at which employees ripped stickers with the IBM logo off computers in unison. Employees were encouraged not to hang on to old legacies. A "trash bin project" was established to give former IBM staff members the opportunity to submit examples of things they did at IBM but did not want to continue doing. Also, management articulated a core set of organizational values to forge common ground and provide guidance on how groups should interact in the new merged company.

In addition to scrapping legacy products and processes, leaders organized Lenovo employees under a unified global identity. Lenovo has no global headquarters but brings its executives together frequently in different cities around the world. After the merger, Lenovo's CEO, Bill Amelio (an American), lived in Singapore while the chairman, Yang Yuanqing (a Chinese), lived in Raleigh, North Carolina. Joining the senior executive ranks was a blend of Americans and mainland Chinese, with members hailing from Hong Kong and cities and countries around the globe thrown into the mix. The sense of being part of a single "global community" was reinforced by efforts to treat all employees as part of one group rather than distinct groups. In their communications, senior leaders made intentional efforts to avoid using distinct group labels such as legacy Lenovo, legacy IBM, and new hires but to use the shared label of Lenovo employees instead.

These tactics and others made room for a new Lenovo story line to emerge. The narrative is that of a "New World Culture" that capitalizes on ideas everywhere and draws upon talents, visions, and concerns of employees and stakeholders around the world. As an executive told us from Beijing, "Our New World Culture reminds us that we seek to create something new that is a valuable combination of our past heritage. We think our culture is unique, allowing us to leverage the strengths of East and West."

Clearly, the road ahead for Lenovo will be full of both challenge and opportunity. The company's financials have been hit hard by the global recession. As a result, Amelio was asked to step down when his three-year contract expired in 2009. Yet there are also encouraging signs. In its earnings report for the third fiscal quarter ending December 31, 2009, Lenovo reported its highest ever worldwide market share (9 percent). During that quarter, Lenovo's worldwide PC shipments increased 42 percent year over year. In comparison, industry PC shipments increased 17 percent world-wide during that period. Perhaps more telling is the recognition among consumers and analysts that Lenovo is offering increasingly innovative products tailored for a worldwide market. At the 2010 International Consumer Electronics Show (the largest consumer technology trade show), Lenovo took home eight media awards for a range of innovative new products. These indications suggest that leaders at Lenovo are crafting a new organizational identity—one that includes and transcends both East and West, legacy Lenovo and IBM—on the way to becoming one of the world's most formi-dable computer companies.

The Practice of Mobilizing

At the turn of the twenty-first century, who would have imagined that an IBM programmer would report to a manager in Beijing rather than Armonk, New York? Yet that is exactly what happened after the merger. As dramatic as this was, the response by leaders throughout the newly merged company was just as sweeping. After the merger, Lenovo leaders established the practice of mobilizing to craft a common purpose and shared identity across groups. By reframing boundaries, Lenovo leaders are creating space for a new organizational story line to emerge that combines and transcends aspects of both companies. Granted, rarely does a merger tran-spire in which the phrase "combining the best of both companies" isn't uttered by senior executives from the acquiring company. Yet the reality is that in many companies, the words remain largely that—lip service. Largely for this reason, over 80 percent of the expected value from mergers and acquisitions typically fails to occur, and three of every four joint ventures fall apart after the initial honeymoon period.[3]

In sharp contrast, leaders at Lenovo are taking a number of steps to forge common ground by bringing together the best of East and West. Crafting symbols, envisioning an inspiring future, and creating new organizational values all serve to build intergroup community. Today's most successful companies—think Google, Nordstrom, Southwest Airlines—are places of community. Intergroup community within an organizational context is the "social glue" that binds groups together. Community is about the experience of belonging emotionally, spiritually, and psychologically to a larger group. Each group identifies with a collective that is larger than its individual group alone. It is also about the sense of ownership that develops when groups feel that they belong. When community exists, groups may have widely different sets of experience, values, and expertise, yet they feel committed to taking joint action on behalf of a larger common purpose. As we see in the story of Lenovo, mobilizing enables groups to set aside their differences and work toward accomplishing a higher shared purpose.

For you and leaders in your organization, mobilizing is also a powerful and galvanizing means to reframe boundaries and build community between groups to solve problems or accomplish a collective goal. Your Nexus Challenge may be to find a way to craft a vision that engages the hearts and minds of groups at all levels. It may be to create a more inclusive and engaging organization for diverse groups. Or it may be to get divergent stakeholder groups to rally around a change in organizational strategy. Regardless, to navigate today's shifting leadership landscape, you must find new ways to reframe old dividing lines as new and fertile ground where community can grow.

Reframing Boundaries

The practice of mobilizing is used to craft a common purpose and shared identity across groups. As illustrated in Figure 7.1, mobilizing encourages groups to "move outside" their smaller group identity and "move inside" a new, larger, more inclusive identity that is shared by all. Mobilizing enables groups to reframe the differences that divide them into factions and coalitions so that they can work productively together. Reframing occurs by creating a larger identity (a vision, goal, or task) that is mutually valued and inspires joint action. The result is intergroup community: *a state of mutual belonging and ownership that develops when boundaries are reframed and collective action is taken.* Developing intergroup community through the practice of mobilizing is the fourth step toward the Nexus Effect.

Figure 7.1 Mobilizing.

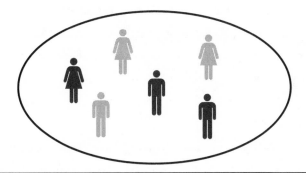

When this step is in place, groups are able to build shared direction, jointly coordinate resources, and take collective action even when forces start to pull them apart.

Mobilizing is designed to activate a shared and inclusive identity in which "everyone can belong." The positive value of "recategorizing" or reframing group boundaries has been supported consistently by research over the last 20 years.[4] Recall from the Robbers Cave experiment, for example, how the boundaries between two competing groups were reframed after the boys were given chances to cooperate on a mutually valued goal such as fixing the truck that was to deliver food to the camp. Mobilizing can be used to do this with real groups in real-world settings.

Mobilizing is similar to connecting in that both practices enable you to forge common ground. A distinction, however, is that whereas connecting builds common ground by breaking down identity differences, mobilizing creates a new and larger identity that is inclusive of all group members. Thus, connecting is about suspending the dividing lines between individual group members, whereas mobilizing is about redrawing the lines to include both groups. Crafting a single, integrated identity out of multiple, often competing and conflicting identities requires a delicate balancing act. Consider the story of *Brandon Leung*, the chief executive of *Faith Community Services (FCS)*, a nonprofit organization in Asia. As a Center for Creative Leadership team worked with Brandon over a period of time, we saw firsthand the power of identity to bind an organization together as well to create blind spots that threaten to tear it apart.[5]

Brandon took the helm of FCS after 12 years of management experience in the corporate sector, serving most recently as operations director for a large manufacturing firm. Trained as an engineer, with a sharp mind and a dedicated work ethic, Brandon thought that leading FCS, with its smaller scope and scale, would be a relatively clear-cut transition for him. Yet after just a year, it seemed that the very leadership tactics he had applied with success in the corporate world were starting to unravel with unintended consequences.

In his previous organization, Brandon developed a reputation as a visionary leader capable of building organizational commitment. He witnessed how a strong organizational identity can bind groups together toward a common purpose. At FCS, he again saw an opportunity to renew and strengthen organizational community by creating a strong organizational identity. He sensed that the staff suffered from low morale, unfocused direction, and a diminished sense of purpose under his predecessor. Specifically, Brandon believed that the Christian faith at FSC was a force that would take the organization to higher levels of engagement and performance. Acting on that belief involved taking a risk. Since FCS was a nonprofit organization, the educational programs and services it provided were secular in nature and served a multifaith community. In addition to Christianity, the employees at FCS had different faith traditions, including Islam, Hinduism, Taoism, and Confucianism, among others.

Brandon's key initiative toward strengthening common purpose and identity was the introduction of "Envision FCS," a series of staff meetings for all employees at which he would use examples and principles drawn from the Bible to share his leadership perspective and direction for the organization. Though recognizing that not all FCS employees were Christians, Brandon wanted to draw on faith as a "North Star." Rather than pointing everyone in a common direction, however, the Envision FCS meetings split the organization in two. A highly vocal minority of non-Christians filed a petition in protest. Several employees, including a highly talented and creative Muslim manager, threatened to resign.

Mobilizing in Action

As an outsider looking in, it may appear obvious to you that Brandon's decision was a catastrophe in the making. Yet his story offers an important note of caution. Asking groups to set aside their differences to work toward a common cause is a timeless and universal approach used by leaders. It is one of the most powerful means to bind people together to take collective action. How often have you found yourself entering the fray in a meeting by asking disputing groups to "work together for the common good" or "put aside your differences and go for the win-win"? It is one thing to do this effectively when groups are relatively similar in values, needs, and interests. It is quite another when you find yourself trying to bridge groups with deep and long-standing differences: people with clashing religious beliefs, former competitors, or even bitter enemies. In these situations, you need to find a way to create a shared identity that is large enough to be unifying for all the groups yet specific enough for joint action to be taken. The following tactics will help you negotiate this delicate balance.

Mobilizing Tactic 1: Craft a Galvanizing Vision, Mission, or Goal That Rallies Groups to Take Collective Action

In every organization the CCL team worked with in our research around the world, we encountered leaders who sought to forge common ground by calling upon a higher goal. In nonprofit organizations, an inspiring mission or vision created a built-in superordinate goal to bridge various functional, demographic, or stakeholder groups. In education, medicine, and other helping professions, reframing boundaries works best by calling on a shared professional identity. For example, in a hospital in Jerusalem, we witnessed how the professional calling of "caring for those in need" enabled Palestinian and Jewish nurses to work constructively together despite the long-standing history of violence and conflict between those two groups.

In the corporate arena, however, staking out common ground often focuses more on strategic or competitive goals: winning market share, hitting financial targets, being first to market with an innovative product or service, and outperforming a competitor. For example, nothing builds community better at Apple than going toe to toe with PC computer companies. Tactics such as these forge common ground by focusing on a common enemy and emphasizing what is positive and distinctive about one organization compared with its competitors.

Mobilizing Tactic 2: Build Shared Identity by Identifying Common, Inclusive Values

Although a vision or goal helps point groups in a common direction, a shared set of values helps groups internalize the core behaviors and beliefs needed to get there. After the merger, Lenovo articulated its identity of "who we are and how we work" by defining four core values: serving customers, innovation and entrepreneurial spirit, integrity and trust, and teamwork across cultures.

Importantly, those values were reinforcing for both the Chinese and the Americans. In particular, the Chinese felt motivated by the value of teamwork across cultures in light of the fact that Lenovo was shifting from a largely domestic to a more globally integrated company. Meanwhile, the Americans were particularly motivated by the value of innovation and entrepreneurial spirit. Many felt a newfound freedom to innovate and experiment now that they were no longer within the confines of "Big Blue." Creating an identity that is inclusive doesn't necessarily mean that all groups will value the same things for the same reasons. Rather, your goal as a mobilizer is to envision an identity that is broad enough to hold the different values and views of multiple groups yet focused enough to lead to collective action.

Mobilizing Tactic 3: Develop a Culture in Which "Everyone Belongs"

"Culture is *the* engine," explains Yolanda Conyers, Lenovo's vice president for global integration and diversity. "Other companies view culture as the program of the week. Culture propels us. We cannot be successful without our culture." At Lenovo, a New World Culture is something in which all groups can feel they are a part. It is not the old Lenovo or IBM culture or the traditional Chinese or American culture but a new culture that everyone at Lenovo creates together. That said, creating and changing organizational culture begins with you and the other leaders in your organization.

"Culture change is a show-up, stand-up, participative, put-yourself-on-the-line personal process," our colleagues John McGuire and Gary Rhodes write in their book *Transforming Your Leadership*

Culture. "You can no more delegate, defer, or demand culture change of others any more than you can delegate someone else to eat your food or drink your water."

When the former chairman Yang Yuanqing replaced Bill Amelio as CEO in 2009, he came into a leadership executive meeting and announced to his team that "our culture starts with me." He followed that up by making an unconventional move: He asked to have himself assessed by a 360-degree feedback assessment on how he was living up to the New World Culture. In China, direct feedback is not a common practice, especially at the senior leadership level. Six months later, he went back to the same people who assessed him and asked them to do it again. Now the entire executive team is going through this process. To make culture the "engine" that drives groups to work collaboratively together, our advice is this: Culture starts with you.

Mobilizing Tactic 4: Craft Shared Symbols or Artifacts to Represent Who "We" Are and What "We" as a Collective Believe

Throughout human history, symbols, artifacts, and icons have served as a powerful force for clans, tribes, cultures, nations, and organizations to express who they are and what they believe in. Similarly, you and the leaders throughout your organization can draw on symbolism to create meaning and transcendent purpose. When employees around the world ripped off old IBM stickers and replaced them with new Lenovo logos, that act symbolically represented that something old was being replaced by something new. Additionally, the "trash bin project" enabled former IBMers to physically "trash" old traditions, habits, and ways of working that they wanted to leave behind (such as those which impeded experimentation and innovation) in joining the new company.

Crafting and calling upon symbols, artifacts, and icons is a double-edged sword. A well-chosen symbol can serve as a galvanizing force to forge common ground. A poorly chosen symbol, however, can tear groups apart. This is unfortunately what happened at FCS. As part of Brandon Leung's efforts to renew a sense of organizational mission and purpose, he had Christian symbols placed throughout the building. Although those symbols resonated with many in the office, they alienated others. If you let yourself wander for just a moment, your mind will be flooded with any number of powerful symbols, some with highly positive associations and some with exceedingly negative ones. We encourage you to recognize the power of symbols and use them thoughtfully by keeping the values and interests of different groups in mind.

Mobilizing Tactic 5: Narrate Stories in Which Everyone Plays a Part

Both narrative and analysis are modes of communication in organizations. Analysis breaks down complex topics into smaller component parts. It is associated with left-brain thinking processes such as logic, reason, and objectivity. In contrast, narratives (i.e., stories) are a means for synthesis, stating how things fit together and conveying shared values, emotions, and aspirations. Stories are associated with right-brain thinking such as meaning, emotion, and subjectivity. Analysis and narrative both play an important role in business. Yet when it comes to crafting shared purpose and meaning, a compelling story probably will prove more useful than any number of objective statistics or data points.[6, 7]

The creation of a New World Culture at Lenovo is in essence a narrative. It communicates who "We" as a merged organization are becoming. It transmits values to guide and instruct behavior. It seeks to spark action and a common fate, and it encourages disparate groups to work together as members of a shared community.

We encourage you to harness the power of narrative. Stories are signposts that enable you to point the way to new and alternative futures in which "everyone belongs." They invite disparate groups into a shared conversation in which groups can construct a common purpose. As we describe in the next section, your role as a mobilizer is to narrate the story of an inclusive shared identity of which you are a critical part.

The Leader's Role in Mobilizing

Your role as a mobilizer is to craft a common purpose and shared identity across groups. Through tactics such as creating collective goals, calling upon shared values, developing a culture in which everyone belongs, crafting symbols, and narrating stories, you can reframe boundaries and build intergroup community. As we saw in the story of Brandon Leung at FCS, crafting a single, integrated identity out of multiple, potentially competing identities is a challenging task.

Caution: The Pitfall of Mobilizing

The boundaries that separate groups are rooted in identity and thus are charged with emotion and meaning. Therefore, we advise you to be careful not to put members of divergent groups in a position in which they must abandon core aspects of their identity on behalf of the larger shared identity. Not only does this raise basic issues of ethics, it is a strategy that cannot sustain itself over time. As described earlier in this book, identity is importantly linked to our self-concept. When our self-concept is threatened, we instinctually react to that threat—either real or perceived—by pulling back and reaffirming our differences.

In the story of the faith-based FCS, we witnessed how Brandon Leung rightly recognized the binding power of a strong organizational identity but didn't expect the backlash stemming from deep-seated religious beliefs. The lesson from Brandon's story is that mobilizing requires creating a shared identity that is large enough to be unifying for all the groups you seek to bring together.

In the past, when groups often had a high degree of similarity, it was relatively straightforward for a leader to create a vision or goal that inspired collective action. In today's shifting leadership landscape, however, it is not enough to hold a vision of the future no matter how refined your skills may be for communicating that vision effectively. More important yet, it is not enough to hold a vision that is unifying for some groups but potentially divisive or polarizing for others. Forging common ground today is more complex than simply stating, "I lead and you follow." Thus, your role as a mobilizer is less about a personal quality you have (i.e., charismatic, persuasive, articulate) and more about your ability to narrate the creation of a shared purpose within and across colliding groups.

Leaders at Lenovo, for instance, are creating a new future identity that is shared by all while taking care not to alienate or threaten the legacy identities of the previous two companies. Former IBMers in the United States are attracted to the innovative and entrepreneurial aspects of the New World Culture, and former Lenovo employees in China are attracted to being part of a company that is competing successfully on the global stage. The shared identity creates room for a transcending organizational story line to emerge. The story line is not just about how the organization is changing but about how the people who work in the organization are changing too. The result, though still a work in progress, is the emergence of a community in which everyone has a role in creating a new and globally integrated computer company.

Recent research offers new insights into how you can walk the fine line required to bring diverse groups, factions, and coalitions together to mobilize collective action. Social psychologists Stephen Reicher, Alexander Haslam, and Nick Hopkins suggest that a central task of leadership today is to define what groups stand for—who they are and how they should act—and to define yourself within the context of this shared identity. This requires you to become, in their words, an "entrepreneur of identity."[8] To illustrate, during his historic campaign for the presidency, Barack Obama would regularly open a speech by placing his own story within the larger context of the issue and people he sought to address: why he was there, where he had came from, and the events that influenced the way he thinks about a certain issue today. As a person with a highly unique background to run for president, he didn't leave it to the media or his competition to define who he was. Rather, as an entrepreneur of identity, he continually linked his own story—his challenges and hopes—to the same challenges and hopes faced by the American people. In large part by effectively telling his story, President Obama created a social movement that was much larger than he but in which he played a critical part.

You too can bring disparate groups together to tackle tough problems, create innovative solutions, or envision transformative new strategies for your organization or community. By crafting common purpose, you can reframe boundaries and develop intergroup community. Your role as a mobilizer is to narrate an unfolding purpose in which multiple groups play a part. This in turn helps foster a sense of community characterized by powerful feelings of

Table 7.1 Mobilizing Summary

Definition What is mobilizing?	Craft common purpose and shared identity across groups to *reframe boundaries and develop intergroup community.*
Rationale Why does mobilizing work?	With *mobilizing,* groups "move outside" their smaller group boundary and "move inside" a new, larger boundary that is shared by all. Mobilizing enables groups to set aside the differences that divide them into factions in order to forge common ground and work work constructively together.
Tactics How is the practice to be accomplished?	1. Craft a galvanizing vision, mission, or goal that rallies groups to take collective action. 2. Build shared identity through identifying common, inclusive values. 3. Develop a culture in which "everyone belongs," a culture in which groups feel a sense of belonging and ownership toward taking joint action on behalf of a larger common purpose. 4. Craft shared symbols or artifacts to represent who "We" are and what "We" as a collective believe. 5. Narrate stories in which everyone plays a part. Utilize the power of story to narrate a new, unfolding purpose in which everyone, including you, play an important part.
Outcome What is the result?	*Intergroup community*—the state of belonging and ownership that develops when intergroup boundaries are reframed and collective action taken.

belonging and ownership. When you enable groups to feel a sense of community, you help unleash their collaborative potential to achieve things far greater than what they could accomplish if they acted alone (see Table 7.1).

Mobilizing and Your Nexus Challenge

Crafting a common purpose and shared identity across groups enables you to develop intergroup community. The questions below will help you apply the practice of mobilizing to your unique Nexus Challenge as well as other challenges and opportunities you face in forging common ground between groups.

Discern: Assessing the Current State

Mobilizing reframes boundaries to develop intergroup community. On a scale of 1 to 10 (where 10 is the highest), how would you rate your team or organization on intergroup community?

Intergroup community increases the more the following is true:

- Common purpose exists between groups, such as a common vision, mission, goal, or strategy.
- There is a mutual feeling of belonging. Each group believes it is part of an identity with a larger collective than that of the individual group alone.
- Groups feel a sense of collective ownership. Each group is committed to taking joint action on behalf of a larger common purpose.

Reflect: Exploring New Approaches

How can you call upon common goals, collective values, shared symbols or artifacts to enable groups to rally behind a common purpose?

What steps can you take to create a more inclusive and collaborative culture in which all groups feel a sense of ownership and are committed to taking joint action on shared goals?

What is your unique "story" as a leader within your organization—who you are, how you came to be, where you are going, and the unique role you play? The more you do to craft your own story, the easier it will be to enable the larger group to craft its story. How can you craft your own story in ways that help the groups you lead do the same thing?

Apply: Taking Action

What is one idea, tactic, or new insight you've learned about mobilizing that you could apply to your Nexus Challenge?

PART 4

DISCOVERING NEW FRONTIERS

A frontier is a place of emergent new possibility. It represents the outer limits, the location where the most innovative and transformative opportunities reside. In the arts, new frontiers are discovered through the creative integration of different media, disciplines, and styles. In business, the intersection where different ideas, perspectives, and areas of expertise collide and link is the place where new and innovative frontiers reside. What if your team and organization were capable of discovering new frontiers for creative collaborations and breakthrough innovation, redefining a market, or reinventing the organization to thrive? These are the questions we'll explore in Part 4.

As you'll recall, Parts 1, 2, and 3 of this book described the six leadership practices that lead upward to the Nexus Effect. Part 2 described how safety and respect are realized through two practices—buffering and reflecting—that enable you to manage boundaries. These practices tap into the powerful human need for differentiation and uniqueness. In Part 3, we discussed how trust and community are the outcome of two additional practices—connecting and mobilizing—that enable you to forge common ground between groups. Distinct from managing boundaries, forging common ground taps into the equally powerful human need for integration and belonging. In Part 4, we'll integrate the two strategies of managing boundaries and forging common ground. That is, we'll explore the frontier where these two fundamental human needs—differentiation and integration—intersect in transformative new ways.

In Chapter 8, we'll learn how the practice of *weaving* involves interlacing boundaries between groups. Weavers draw out and integrate group differences within a larger whole to advance intergroup interdependence. We'll travel to India to observe how the CEO of the nonprofit organization CRY interlaced boundaries between different regional groups to lead a successful change in organizational strategy in service of the organization's mission.

In Chapter 9, we'll explore how the practice of *transforming* can be used to cross-cut boundaries between groups. Transformers bring multiple groups together in emergent new directions to enable intergroup reinvention. We'll see how Mark Gerzon, one of the world's foremost authorities on intergroup leadership and mediation, is cross-cutting boundaries to create an alternative future for the current climate debate. Combined, weaving and transforming enable you to discover new frontiers by tapping into the transformative potential of differences (see Figure P4.1). It is here, at the juncture where similarities and differences meet, that the most advanced and innovative opportunities await.

Figure P4.1 Discovering new frontiers.

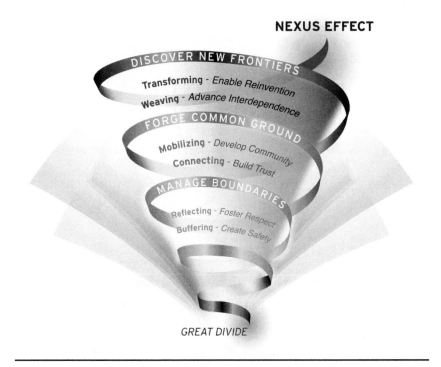

CHAPTER 8

WEAVING: ADVANCING INTERDEPENDENCE

In 1979, a young man by the name of Rippan Kapur and six friends gathered around a dining table in Mumbai, India, to discuss an extraordinary dream—a dream that no Indian child would be deprived of the basic human rights of survival, participation, protection, and development. With 50 Indian rupees and a collective resolve to do something to improve the situation of underprivileged children, CRY (then known as Child Relief and You) was born.[1]

In its early years, Rippan's steadfast determination drove CRY. The organization made significant steps toward becoming the recognized "link" between the millions of Indian citizens who could provide resources and the thousands of resource-strapped nongovernmental organizations (NGOs) that wanted to help children but lacked resources. Then, in 1994, at the young age of 40, Rippan passed away.

Fast forward to 2004. CRY had experienced a number of difficult transitions in the intervening decade. Two CEOs had come and gone. In light of CRY's democratic and collective culture, those CEOs' top-down strategies were rejected summarily by the staff. Many recognized that a new strategic direction was needed, yet there was no consensus on how to get there. CRY spans 17 of the 28 Indian states and is a microcosm of the tremendous diversity of that vast nation, including regional differences in language, ethnicity, religion, and caste. A new way forward was needed that would integrate those variations both within the organization and among the constituents it served yet offered a clear and aligned future direction. How would CRY keep Rippan's dream intact yet project it boldly forward into a dynamic and rapidly changing India?

The charge to lead the strategic change fell to newly appointed CEO Ingrid Srinath and her management committee. At the onset, Ingrid was acutely aware that the task required her to adopt a radically different model of leadership. Ingrid joined CRY after 11 years of leadership in the hard-charging world of corporate advertising. When asked to describe her leadership style, she candidly summed it up in two words: "impatient and unreasonable." Organizational change would take root at CRY, Ingrid reasoned, only if the diverse experience and expertise of all groups was called upon and ultimately combined: "We can't create a movement [for children's rights] with over a billion people in India until we first create that movement and that understanding within our own diversity." Guided by the principle that all groups within CRY had to be brought along on the "change journey," Ingrid and her team used the practice of weaving to achieve phenomenal success.

Institution building was the name CRY adopted to create an umbrella framework to drive the strategic change process. Over a two-year period, institution building involved a series of cross-regional, cross-boundary activities and dialogues. Though the topics were wide-ranging, the purpose was to explore intergroup differences and similarities as they related to the larger strategic change initiative. To transform the ethnic, gender, region, class, and caste barriers that divided children in India, the diverse regional groups that constituted CRY first needed to understand and integrate those divisions within themselves. "We need to eat our own bird food," explained Shekhar Manekar, one of the human resources (HR) leaders who orchestrated a number of the change processes. "Our philosophy is that whatever we take out there [into the broader society], we need to have first digested fully in here [within CRY]."

During an institution-building session, staff members were encouraged to explore their differences and how those differences separated privileged Indian children from the underprivileged in the larger society. All topics were open for discussion: religion, gender, language, sexual orientation, caste, class, poverty. "This method allows us to work with identities and scripts that people have written for them and look at how these scripts can actually change," says Shekhar. "With this new understanding, we as an organization begin to internalize how we can facilitate this change in society itself, whether addressing issues of regionalism, sexism, or nationalism."

As the strategic change initiative progressed, Ingrid and her management committee built on the momentum created through institution building by developing an innovative strategy-planning process. India is a vastly different country as one travels north to south and east to west in everything from dialects, to social attitudes, to the amount of spice in the food. Ingrid knew that within this diverse context a traditional strategic planning process wasn't going to work. Rather than cascade a strategy down through a chain of command, they developed a process that integrated the distinct regional identities across the organization. The first step involved developing a statement of strategy at the regional level. Ingrid and her team traveled to each region to work with the staff on scenario planning. The scenarios asked the staff to imagine India with respect to children under two conditions: "as it is now" and "as it should be in the future." Out of this activity, each region drafted statements of strategy concerning how it could close the gaps between the current and the desired future conditions. The second step involved Ingrid and her team completing the same process, but at an organizational rather than regional level. The last step involved bringing together members of the regional groups and the management committee to integrate the regional and organizational plans. The final version is what emerged after the groups cooperated to synthesize regional and organizational variations in support of an integrated change strategy.

Through a systematic and thoughtful process of interlacing geographic and demographic boundaries, Ingrid and her management committee engaged the entire organization in leading strategic change. In April 2006, CRY came together to celebrate its collective achievement. On that day, all 191 employees witnessed the formal changing of CRY's name from Child Relief and You to Child Rights and You. CRY's new strategy called for a bold pivot from supporting grassroots relief to championing and advocating for child rights at all levels of society. A "child rights" approach would position CRY to get more directly to the root of the problem and bring about lasting change. True to Ingrid's guiding principle, all groups in the organization were brought along on the change journey. One employee poignantly described the event like this: "It was a day in which everyone experienced a collective vision. Out of our differences emerged a new way forward. The power of a collective vision is something you are lucky to experience once, maybe twice, in your entire professional career." In the same year CRY went on to affect the lives of nearly 500,000 children through advocacy and initiatives in more than 5,000 villages throughout India.

The Practice of Weaving

In leading a successful organizational change initiative at CRY, Ingrid Srinath and her management committee used the practice of weaving to dramatic effect. In the way yarn or threads are braided to create a tapestry or rug, Ingrid interlaced groups across regional boundaries to realize a change in organizational strategy.

Since the 1990s, research studies have suggested that failure rates for organization-wide change efforts range from 66 percent to 75 percent, with one study finding that only one-third of enterprise change initiatives achieve any success at all. The reasons for these dismal statistics are many, but one common factor is this: Most change initiatives endorse an "outside-in" change philosophy, focusing on external systems, structures, and processes and largely ignoring the critical role people and culture play in attempts to enact systemic change.[2] Had Ingrid and her management committee adopted a similar externally focused approach, a method familiar to Ingrid from her days in corporate advertising, the odds of leading a successful change would have been equally slim.

Ingrid took a different approach. She understood that the change from "relief" to "rights" would occur at CRY only if it was led from the "inside out." Inside-out change meant upholding the different internal values, beliefs, and relationships across CRY's varying regions and then strategically integrating them. In so doing, Ingrid fostered positive interdependence across regional groups. Groups became mutually dependent, recognizing that they needed to rely on other groups. Each group had part of the answer, but no group had the entire answer. Similarly, to identify the best solution for going forward, regional groups at CRY engaged in collective learning. In the same way that the practices for managing boundaries (buffering and reflecting) focus on differentiation, people inquired and actively sought information across other groups. By more deeply understanding their own identity differences, regional groups gained critical new insights into how those differences divided privileged from underprivileged children in India.

But CRY didn't stop there. In the same way the practices for forging common ground (connecting and mobilizing) focus on integration, the groups then sought to synthesize their differences within a larger and shared whole. Disparate sources of information were woven together to create new possibilities and solutions. Indeed, it was through the creative integration of widely varying experiences, backgrounds, and expertise that the inspiration and source for the eventual strategic change ultimately were realized.

CRY is a remarkable organization doing remarkable things. Organizations characterized by interdependence across boundaries are rare. In fact, in CCL's research behind this book, we were unable to identify a single large, publicly held company where interdependent boundary spanning collaboration was an everyday occurrence.

That said, executives of Fortune 500 organizations were unanimous in calling for more collaborative approaches to leadership in their organizations. With candor—recall the 79 percent self-reported gap between importance and effectiveness in boundary spanning capabilities—those executives recognized that they were not exempt from the need to develop new leadership approaches.

Despite recognizing that these changes won't happen overnight, you can begin creating an environment for greater collaboration today by applying the practice of weaving. Even if your organizational structure tends to be a barrier to cross-organizational collaboration, remember that collaborating by differentiating and integrating differences is part of human nature. As our CCL colleague Edward Marshall wrote in *Transforming the Way We Work*, "Collaboration is the way people naturally want to work together." Whatever your Nexus Challenge—fostering organizational learning capabilities, accelerating change in systemwide strategies, launching new joint ventures—you can use the practice of weaving to interlace boundaries and realize exciting and innovative new possibilities.

Weaving Boundaries

As illustrated in Figure 8.1, weaving occurs when group boundaries "interlace" yet remain distinct. Each group has a unique role or contribution that is integrated in service of a larger whole that is shared. To interlace means to cross one thing over another as if the two were being woven together. Think about how making a woven rug involves interlacing different threads or yarns. Each thread remains distinct, yet when they are woven together, a larger whole is

Figure 8.1 Weaving.

created—an intricate rug. As another example, think about Russian *matryoshka* dolls, the hollow wooden toys in which smaller dolls are nested inside larger dolls. When children play with these toys, each doll is unique, with its own personality and characteristics. Yet at the same time each doll can be nested within a larger doll so that all the dolls add up to a whole. Each doll has unique properties, but the full value is realized only in the complete and integrated toy.

Weaving intergroup boundaries is similar in that it encourages groups to have their own distinctive identity and purpose (Us and Them) and at the same time to integrate each group within a larger organizational whole (We). Weaving both meets fundamental needs and capitalizes on the potential that exists when both are met simultaneously. Weaving meets the need for differentiation or uniqueness by respecting varied experience and expertise, yet it also meets the need for integration by forming new combinations grounded in existing knowledge. The result is intergroup interdependence: *a state of mutual dependence and collective learning that develops when boundaries are interlaced within a large whole.* Advancing intergroup interdependence through the practice of weaving is the fifth step toward the Nexus Effect. When this step is in place, groups are capable of cocreating a shared direction, aligning and realigning resources as business requirements change, and exploring diverse perspectives that enhance the effectiveness of the larger organization, not just the individual groups.

Research demonstrates that creating "subcategories" by activating both a group identity and a collective identity can be more effective than strategies that activate a group or collective identity alone.[3] In this approach, members of disparate groups play different but complementary roles in contributing to a common goal. That is, boundaries between groups are maintained, but within a larger whole. Weaving is an inherently more complex practice than those we've discussed thus far because it taps into human needs for both unity and separation. To grasp the distinctions, let's look at how Mechai Viravaidya, a longtime social activist, led what has been widely deemed as one of the world's most successful campaigns to save lives through AIDS awareness and education.[4]

In the late 1980s, Viravaidya, affectionately known as Mr. Condom, anticipated that AIDS would become a crisis in Thailand but was aware that trying to broach the subject was not going to be easy in conservative Thai society. He also realized early on that effectively curbing the spread of AIDS in Thailand would require having many different groups with diverse interests work together. It looked like an uphill battle. In addition to religious concerns, the tourism industry was concerned that visitors would be scared off by this highly publicized education campaign on AIDS.

Mechai reached out to groups outside the government, especially those with wide influence in Thai society. He had success with

Buddhist monks and the military. "In Thailand it is critical to get religion on your side," Mechai explained in an interview. "The Catholics were tough, but we won over the Buddhists." He took the highly unconventional step of asking Buddhist monks, an important moral authority in predominately Buddhist Thailand, to bless batches of condoms before they were sent out for distribution. In addition, some religious associations trained monks and nuns to work in the areas of prevention and treatment. In 1989, Mechai persuaded General Chavalit Yongchaiyudh, the army chief and acting supreme commander, to agree to make 126 military-run radio stations and two television networks available for the AIDS prevention campaign. The general also presided over the testing for AIDS of all the military's personnel, including its temporary civilian staff.

When the Thai prime minister appointed Mechai as the country's AIDS czar in 1991, Mechai positioned AIDS as a societal and national challenge rather than an issue handled by the health ministry and confined to a small group of citizens. He persuaded the prime minister to take the helm of the national AIDS committee. This was an important symbolic move that also afforded Mechai, by extension, the power of the pulpit with the government ministries. He used the office to engage and direct a variety of groups— including government departments, schools, television and radio stations, nongovernmental organizations, and the business community—to support the AIDS education campaign. "Every group was involved," Mechai explained. "Government, business, religion, the military, the police, everyone. Each had a role to play in the fight to save lives." The results of Mechai's efforts speak for themselves. According to the United Nations, in the years between 1990 and 2004, the number of new AIDS infections in Thailand declined by

90 percent. In addition, separate analyses conducted by the World Bank estimated that during that period, over 7.7 million people were prevented from contracting the disease in Thailand.

Weaving in Action

The practice of weaving enables a leader to draw out and integrate group differences within a larger whole. Below are several tactics you can use to advance interdependence where boundaries collide, intersect, and link.

Weaving Tactic 1: Clear the Path—Remove Group Barriers, Roadblocks, and Obstacles That Get in the Way of the Larger Collective Goal

At the onset of AIDS awareness campaign in Thailand, Mechai Viravaidya was well aware of the sharp resistance he would face across a wide range of religious, political, business, and educational groups. Significant borders, grounded in identity differences, were standing in the way. However, he also understood that each group at heart supported the larger goal of saving lives through AIDS awareness. Mechai needed to find a way to utilize differences because each group was able to reach different segments of society. He also had to connect and link those efforts on behalf of the larger goal. Ultimately, he succeeded through approaches that were as effective as they were unconventional.

First, as described above, Mechai got "religion on his side" by having Buddhist monks bless batches of condoms before they were distributed. Buddhist scripture includes passages about how birth causes suffering. To prevent unwanted suffering, you need to prevent unwanted birth. A blessing from monks helped meet both needs while addressing complex values within the religious community associated with the morally sensitive topic of human sexuality.

Next, he worked to remove roadblocks across the political community. Although the majority of politicians recognized the importance of curbing the spread of AIDS, there were differing views on how to do that. The contrary opinions were due in part to different beliefs and values concerning how the disease is transmitted. To bring a conclusive end to the debate, at a major news conference Mechai drank from a glass that had been used by an AIDS patient. That headline-grabbing event finally brought home to wary politicians and the constituents they served the fact that AIDS cannot be transmitted by casual contact.

Finally, Mechai reached out to remove obstacles within the educational community. Educators were largely supportive of including AIDS awareness in the school curriculum but had concerns about doing it in an age-appropriate manner. Mechai worked with teachers to create educational songs. For example, in the grade schools, they developed a new "ABC" song in which letters of the alphabet were represented by different types of contraceptives. Students learned the alphabet while simultaneously learning about family planning.

Granted, Mechai's brash and irreverent personality, not to mention his knack for the dramatic, stands outside the traditional business executive mold, but his extraordinary results offer lessons to us all. By removing limiting borders between groups, you can tap into and integrate differences to exploit new frontiers.

Weaving Tactic 2: Let Different Groups Be Different Groups—Draw Out, Utilize, and Capitalize on Differences

In Thailand, Mechai Viravaidya enabled different groups to play a role in the AIDS awareness campaign. In India, Ingrid Srinath and the management committee recognized that they needed to capitalize on the distinct knowledge sets of the organization's regional groups to create a unified strategy at CRY. In both instances, different groups were encouraged to be, in fact, different groups.

This simple idea turns conventional thinking about leading change on its head. The dominant view in management research and practice is that the key to leading organizational change is alignment: getting "buy-in" from all groups and getting "everyone on the same page." Alignment is important, but the rush for integration doesn't have to come at the expense of enabling the productive use of differences. In contrast, the view at CRY was that unique perspectives and experiences were the key to accelerating strategic change. Vimmi Budhirija, who along with Shekhar Manekar helped lead the change process, put it like this: "The organization must be willing to learn with you, to give everyone at CRY the freedom and space to experiment, to bring in different ideas and new ways of doing things." The leaders at CRY knew that it was only through embracing identity differences that breakthrough change could occur. They knew that it was more challenging to hold on to those differences than to minimize them, but they also knew that this was the only way to tap into the best each group had to offer.

As part of the two-year institution-building process, members of different groups frequently were brought together for intergroup dialogues in which they were asked to "bring their differences into the room." For example, one dialogue focused on better understanding the unique hurdles and obstacles faced by underprivileged girls in India. Both men and women openly described their differing life experiences as it related to gender. For one of the male employees, this dialogue helped shift his perspective: "For me, it was a complete eye-opener. So many of the things around us every day we never stop to consider. It [the dialogue on gender] has helped me to start asking new questions."

Similarly, as part of the strategy-planning process, each regional group was asked to create a distinct regional plan. Differing and sometimes conflicting regional plans were not seen as a problem to avoid. Instead, they were embraced and ultimately enabled CRY to consider a broader and fuller range of options to move the organization forward. Letting different groups be different enabled employees at CRY to broaden their horizons while better understanding the needs of those they served (in this case disadvantaged Indian children). Because the need for both differentiation and integration was met, new and well-vetted ideas emerged that would not have been possible if groups had instead "left their differences at home."

Weaving Tactic 3: Connect the Dots—Link Group Expertise, Experience, and Actions Back to Larger Collective Goals

The greatest advantage of unique group knowledge and expertise is realized when it is applied to solving a larger problem or creating a new solution that benefits the organization as a whole. At CRY, for example, unique regional knowledge and expertise were linked systematically and explicitly to the larger strategic change goal. Unfortunately, this step is often sidelined in organizations. As a case in point, consider the widely used organizational approaches of affinity groups and communities of practice.[5]

Like the leadership practice of weaving, both techniques seek to foster the development of unique group knowledge and a shared identity. A "working parents" affinity group, for example, creates a space for parents to share their successes and struggles in managing the role demands of both work and parenting, and a "fringe technologies" community of practice allows a group of tech-savvy employees to develop shared knowledge around a topic of interest. Yet in these instances it is likely that systematic efforts are not made to connect the unique group knowledge or expertise to broader organizational goals. In this scenario, both groups and the organization lose out. Group engagement falters over time as group members feel their input and ideas are not valued by the organization. Also, the unique knowledge of these groups is kept within the group and not brought to bear on larger organizational problems.

Again, remember the *matryoshka* dolls. What makes this toy stand the test of time is that each doll is unique, yet its full value becomes apparent only when each piece is connected to the larger whole. There are any number of different ways to link unique group knowledge and experience back into the larger organization. See the sidebar below for a few suggestions to get you started.

How to Uncover New Sources of Value by Linking Groups to the Larger Whole

To create opportunities for groups to share and integrate their unique knowledge, perspectives, and experiences with the larger organization, you can do the following:

- Create an "affinity group fair" in which time is set aside for multiple affinity groups to report on the topics and issues they've been discussing in their regular meetings and how those issues could be applied to help solve current organizational problems.
- Set up a community of practice "fishbowl" in which anyone in the organization can come, listen in, and contribute to a community of practice meeting. To illustrate this, take the "fringe technologies" community of practice mentioned above. You can set up a meeting so that the community members sit in a circle together (they represent the fish) with noncommunity members sitting outside the circle (they represent the fishbowl). Schedule the meeting to last an hour and let the community members engage in a conversation about new cutting-edge technologies for 30 minutes or so. Then take 20 minutes to have the noncommunity members comment, reflect, ask questions, and identify themes based on what they heard. Reserve the last 10 minutes to identify any specific ideas, action steps, or recommendations that can be applied to larger organizational problems or goals.

> • Conduct an after-action review by bringing the groups involved with a successful organizational initiative together. Have the groups share what they identified as being the key success factors in light of their unique vantage points.

Weaving Tactic 4: Foster an Interdependent Group of Groups

In today's shifting leadership landscape, teams look less like teams in the traditional sense of the word and more like groups that come together, get their work done, disband, and recombine with other groups. Yet they still need to have a clear identity, purpose, and set of deliverables. In line with this business reality, you can take steps to help teams foster dual identities. Think of this as a "group of groups," or "different groups working on the same overarching team."

In this scenario, groups have distinct goals yet also share a larger goal that requires them to work together. As Chris initially described in the Preface, my travels to interview employees in a number of CRY regional offices—Bangalore, Delhi, Kolkata, Mumbai—revealed that each office had its own unique energy and vitality. Yet in my conversations, employees spoke with a clear sense of the whole of CRY. Staff in Delhi spoke about unique issues in Bangalore, and employees in Kolkata felt connected to the staff in Mumbai. I realized that the aliveness of each office was in part dependent on its inter-connections to other offices and the larger mission of CRY.

You too can foster dual identities by calling out each group's unique purpose and defining how that purpose contributes to a larger organizational goal. You also can take steps to specify how the interdependencies across groups combine to support a larger systemic goal. Recent research shows that in multiteam work environments, systemwide performance increases as the level of interconnection across teams increases.[6] Similarly, you can help define the way teams need to work together across boundaries to increase not just team performance but the performance of the organization as a whole.

Weaving Tactic 5: Create Interdependent Goals That Groups Cannot Achieve on Their Own

The most important business challenges we face today are interdependent: They can be solved only by groups working collaboratively. Yet all too often we find groups in the same organization working independently or, worse, at cross-purposes. This is problematic because the way we work has to match the nature of the goal we want to achieve. When the goal is interdependent, you can create the conditions for groups to capitalize on their distinctive resources to succeed. In these situations, it is the health of the whole that ultimately determines the success of the different groups.

As one of the explicit outcomes of institution building at CRY, employees were held accountable for developing institutional stances. A stance is an organizational point of view on the key issues related to the organization's mission. In the transformation from a relief to a rights-based organization, these stances became the foundation for CRY's advocacy positions. "We seek to develop a stance," explains Shekhar. "It's not about saying we want everyone in the same color but rather saying how can we bring our different perspectives together to develop a collective point of view." These stances integrated the best ideas and novel perspectives of CRY's different regional, functional, and cultural groups. Similarly, in the strategy-planning process, regional leaders had to work closely with Ingrid and the management committee to reconcile regional variations in support of an enterprise plan. "Rather than create an organizational strategy forcing the regions and functions to comply," says Vimmi, "our process is to come together and negotiate spaces." By negotiating spaces, CRY is able to develop strategic plans that embrace regional differences yet create a coherent and integrated path forward.

The Leader's Role in Weaving

When you draw out and integrate group differences within a larger whole, you are using the practice of weaving. Through tactics such as removing group barriers, capitalizing on differences, linking group expertise, fostering a group of groups, and creating interdependent goals, you can interlace boundaries and advance intergroup interdependence. To make a tapestry, blanket, or rug, an accomplished weaver brings together different threads to create larger patterns and designs. Just as a weaver seeks to integrate different threads, you can knit together the differences between groups. Whereas it is the intersection of colorful threads that enables a weaver to create a fine rug, it is the intersection of ideas across your organization's functions, regions, or demographic groups where your next big product or service can be found.

When leading strategic change at CRY, Ingrid Srinath acted as a weaver to integrate the varied experiences, backgrounds, and expertise of different regional groups. She traversed India to attend regional meetings on a regular basis and actively participated in both the institution-building and strategic-planning processes. Her task was to facilitate constructive conversations that helped draw out and then integrate the widely differing perspectives in the room. "You have to be able to hold both [groups] simultaneously," explained Ingrid. "Rather than leave out one or the other, or alternate in between, you need to hold the interests and needs of both." In essence, Ingrid created a space to hold multiple groups—both their distinctions and their overlaps—to create a new synthesis that ultimately became the new organizational change strategy.

In leading strategic change, Ingrid recognized that change would have to start with her. "Honestly, I would have preferred to handle the transition autocratically and unilaterally and be done with it," she shared with Chris at a breakfast meeting in Mumbai. "But investing the time and effort to bring everyone along pays off because there is a genuine acceptance of the need for change. The sustainability is so much greater because it becomes fully internalized." In enacting the practice of weaving, you too may find yourself having to change. You cannot tell groups to be interdependent. You can only create the conditions, time, and space for interdependence to develop and serve as a role model every step of the way. This will require you to continue to expand your capabilities in two important arenas: leading conflict and managing adversity.

Weaving involves vigorously drawing out and threading together differences. Inevitably, conflict will arise as diverging values and opposing beliefs come into direct contact. In these moments, you will need to mediate and reconcile constructively between differing points of view. We recognize that it is often tempting to gloss over differences, especially when they have the potential to crack open a

Great Divide. However, as we can see in the following story from CRY, engaging rather than bypassing differences often unlocks new ideas and possibilities.

Once, in a CRY institutional building dialogue, a Brahmin (a member of the highest caste) shared a story about the appalling treatment a Dalit worker (a member of the lowest, untouchable caste) received in his home when he was a child. Just as there are any number of "undiscussables" in your own culture or organization, the issue of caste is highly polarizing in India. Instantly, the tension in the room became palpable. Rather than hope the moment would pass, a management team member stepped into the divide. He encouraged members of different groups and of all castes to think about the story of the Dalit worker in terms of its broader societal implications for children, that is, to focus on the story rather than the storyteller. Space was created for beliefs to be challenged and unexplored assumptions to be tested. "CRY is one of the rare organizations that actually support and encourage such discussions," explained one of the employees in the meeting. "We can have a debate or a heated argument and not be judged or victimized." By constructively engaging differences, the management team member helped the groups better understand the larger societal practice—caste in India—which in turn opened up an important conversation with direct relevance to the mission of the organization.

Caution: The Pitfall of Weaving

In a well-known fable, a group of blind men touch an elephant to discover what the animal before them is like. Each man touches a different part, but only one part. When they describe to one another what they felt, they fall into complete disagreement. The man who feels the tail says the elephant is like a rope, the one who feels the trunk says the elephant is like a tree branch, and the one who touches the ear says the elephant is like a hand fan. The men find themselves at a standstill, as they aren't capable of linking their different perspectives to create a larger whole.

This fable illustrates the pitfall of weaving. All too often, competing or divided groups are brought together to accomplish a higher purpose, yet they "see" the world in such different ways that accomplishing shared progress toward a common end is difficult. You need to balance these tensions by not overweighting or underweighting the value of any one group relative to another. That is, you need to enable groups to occupy different but *equally* valued roles. By helping disparate groups see that they are different in important ways and that those differences are crucial to the success of the whole, you can resolve the blind men's dilemma.

Drawing out differences, reconciling conflict, and attempting to synthesize varying values and points of view is exhausting work. To play the role of weaver, you probably also will have to develop new ways to manage adversity. Integrating boundaries and advancing interdependence require you not only to manage the thoughts and feelings between divided groups but also to understand how those contradictory thoughts and feelings reside within yourself.

Ingrid candidly described these realities like this: "When you anchor the institutional building and strategy-planning sessions, you can end up putting all of the stress in the room onto yourself. First your back gives in, then your neck, and then finally your brain just shuts down." But then she went on to describe the payoff: the day in April 2006 when all 191 CRY employees assembled to recognize their name change from Child *Relief* and You to Child *Rights* and You and the change in strategy that represented. "We have led this change from the inside out, and that is why it will stick," Ingrid explained. "The name-changing event was actually about recognizing the change that had already happened rather than a launch of a new change initiative."

We encourage you, like Ingrid, to develop new capabilities in the practice of weaving. If you draw out and integrate group differences, new frontiers will be discovered where groups will achieve inspiring results far beyond what they could achieve alone (see Table 8.1).

Weaving and Your Nexus Challenge

Drawing out and integrating group differences within a larger whole enables you to create the conditions for intergroup interdependence. The questions below will help you apply the practice of weaving to your unique Nexus Challenge as well as other challenges and opportunities you face in discovering new frontiers between groups.

Discern: Assessing the Current State

Weaving interlaces boundaries to advance intergroup interdependence. On a scale of 1 to 10 (where 10 is the highest), how

WEAVING: ADVANCING INTERDEPENDENCE

Table 8.1 Weaving Summary

Definition What is weaving?	Draw out and integrate group differences within a larger whole to *interlace boundaries and advance intergroup interdependence*
Rationale Why does weaving work?	With *weaving*, groups "interlace" their boundaries, yet remain distinct. Each group has a unique role or contribution that, when interlaced, adds up to a larger whole. Weaving capitalizes on both the power of differentiation (i.e., varied experience and expertise) as well as integration (i.e., belonging to a larger identity).
Tactics How is the practice to be accomplished?	1. Clear the path. Remove group barriers, roadblocks, and obstacles that get in the way of the larger collective goal. 2. Let different groups be different groups. Draw out, utilize, and capitalize upon differences. 3. Connect the dots. Link group expertise, experience, and actions back to larger collective goals. 4. Foster an interdependent group of groups. Help teams develop dual identities as members of a group that are also part of a larger group (i.e., different groups working on the same, larger team). 5. Create interdependent goals that individual groups cannot achieve alone. Create opportunities to enable groups to integrate their distinctive resources in order to succeed.
Outcome What is the result?	*Intergroup interdependence*—the state of mutual dependence and collective learning that develops when intergroup boundaries are interlaced within a larger whole.

would you rate your team or organization on intergroup interdependence?

Intergroup interdependence increases the more the following is true:

- Groups are mutually dependent; each group recognizes that it must rely on other groups to resolve a problem or generate a solution.
- There is an affinity for differences; groups actively seek to explore, understand, and capitalize on their differences.
- Groups seek synergies across their differences and look for creative ways to integrate those differences.

- Groups engage in collective learning; people inquire and actively seek information across groups to facilitate continuous learning.

Reflect: Exploring New Approaches

How can you more intentionally facilitate collaborative conversations that encourage groups to explore and then integrate and capitalize on their differences?

How comfortable are you with leading through conflict? Do you tend to see conflict as healthy and constructive or as something you'd rather avoid? How can you welcome the clash that inevitably occurs when differing intergroup values, interests, and perspectives collide and view this more as an opportunity to embrace than as a problem to avoid?

How adept are you at managing adversity? Drawing out differences, reconciling conflict, and synthesizing values and points of view require flexibility and resiliency but also a steadfast belief in one's core values and identity. How can you take steps to ensure that you are taking care of yourself emotionally, physically, and spiritually so that you can manage adversity better?

Apply: Taking Action

What is one idea, tactic, or new insight you've learned about weaving that you could apply to your Nexus Challenge?

CHAPTER 9

TRANSFORMING: ENABLING REINVENTION

The sixth and final practice—transforming—is about inter-group reinvention: the state of renewal, alternative futures, and emergent possibilities that develops when intergroup boundaries are cross-cut in new directions. It is about what is possible when groups create a new identity and transform the boundaries between them. When this occurs, problems that were previously intractable are resolved and solutions that felt far beyond reach become not just viable but fully realizable.

The practice of transforming involves bringing multiple groups together in emergent new directions. When boundaries are cross-cut, new identities and new possibilities associated with those identities emerge. To cross-cut means to cut against the grain or on the bias; transforming occurs when time and space are provided for members to cut against the grain of their respective boundaries, opening themselves up to change. Transforming is highly complex in practice. The tactics for cross-cutting boundaries are practically infinite, as are the possibilities that can be realized. Thus, the best way to understand this final practice is to observe several transformers in action.

In the pages that follow, we'll introduce you to Butch Peterman, Margaret Jenkins, and Mark Gerzon. First, we'll see how Butch and Margaret are bringing groups together to reinvent their organization and community, respectively. Next, we'll describe in greater detail the practice of transforming. We'll close the chapter by taking an in-depth look at the tactics of a master transformer. From corporate CEOs to heads of governments, Mark has partnered with key decision makers on every continent to transform limiting borders into new frontiers.

Three leaders with three unique stories, yet at an organizational, community, and societal level, Butch, Margaret, and Mark are helping collectively to create alternative futures that are as exciting as they are necessary.

Transforming an Organization: Butch Peterman and Abrasive Technology, Inc.

Loyal "Butch" Peterman, the founder, owner, and president of Abrasive Technology, Inc. (ATI), looked at the increasingly competitive market and the inflexibility of his manufacturing company's operations and placed a bet on the future. His company would transform from a functionally organized manufacturer with strict division of labor to an innovative, customer-focused "process-centered" organization.[1] In a globally integrated manufacturer of precision grinding and tooling products, Butch knew those changes required much more than rearranging the organizational chart. It would be necessary to ask the people at ATI to change how they defined themselves and their company. Both the identity of distinct functional groups and the leadership culture would have to be reinvented.

The work began with tossing out the use of traditional supervisory and managerial roles. New nontitled roles were created around core tasks. All employees were assigned a process, and each process had a continual-improvement process engineer and a coach to assist it both with its work and with personal growth and development. Individuals were thought of not as employees but as associates with full responsibility for managing themselves and their work in collaboration with the process coach and other process members.

Today, processes are team-oriented at ATI. Coaches have replaced supervisors. Horizontal cross-training and role flexibility are the norm. Differences in experience and expertise are explored to find the best solutions, and associates are rewarded for individual, team, and overall organizational success. Over the course of several years, ATI has sustained its market position while experiencing marked improvements in its operations and culture. Although the work of reinvention continues, some of the outcomes realized to date include the following:

- Employee turnover rates that have dropped from double-digit yearly percentages to nearly zero
- A 50 percent reduction in product returns year after year for five years running
- Zero recruitment costs as a result of 100 percent internal referrals of new hires

- Low-performing plants now operating at companywide standards
- A highly advanced talent management system that includes peer reviews; individual-, group-, and organization-level compensation; coaching; and assessment and learning systems

Transforming a Community: Margaret Jenkins and Small Town America

When Margaret Jenkins's neighborhood held two pancake breakfasts on the same Saturday three blocks apart, she decided it was time to act.[2] Several weeks earlier, a rift had opened up concerning future residential development in the neighborhood. Should the community support a proposed project to build low-income town houses in the neighborhood, or should it raise the battle flag and oppose the project head on? Divergent perspectives on this question split the neighborhood in two. Ugly and heated arguments concerning age and class pitted neighbor against neighbor. Margaret recognized that the faultline ran much deeper than which group had the better pancakes. It was about the identity of the neighborhood both in terms of what it traditionally had been and, more important, what it was becoming.

After the dueling pancake breakfasts, Margaret initiated a transformation in her neighborhood that would turn a deep divide into an exciting new future. In packed-to-the-walls meetings, neighbors came together to share their stories and listen to the stories of others. Margaret's role was to create space for two things to occur. First, she ensured that different views and diverse perspectives were included in the dialogue. Invitations sent out for the initial meeting simply stated, "You are welcome to come envision the future of our neighborhood." Then, at the meetings, Margaret kept the conversations future-oriented (imagining the neighborhood five years later) rather than present-oriented (engaging in the current debate about the pending development). Everyone felt welcome to attend and participate. "The future," Margaret said, "is something that everyone in the neighborhood cares about, no matter what side of the fence they are on."

Second, she used a number of approaches to bring different groups into contact with one another in different ways. In some meetings, everyone in attendance—young and old, white-collar and blue-collar—sat in a large circle. In others, Margaret mixed everyone up into smaller groups for more personal conversations. "Getting neighbors talking, side by side, cross-fertilizing points of view is the name of the game," Margaret explained. "My goal here is to create an environment in which people can collectively imagine a new tomorrow." As stories continue to be shared and new perspectives emerge, there is great potential for neighbors to create a new tomorrow that is not just an improvement on the old but potentially something very different altogether.

Transforming Boundaries

The practice of transforming is used to bring multiple groups together in emergent new directions to "cross-cut" boundaries. In Figure 9.1, the boundaries between three groups overlap so that over time and repeated interaction, a new and distinctive group identity is formed. What happens with the practice of transforming is that when boundaries are cross-cut over time, identity-based

Figure 9.1 Transforming.

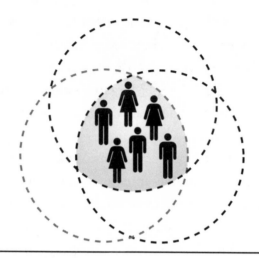

values, beliefs, and perspectives between groups shift and change in fundamental and often transformative ways. The result is intergroup reinvention: *the state of renewal, alternative futures, and emergent possibilities that develops when boundaries are cross-cut in new directions.* Enabling intergroup reinvention through the practice of transforming is the sixth step toward the Nexus Effect. When this final step is in place, groups are uniquely able to cocreate emergent direction, align collaborative action, and renew, reenvision, and reimagine themselves and their environment in ways that enable them to thrive in a dynamic world.

Transforming is similar to weaving in that both practices enable you to discover new frontiers by intersecting similarities and differences and establishing a delicate balance between the needs for unity and separation. A crucial distinction, however, is the way in which the two practices are used to alter boundaries between groups.

Weaving seeks to keep existing identities intact and create a new synthesis derived from current experience and expertise. Think of how in knitting a rug, a red thread remains red even when interwoven with yellow and blue threads. The new synthesis is the "top level" or "larger whole" that unifies the component parts (the finished rug). Recall how Ingrid Srinath used weaving in leading the change in organizational strategy at CRY. The larger whole—the creation of a new organizational strategy—evolved from creatively integrating the different but intact experiences, knowledge, and backgrounds of CRY's regional groups.

Transforming, in contrast, makes no claim to discovering a unifying whole. Rather, current experience and expertise are used only as a starting point toward new, emergent, and often undefined ends. When the goal is reinvention through transforming, you must accept that you don't know exactly how things will turn out. With transforming, you bring multiple groups together in limitless new ways and then see what happens. All the tactics described for the previous five practices also can be used in the practice of transforming, along with many others. In this way, transforming can be thought of as a gestalt, the integrated totality of the tactics in this book for managing borders, forging common ground, and discovering new frontiers. At Abrasive Technology, Inc., Butch Peterman is enabling reinvention by using multiple tactics—nontitled roles, team-oriented production processes, horizontal cross-training—to enable employees to reimagine themselves and their relationships with one another. In a small-town neighborhood, Margaret Jenkins is creating an invitational space for groups to come together "on each side of the fence." Her intent is not simply to mend or repair the fence but to have neighbors reinvent the fence altogether.

Both Butch and Margaret are enabling reinvention by bringing different groups together in different ways. Yet the groups involved and the methods used couldn't be more different. So it is with the practice of transforming. It is the explicit goal and intention of transforming that defines it as a practice and enables it to stand alone: to cross-cut boundaries of identity and realize the new possibilities that emerge from those identities. When the boundaries between groups are cut "against the grain," the identity-based values and beliefs of those groups change in fundamental and often transformative ways. When groups change who they are and what they believe, exciting alternatives and futures emerge.[3]

Our thinking about transforming merges contemporary concepts in the fields of social psychology and organizational development. In social psychology, Marilynn Brewer, a professor at Ohio State University, argues that identity categories in the broader society become problematic when they are related to subcategories within organizations.[4] For example, stereotypical social categories often overlap with functional groups, such as "German engineers" and "British accountants." Brewer's concept of cross-cutting attempts to break down these distinctions by creating, for example, mixed teams that include engineers and accountants from both countries. The result is that organizations have greater representation and increased interaction across multiple layers and functions. The key idea in Brewer's work is that by cross-cutting boundaries, we can change *who* we bring together in organizations and communities.

In the field of organizational development, there have been significant recent advances in methods for bringing multiple groups together across boundaries. Typically called large-group methodology, these approaches are known by names such as action learning, future search, intergroup dialogue, open space technology, and World Café.[5] Each of these methods is unique, but all hinge on changing the structure of the ways in which people and groups meet. The key take-away from these methods is that *how* you bring groups together is just as important as, if not more important than, the issue, problem, or topic of conversation you put before them.

Combining ideas from the fields of social psychology and organizational development, the practice of transforming seeks to bring together different people (the *who*) using different approaches (the *how*) to cross-cut boundaries of identity and enable intergroup reinvention. As we see in the stories of Butch Peterman and Margaret Jenkins, the practice of transforming can be used to help groups change their identity: who they see themselves to be and how they define their group. Transforming does this by creating an environment where existing identities and perspectives are open to inquiry, discovery, and change. When intergroup identities change, the boundaries associated with those identities change too. Borders that once served to divide groups now serve as frontiers to unlock new and emergent opportunities.

Next we share with you a story from Mark Gerzon about what is perhaps the most pressing transformational issue of our time: the global challenge presented by climate change and energy security. As president of Mediators Foundation, Mark says that his mission is "to foster global leadership for a peaceful, just and sustainable world by identifying, supporting and connecting visionary leaders working in the best interests of our small planet." Mark was afforded a unique opportunity to live out his mission at a pivotal event in the climate debate at a conference center in Colorado's Rocky Mountains.

Transforming in Action

In the early 2000s, former American vice president Al Gore emerged as the most prominent crusader against global warming and the greenhouse gas emissions that were said to be the cause of it. At the same time, a faction of critics, mostly on the conservative side of the political spectrum, arose to challenge and debate the claim of climate change; they argued there was no scientific evidence for it and it was just alarmism on the part of liberals. The two groups polarized into what could be called the "green wing"—Gore and his supporters who believed that the environment was being destroyed—and the "industry wing"—a group consisting of the Competitive Enterprise Institute, energy interests, and others who said that the threat of global warming either wasn't real or was being vastly over-blown and that efforts to counteract it would endanger jobs and economic growth. Some members of the industry wing went so far as to take out attack ads against Gore and the green wing.

To help create trust and ultimately pave the way for reinvention between those two factions, Joseph McCormick, cofounder and chairman of Reuniting America, worked for several years to convene a transpartisan retreat. When the pieces finally came together in 2004, Joseph knew he needed the most experienced intergroup facilitators he could find to make the retreat a success. He chose Mark Gerzon and Bill Ury, the director of the Program on Negotiation at Harvard Law School and the coauthor of *Getting to Yes: Negotiating Agreement without Giving In.*

In contrast to the stories you've read throughout this book, we want you to hear this one in Mark's own words.[6] We've taken the liberty of organizing the narrative according to five tactics you can draw on to cross-cut boundaries and enable reinvention. Consistent with the practice of transforming, these tactics overlap with other tactics you've read about for managing borders, forging common ground, and discovering new frontiers. Mark chose to do these five things in this situation, but remember that the tactics for transforming are as limitless as the types of groups you may strive to bring together.

Transforming Tactic 1: Bring the Whole System into the Room: Gain Representation across All Groups and Ensure Maximum Diversity of Perspective

In cross-cutting boundaries, you need to make a concerted effort to ensure that you have representation from all groups. In the run-up to the transpartisan retreat, Mark went to great lengths to encourage a broad and inclusive group of people to attend, allow all points of view to be heard, and bring the full range of the system into the room. As he describes it:

> We brought together a whole range of people—there were thirty people in the room. We had Al Gore representing the "green wing." We had the Competitive Enterprise Institute representing the "industry wing." There were participants from the Christian Coalition and some of the evangelical groups that were concerned about the environment. We brought together people from other conservative organizations and people representing the energy conglomerates, such as the American Gas Association. And then we had some of the renewable-energy proponents. So we had a microcosm. I

would say we had a very good microcosm of the climate-change and energy-security issue. If you don't get the full range of the right people in the room, you won't make the progress you hope for.

Transforming Tactic 2: The Way You Frame the Issue Is the First Act of Leadership

In bringing multiple and often opposing groups together, the way you position issues is critically important. Similar to the inclusive invitations that Margaret Jenkins sent out to welcome people to attend the first neighborhood meeting, the way you frame an issue needs to take into account the identities of all the groups that span the divide. Mark made a point of referring to the event as a "transpartisan retreat on climate change *and* energy security." He translates his remark this way:

> I kept stressing climate change and energy security because that was the only way to get all the right people in the room. If we had called it just "climate change," many of the people would not have come because it would have sounded as though the issue had already been settled. And this is one of the things that I always teach: how you frame the issue is one of your first acts of leadership.
>
> I would say that the state of the earth and the state of mankind hang in the balance between those two wings of the climate change and energy security debate. Much depends on how those poles actually deal with each other in coming generations. If we don't find a new way to develop that is sustainable, we're sunk.

Transforming Tactic 3: Give Equal Space to All Groups— Give All Groups an Equal Opportunity to Create and Envision an Alternative Future

Including people from all parts of the system and framing issues in an open and invitational way are two tactics for setting the stage for cross-cutting boundaries. Now that you are ready to bring competing and divided groups into direct contract, another tactic to consider is to give all the groups equal time and space to participate. As Mark states, this enables you to model respect and fairness for everyone:

> I needed to model respect for everybody. I needed to model fairness. I needed to model equal time for speakers on both sides of the issue. For example, we had two full nights during the three-day retreat. So we gave Al Gore one night, and he showed his slide show that later was expanded into the documentary film *An Inconvenient Truth*. He showed it to everybody, including the people who were taking out the attack ads against him. The next night, we gave the speaking forum to Fred Smith, head of the Competitive Enterprise Institute. And it was very clear that each side would have one evening, that both of the poles would have a shot.

Transforming Tactic 4: Allow All Groups to Confirm Their Core Values

Another tactic for cross-cutting boundaries is finding avenues that allow members of disparate groups to confirm their core values. At one level, this allows people to feel more grounded and secure.

At another level, it allows people to realize that despite their differences, members of both groups have decent and principled values that sometimes overlap. Mark describes putting this tactic into action:

> You begin by allowing people to affirm their core beliefs. As we have worked with transpartisan groups over the years, we have always given them an opportunity to affirm their core values. That makes them feel safer. So if everybody gets to say: "This is a core value I hold. I'm glad to be here, but I'm not changing my mind. When I leave, this is still going to be my core value," you could call that their nonnegotiable "yes." It's very important that when people start speaking, they're speaking about core values, not positions. Because if they start speaking about positions before you've built an environment amenable to negotiation, then they're stuck on those positions. So I try to get them to talk about their core values and to demonstrate their passion about those core values. And what you will find is that most people's core values are decent values. So you can have groups representing the entire American political spectrum, and people would have values such as justice, freedom, liberty, human rights. Nobody says, "My core value is racism or inequality." So you put the core values out there.

Transforming Tactic 5: Create a Channel for Both Positive and Negative Energy to Flow

The previous tactic highlights the importance of affirming core values. Now, as you seek to discover new frontiers, you have to draw out both similarities and differences. This final tactic can be used to create a channel for positive and negative energy to flow. The idea, as Mark explains, is to attempt to structure interactions around two channels or strands.

> I usually try to structure things around two strands, what I would call a "consensus" strand and a "conflict" strand. The conflict strand is where people across the spectrum come together and identify areas where they think they just won't be able to work together. The consensus strand is where people work to find areas where they might be able to work together. And we'll make a list of each strand. I try to establish a container where there can be that positive energy, what you could call yes energy, consensus energy. Then I try to give the negative energy, the conflict energy, a channel to move in. And I honor both of them. So with the two channels the groups can say: "In the morning we're going to have small groups where we're looking at areas of consensus. And in the afternoon we're going to have debates around issues A, B, and C that clearly are areas where we disagree."

Reinvention is an unfolding process without a definitive start or stop. No single moment or event, such as the transpartisan retreat, is sufficient to transform or resolve a challenge as daunting as climate change and energy security. Yet something distinctly changed in the nature of the climate debate back in 2004 in that Rocky Mountain conference center. Al Gore indicated that the industry wing had sensitized him to the legitimate concerns of conservatives regarding the way he had been talking about climate change. Climate change could be fought while still honoring the needs of businesses, he said, and in the future he would be clear on the critically important role of the private sector. As for the industry wing, its members came to concede that climate change may indeed be real, though they remained concerned that Gore and his supporters were exploiting it for political purposes.

Whether people someday will look back at those events in the Rocky Mountains as one of the tipping points in the climate debate within the United States is uncertain. Yet what is clear is that by bringing multiple and opposing groups together in new directions, the transpartisan retreat created new levels of awareness and understanding. In the ensuing months, the retreat set the stage for a number of follow-up meetings in which energy and climate were discussed without nearly the same amount of animosity that had characterized previous exchanges. Those conversations continue to this day.

The Leader's Role in Transforming

Your role as a transformer is to bring multiple groups together in emergent new directions to cross-cut boundaries and enable reinvention. Butch Peterman is cross-cutting boundaries at Abrasive Technology, Inc., to create a process-centered organization. Margaret Jenkins is cross-cutting boundaries to enable neighbors to imagine a new identity for the neighborhood that is not just an improvement of the old but potentially something very different altogether. And Mark Gerzon is cross-cutting boundaries to enable people, in his words, "to transcend partial, fragmented identities and embrace a wider, more integral vision of the planet."

As Butch, Margaret, and Mark will tell you, transforming is highly complex in practice. There are infinite possibilities for how you can bring multiple groups together in new ways. Reinvention is a time-consuming process that by definition is never fully completed. And transforming involves letting go of the past and the present and putting the weight of your efforts toward an emerging future.

Caution: The Pitfall of Transforming

In past chapters, we identified pitfalls you may encounter when enacting each of the boundary spanning practices. We offer these words of caution on the basis of the various ways each practice seeks to alter the nature and composition of boundaries between groups. This creates both good news and bad news in terms of the pitfalls for transforming. As this final practice can be considered a gestalt of the other five practices, the bad news is that all the pitfalls described in the previous chapters also apply to transforming. Feelings of threat, leadership trade-offs, complex in-group–out-group dynamics, and colliding values and beliefs can easily surface in the process of cross-cutting boundaries between groups. The good news, however, is that when relationships between groups are characterized by the outcomes of the other five practices—safety, respect, trust, community, and interdependence—a solid platform is intact for the practice of transforming. As a transformer, you will need to continue to cultivate your awareness of complex intergroup dynamics and learn ways to navigate the paradoxical tensions between unity and separation when groups collide, intersect, and link.

Transforming asks groups to open up their current identities to change. Current ways of understanding the world are considered starting points toward something new rather than end points that cannot be altered. Perhaps nowhere are these complexities felt more than they are in virtual and globally dispersed teams. These teams are assembled to achieve results even though their members often embody the deepest differences in the world. Sometimes they are capable of cross-cutting their boundaries to discover new frontiers. Yet more often than not, limiting borders constrain their ability to realize inspiring results.

Giving you made-to-order advice on how to lead in this environment takes us as authors to the frontier of our own current knowledge and experience. We are all collectively making it up as we go. However, returning to Mark Gerzon one final time, we find new insight. Mark has a favorite quote. It's from Albert Einstein, and Mark likes to carry a large Einstein poster with him in his travels around the world with this quote emblazoned at the bottom: "Problems cannot be solved at the current level of awareness that created them." We think this truth offers great potential for how you can become a transformer of boundaries.

We invite and challenge you to continue to grow and to develop yourself and the groups around you toward ever-higher levels of awareness. When our collective awareness expands, we are capable of thinking and acting beyond the boundaries that once limited us. This requires a paradoxical combination of deep humility and steadfast determination. Humility enables us to see the limits of our current identities within ourselves and in the groups we seek to bring together. Steadfast determination provides the inner intensity needed for transformation and a deep faith in the potential of the human spirit. We see these dualities come together in these final words from Mark Gerzon:

There was a crucial moment in the Gore event where I didn't know what to do. Two people had spoken on opposite sides of the issue. One had spoken eloquently about his view that the United States was going to have trouble leading the whole area of climate change because America was the most hated and most selfish country in the world. And he was obviously on the left, the "green wing." And then someone else, someone very close to President Bush, spoke and said that he refused to sit silently while the United States was described as hated and selfish. He said America was the most loved and most generous country in the world and that no country had done more for the world than the United States.

So after those two polarized statements, both of which had these two men with tears in their eyes, it was like, what do you do then? You could feel the room polarized around those two positions—America is selfish and hated, and America is generous and beloved. And the only proper response to that moment was humility—humility and silence. And that's what I did. I said: "Let's just take a moment of silence and hold these two men in our hearts. That's why we came here." And it was a very powerful moment.

And after some time had passed, I said: "Thank you for that silence. Thank you for holding these two men in your hearts. Now, who would like to speak?" I asked four people to speak, and I picked them carefully so they were across the spectrum. And they spoke with such wisdom and such appreciation for paradox. Before the silence it was as though we were being pulled apart by magnets. But after the silence there was a feeling of sacred wisdom.

Transforming and Your Nexus Challenge

Bringing multiple groups together in emergent new directions enables you to tap into an ongoing source of new possibilities that paves the way toward intergroup reinvention. The questions in column 1 of Table 9.1 will help you to apply transforming to your

Table 9.1 Transforming Summary

Definition What is transforming?	Bring multiple groups together in emergent, new directions to *cross-cut boundaries and enable intergroup reinvention.*
Rationale Why does transforming work?	With *transforming*, groups "cross-cut" their boundaries. When groups cut against the grain of their respective boundaries over time and continued interaction, new identities and new possibilities emerge. Identity-based values, beliefs, and perspectives between groups shift in fundamental and often transformative ways.
Tactics How is the practice to be accomplished?	1. Bring the whole system into the room. Gain representation across all groups and ensure maximum diversity of perspective. 2. How you frame the issue is the first act of leadership. Ask groups to leave behind old boundaries and place the weight of their efforts toward an emerging future. 3. Give equal space to all groups. Give all groups equal opportunity to create and envision new possibilities. 4. Allow all groups to confirm core values. Enable all groups to affirm both their core differences and similarities. 5. Create a channel for both positive and negative energy to flow. Channel both positive and negative energy to realize transformative opportunities.
Outcome What is the result?	*Intergroup reinvention*—the state of renewal, alternative futures, and emergent possibilities that develops when intergroup boundaries are cross-cut in new directions.

unique Nexus Challenge as well as other challenges and opportunities you face in discovering new frontiers between groups.

Discern: Assessing the Current State

Transforming cross-cuts boundaries to enable intergroup reinvention. On a scale of 1 to 10 (where 10 is the highest), how would you rate your team or organization on intergroup reinvention?

The potential for intergroup reinvention increases the more the following is true:

- Groups take advantage of or create opportunities for in-depth interactions in which they recognize existing constraints yet actively focus on creating a different future.
- Identity-based values, beliefs, and perspectives of multiple groups are open to inquiry and transformation.
- Groups invite opportunities for renewing, reenvisioning, and reimagining themselves and their environment as needs change and opportunities arise

Reflect: Exploring New Approaches

How could you take steps to increase representation and interaction across multiple organizational layers, functions, and regions as well as diverse demographic and cultural groups?

How could you more actively create time and space to bring multiple groups together in new directions to imagine cutting-edge possibilities and alternative futures?

What are the borders that confine and limit you? How can you learn to continually evolve your own level of awareness to think and act beyond today's borders and create the future?

Apply: Taking Action

What is one idea, tactic, or new insight you've learned about transforming that you could apply to your Nexus Challenge?

PART 5

THE NEXUS EFFECT

When groups achieve the six outcomes that result from *buffering, reflecting, connecting, mobilizing, weaving,* and *transforming*, they have the potential to achieve the Nexus Effect (see Figure P5.1). When safety, respect, trust, community, interdependence, and reinvention characterize the interactions between groups, those groups will achieve something together above and beyond what they could achieve on their own. In Part 5, we explore the limitless possibilities and inspiring results that exist when groups achieve the Nexus Effect.

In Chapter 10, we describe how John Herrera used all six boundary spanning leadership practices to bring three divergent groups together to create the Latino Community Credit Union, an inspiring example of the Nexus Effect in action. We also further explore your unique Nexus Challenge and examine how the six boundary spanning leadership practices may help you not only resolve this

Figure P5.1 The boundary spanning leadership model.

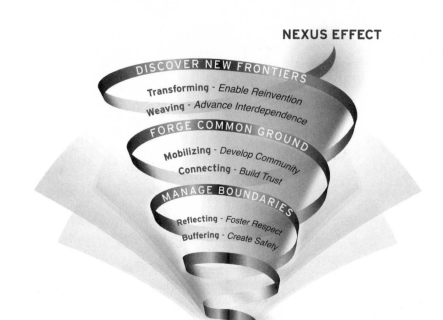

NEXUS EFFECT

DISCOVER NEW FRONTIERS

Transforming - Enable Reinvention

Weaving - Advance Interdependence

FORGE COMMON GROUND

Mobilizing - Develop Community

Connecting - Build Trust

MANAGE BOUNDARIES

Reflecting - Foster Respect

Buffering - Create Safety

GREAT DIVIDE

challenge but tap into the potential that can be found at the nexus between groups.

In the Epilogue, we revisit the stories of the boundary spanning leaders who exemplify each of the six practices. We look into the future to predict what may happen if the possibilities that exist at the nexus between groups are fully realized. What kinds of problems might we be able to solve? What innovative ideas might emerge? And how might organizations serve as catalysts for positively transformative change in business and society as a whole?

CHAPTER **10**

THE NEXUS EFFECT
AND YOU

Throughout this book, we've seen boundary spanning leaders solve problems, drive innovation, and create positively transformative outcomes for their organizations and communities. The stories are extraordinary, but the leaders themselves are often quite ordinary. They confronted challenges much like the ones you may be facing right now in your organization. At Insurance Incorporated in South Africa, Joe and Zanele defined boundaries and created a more psychologically safe environment for their employees by being willing to stand up and speak out. Rick Givens experienced a transformation within himself that paved the way to greater respect for differences and then led a successful change effort by creating a new understanding of the boundaries between immigrants and non-immigrants in Chatham County, North Carolina. In Europe, Daniel Sutton was able to suspend boundaries and build trust across three divergent groups—energy executives, environmentalists, and government leaders—to develop a new, more sustainable plan for their city. At Lenovo in China, leaders from East and West reframed boundaries to craft a new and inclusive organizational identity, positioning the company to become the world's most innovative personal computer (PC) firm. In India, Ingrid Srinath interlaced boundaries between different regional groups to lead a successful strategic change effort and advance interdependence in support of CRY's mission. In the mountains of Colorado, Mark Gerzon crosscut boundaries across groups engaged in a heated debate over global climate in search of transformative solutions and reinvention of a systemic global problem.

Buffering, reflecting, connecting, mobilizing, weaving, transforming—out of these six boundary spanning practices come safety, respect, trust, community, interdependence, and reinvention. As each outcome is achieved and intergroup collaboration increases, leaders move farther up the spiral, transforming the limited and counterproductive outcomes of Great Divides into the limitless possibilities and inspiring results of the Nexus Effect. By establishing a nexus between groups, leaders can create something new and innovative, facilitate a significant change or shift in the organization, or solve a problem that can be dealt with only when groups work collaboratively. Leaders create the Nexus Effect by spanning boundaries and harnessing the energy between groups that is above and beyond the energy created by groups working alone.

The word *nexus* comes from the Latin word *nectere*, which means "to bind." A nexus is a form of connection, a link, or a tie.[1] In scientific terms, a nexus is a specialized cellular connection that enables molecules and ions to pass freely between cells. In technological terms, Nexus was the name given to the world's first Web browser, developed by Sir Tim Berners-Lee in 1990. In mathematical terms, Alfred North Whitehead, a nineteenth- and twentieth-century English mathematician and philosopher, described a nexus as a system of relationships in which the whole is greater than its parts. Combining elements at the precise time and in a precise way can result in a multiplicative effect in which $1 + 1 > 2$. For example, in manufacturing, the yield from two machines working together, in concert, is greater than what can be achieved by both machines working independently of each other. The same principle can hold true for organizations, where groups that are able to work collaboratively achieve infinitely more than they would if they worked alone. In this case, the presence of one group enhances the other.

We define the Nexus Effect as *the limitless possibilities and inspiring results that groups can achieve together above and beyond what they could achieve on their own.*[2] Unlike the nearly limitless connections found in biological cells or on the Internet, a collaborative nexus between groups is not something we see happening every day, probably because creating the Nexus Effect is not easy. But you know it when you see it. You can spot it by the energy and sense of resolve you get from talking to someone who has experienced the Nexus Effect. Those people are excited to share their story, the barriers they overcame, and how it once seemed impossible to get where they are today.

This is what we felt when we sat down to have lunch with John Herrera, senior vice president of Self-Help, an organization whose mission is "creating and protecting ownership and economic opportunity for people of color, women, rural residents and low-wealth families and communities." We initially invited John to lunch to learn more about his role in working with Rick Givens, Chatham

County, and the Latino Initiative program. But it wasn't long before John started to tell us the story of the Latino Community Credit Union (LCCU) based in Durham, North Carolina. His passion for LCCU and the pride he felt in overcoming the many challenges he faced were evident as we ate sushi and drank sweet tea. We knew then and there that we'd found a great example of the Nexus Effect or, rather, that it had found us.

In 1999, John was hired by Martin Eakes, president of Self-Help, to expand the organization's mission to the Latino and immigrant community. He was tasked with what seemed like an impossible job: finding a way to provide economic opportunities for some of the poorest people in the community. John received helpful advice from his inspiring mentor, Martin, a MacArthur Foundation "genius" award winner and the recipient of *Fast Company* magazine's 20 Social Capitalists That Are Changing the World award. "Martin told me that great things will happen as long as no one cares who gets the credit," John said. "Martin is a living example of this advice. He is humble to the core, always looking to deflect attention somewhere else. I took his advice to heart."

John decided that what was needed most was a credit union specifically designed to meet the unique needs of an immigrant population, needs that included getting a loan without a credit history or even a social security number. Most Latinos in the community were distrustful of banks and carried their money with them or hid it under their mattresses. This contributed to greater crime in the community as robberies were far too common because Latinos felt that there was no safe place to store their money. Some called them "walking banks" because criminals saw this as easy money.

John believed that if he could build a credit union in which Latinos felt it was safe to invest their money and to trust its leaders, this would contribute to lower crime and the community as a whole would prosper. But other leaders in the banking industry thought John was crazy. Giving loans to poor people was just plain bad business. How could a financial institution put itself in the risky position of providing loans to people who owned virtually nothing? But John was not deterred. He knew what a strong work ethic members of the immigrant community lived by and also knew how important it was for them to get loans. "Without a credit history, you're nobody in this country," he told us.

John began to work with several leaders, in particular with two influential men in the community who over time became both mentors and business partners. He sought the help of Jim Blaine, an older and well-respected white man in the community. Jim was the CEO of the State Employees' Credit Union of North Carolina (SECU), the second largest credit union in the world. He also sought help from Linwood Cox, the CEO of the North Carolina Minority Support Center (NCMSC), a nonprofit coalition of 15 African-American credit unions. Cox was an influential and highly successful African-American man in the community. By working closely with Jim Blaine and Linwood Cox and the different organizations and communities they served, John created a powerful nexus between groups. With their help, John founded the Latino Community Credit Union, the fastest-growing credit union in the country today.

John's story illustrates how boundary spanning leadership can lead to the Nexus Effect. At the nexus between groups, John enacted the six boundary spanning practices to achieve inspiring results.

Many tactics are possible, and the path to collaboration may be anything but linear. In fact, in your own boundary spanning work, you may find yourself taking two steps forward and one step back. Or your starting point may be different if safety, respect, and trust already exist across groups. However, your journey probably will be similar to John's in that you will need to manage boundaries, forge common ground, and discover new frontiers to realize the outcomes of the Nexus Effect. John's inspiring story illustrates how boundary spanning leadership can serve as a catalyst for positive outcomes within organizations and in the broader communities they serve.

MANAGING BOUNDARIES

Creating Intergroup Safety through Buffering

John's path toward the Nexus Effect began with defining a clear organizational mission and thus building a protective wall around the organization's identity. He engaged in the leadership practice of buffering: monitoring and protecting the flow of information and resources across groups to define boundaries and create intergroup safety. John and his team were clear from the beginning that they were a nonprofit organization, not a bank. A credit union differs from a bank in several important ways. Unlike a bank, whose primary mission is to generate a profit, a credit union's primary mission is to provide people with access to loans and affordable financial services. Each member of the credit union is an equal owner of the union, and every member has the right to vote at the annual meeting.

In addition to being a credit union and thus a nonprofit entity, John knew that whatever organization he created had to be one that Latinos in the community trusted enough to take their money out from under the mattress and place it in the care of the credit union. To accomplish this, John created a different kind of credit union, one in which personal interactions and the importance of family were evident in the way business was conducted. From the very beginning, employees at LCCU were encouraged to call members by name, ask how their family members were doing, and take the time to connect with each member on a personal level. To date, LCCU has no drive-through option because the credit union places a high value on one-to-one interaction and the personal touch that occurs when people do business face to face. Each branch also has a playground on-site so that families can let their children play safely while they conduct business at the credit union. John created a place that families look forward to visiting and where members feel welcome, comfortable, and safe.

One of the biggest hurdles John had to face was working within the legal constraints inherent in providing loans and financial services to an immigrant population, many of whose members do not have a social security number. He had to define the boundaries of their business and clearly demarcate practices that were legal and illegal. The reality was that LCCU would need to serve undocumented immigrants; thus, they had to find a way to serve "illegal immigrants" legally. Although it is common practice now, LCCU was one of the first credit unions in the country to encourage members not eligible for a social security number to obtain an Individual Taxpayer Identification Number (ITIN). By obtaining an ITIN, which previously was something used only by wealthy foreign investors, low-income immigrants had a legal way to pay taxes. Also, with an ITIN, undocumented immigrants were able to join the credit union and begin to develop a credit history.

John acted as a buffer by creating a clear and compelling mission for LCCU: to be a unique credit union that caters to the needs of Latino families by emphasizing a personal touch and family values. He established a clear identity for LCCU and showed how it was different from profit-driven banks and credit unions that fail to meet the unique needs of an immigrant population. In contrast, LCCU is run and owned by its members, and many of its staff members are bilingual and bicultural. John defined the boundary that surrounds LCCU. He also acted as a buffer by managing the flow of information in terms of legal and illegal practices. One of John's most important duties as leader, when LCCU was in its infancy as well as now, has been to ensure full compliance with laws and regulations as a state-regulated and federally insured financial institution that serves immigrants. Through buffering, John created the right conditions to allow groups to interact and work across boundaries in a safe environment and created a place where Latinos felt it was safe to store their hard-earned money. As a result, applications for membership skyrocketed and went far beyond anyone's expectations. Early forecasts set an application target of 500 new members a year. This goal was broken within the first two months: LCCU grew at a rate of over 1,000 members a month!

Fostering Intergroup Respect through Reflecting

By clearly defining boundaries between groups, John initiated his journey toward the Nexus Effect, but it was just a start. John knew that if he was going to be successful in creating a different kind of credit union that met the unique needs of an immigrant population, he was going to have to reach out to other communities and credit unions for help. John shared his thinking at the time: "I always felt that we were dealing with a unique community, a very vulnerable community, both financially and emotionally. I figured the more allies we had, the safer we were going to be. When we did a SWOT [strengths, weaknesses, opportunities, and threats] analysis, we realized that other minority groups (such as the African-American credit unions) could potentially be a threat to our goals. But we decided that if we worked with them rather than against them, we could turn this threat into an opportunity." John knew the needs and values of the Latino immigrant community well. But he also recognized how important it was to understand what had made credit unions successful in other communities and learn from the experience of others. For that reason he engaged in the practice of reflecting: representing distinct perspectives and encouraging knowledge exchange across groups to understand boundaries and foster intergroup respect. John did a lot of listening and learning before he created LCCU.

He sought guidance from Jim Blaine, the prominent white businessman who had been highly successful in creating a credit union for state employees. At the time, the state of North Carolina had the fastest-growing Latino population in the country. That created a number of growing pains for the state as Latinos and other groups suddenly found themselves living and working side by side. The explosion in the Latino population created tremendous opportunity for a Great Divide or the Nexus Effect. Reaching across the boundary between the white and Latino communities, John asked

Jim Blaine to become a member of the board of directors he was putting together for the credit union. Blaine was the CEO of the State Employees' Credit Union of North Carolina (SECU), and John knew he could learn a lot from him.

Although John had great passion for creating a credit union for immigrants, he had very little formal business training. He had a degree in agriculture but not an MBA, and so he reached across boundary lines and asked Jim to join the board of directors, hoping that the invitation to get involved would create a path for potential collaboration. John believed that working together would create more opportunities for both organizations than would working against each other. "I needed an insurance policy," John told us. He knew that Jim was a powerful figure in the community and wanted him on his side: "Mr. Blaine is a nationally recognized credit union leader who has confronted banks for their abusive practices that harm consumers. We're going to need somebody on our side who's big enough to pick and win a good fight. And Jim Blaine can win."

The two men spent time getting to know each other and their respective communities and organizations. Jim encouraged John and helped him learn the business. Jim had learned about the credit union business through hard work and resilience and inspired John to do the same thing. They met regularly for coffee and exchanged ideas. Jim shared his experiences and successes, and John shared his vision for LCCU. The two didn't always see eye to eye, but both listened and learned from each other. Over time, both men developed greater respect not only for each other but for the groups they represented. They learned a great deal by using the leadership practice of reflecting, and Jim even learned a bit of Spanish along the way. Jim served an important role as mentor and advisor in the development of the LCCU. John told us, "He let us make our own mistakes but also coached us and taught us." John played an important role as a reflector. He not only learned a great deal from Jim about business in the dominant community by asking questions and listening but also provided Jim with a window into the Latino community and what was unique and different about their two cultures. John and Jim both practiced reflecting by representing the unique perspectives and experiences of the Latino and white communities to each other so that each could better understand the boundary between them. John told us that listening and learning from others was a big part of his early success. It led to mutual respect and a successful partnership between LCCU and SECU and between the Latino and white communities.

FORGING COMMON GROUND

Building Intergroup Trust through Connecting

By enacting the practices of buffering and reflecting, John was ready to move up the spiral toward higher levels of collaboration—to go beyond managing boundaries and toward forging common ground. His next step was to reach across yet another boundary to seek input and assistance from leaders within the African-American community. He asked Linwood Cox for help. As a leader in the North Carolina Minority Support Center (NCMSC), a nonprofit coalition of 15 African-American community development credit unions, Linwood was well respected within the African-American community. At first, Linwood thought that inviting a highly influential man from the white community such as Jim Blaine would be professional suicide. He told John that he was crazy for giving all the power away to the whites. But John didn't see it that way. He figured that the real power came from working together, not separately. He believed that he was increasing the strength and power of LCCU by reaching across racial boundaries.

The three men and others on the board of directors worked hard to generate a business model for LCCU. Over time, the mutual respect that developed as a result of sharing different perspectives and learning from one another evolved into relationships marked by a high level of trust. The racial boundaries that were once prominent faded and virtually disappeared over time. Distrust about who had the most power and influence largely disappeared as group members got to know one another and talked about ways they could work together for mutual benefit and success.

As a result of the relationship that emerged between John and Linwood, LCCU became the first Hispanic credit union to become part of the NCMSC coalition of credit unions, and Linwood asked John to join its board. As trust across the different communities continued to strengthen, Jim and John also established a business partnership that would serve both of their organizations well. SECU ultimately provided the Latino credit union with the capital required to get started. The creation of these partnerships was a tangible outcome of the practice of connecting: linking people and bridging divided groups to suspend boundaries and build intergroup trust. The three men were able to reach across and ultimately break down the racial boundaries that once separated them to develop trusting relationships that paved the way for collaboration. Connecting with people across boundaries is not a simple task. "Once you let folks know that you understand their pain and where they're coming from," John explains, "they open up to talk to you. Once you manage to get that door open, they start to trust you." By building trust, John was able to lay the groundwork needed to forge common ground.

Developing Intergroup Community through Mobilizing

With a solid foundation that included intergroup safety, respect, and trust, John was able to reach farther and higher toward the limitless possibilities and inspiring results of the Nexus Effect. A critical moment arrived when John and Linwood went together, as a united team, before the North Carolina General Assembly to lobby for funding. In the past, the Minority Support Center had asked and typically received about half a million dollars from the assembly, but John thought that if the Latino and African-American communities banded together and asked for funding, the assembly would have to pay attention: "Critical mass. Black and brown—that is the future." John told Linwood that he thought they should approach the assembly together and ask them for $10 million. Again, Linwood thought he was crazy, but he soon was convinced by John that through a show of solidarity, they could win over the assembly.

John described the scene for us: "You see this black man and a Latino man walking together in the hallways of the very conservative General Assembly in North Carolina. Black and brown together. Can you believe it—they gave us five million dollars! That victory in itself consolidated everything I had been dreaming about. There was a sense that day among the government officials. … My God, they've figured it out. Black and brown, they are actually working together. We better help these folks because they are the future."

The award from the General Assembly was a significant victory for LCCU but also for the Minority Support Center. The NCMSC had never received an award that big, and it went a long way toward accomplishing the organization's mission. Both John and Linwood were energized by what they were able to accomplish by working collaboratively and creating a shared group identity—black and brown working together. They engaged in the practice of mobilizing: crafting a common purpose and shared identity across groups to reframe boundaries and develop intergroup community. What once seemed to be a border that separated the two racial communities began to emerge as a new frontier that both groups could mobilize for significant gain. By reframing boundaries, John and Linwood were able to build intergroup community and create a shared identity with a common purpose.

DISCOVERING NEW FRONTIERS

Advancing Intergroup Interdependence through Weaving

Through the practices of connecting and mobilizing, John was able to forge common ground between groups. Whereas managing boundaries taps into the powerful need for differentiation, forging common ground taps into the equally powerful need for integration. Now John was ready to take the final step: moving beyond forging common ground to discover new frontiers. Here, at the juncture of similarities and differences, John was able to capitalize on new possibilities and innovative opportunities. He worked closely with Jim to develop a business model and lending policies that would work for LCCU. Initially, Jim's position was that the lending policies that had worked for SECU would work for LCCU, but John convinced him otherwise. John recalls those early conversations: "I remember in the beginning, Jim said a loan is a loan. No matter if the person is black, Chinese, white, whatever." But John felt strongly that the Latino community was unique and needed lending policies that were different from those of the white community and reflected its own culture. He listened intently to what had worked for Jim with state employees and how the lending policies of SECU had been highly successful but then told Jim he felt LCCU needed different lending policies because Mexico is a cash-based economy. Almost two-thirds of Mexicans do not have a bank account: "In the Latino community, having debt means that you are irresponsible. But Latinos in the United States will take out a loan to buy a used car so that they can get to work every day."

Of course, acquiring debt is important to establish a credit history in the United States; that in turn allows a person to obtain credit for future purchases. Credit is important in the United States and necessary for Latinos and immigrants to play a role in the U.S. financial system. In the end, Jim and John agreed that LCCU lending policies had to be different from those of the SECU, and so LCCU became the first credit union in the country to lend up to $10,000 to members with no credit history. In terms of traditional financial principles, this seemed ludicrous, but John was right. The fact is that nearly 100 percent of the members repaid their loans. LCCU has the lowest delinquency rate of any credit union in North Carolina. Today the delinquency rate is less than 1 percent for LCCU, whereas this figure can be as high as 30 percent for credit unions across the country.

John engaged in the practice of weaving: drawing out and integrating group differences within a larger whole to interlace boundaries and advance intergroup interdependence. He was able to call out and draw on the differences between the white and Latino cultures and combine them into a larger vision of the partnership of SECU and LCCU. Both Jim and John initially held strong positions on the lending policy that should be used, but by reconciling and integrating their differences, they came out with a creative solution—to lend up to $10,000 to new members. This was something that had never been done before but was made possible because both groups learned from the other and wove their differences together in a unique way. The two organizations became interdependent in the sense that they have unique members and thus unique policies but also share a number of policies and operating principles that allow for a successful partnership. Recall too that Jim had a vested interest in the success of LCCU, as his organization provided the initial capital investment to launch the new credit union. Because John and Jim were able to keep in mind both their higher, shared mission and the unique needs of their respective stakeholder groups, they were able to come up with a new way of doing business that in the end provided great financial benefits to both organizations.

Enabling Intergroup Reinvention through Transforming

In creating a nexus between groups, LCCU, SECU, and the Minority Support Center have all benefited far more than they would have if the three organizations worked in isolation. John, Jim, and Linwood, along with their respective organizations, have essentially reinvented what a credit union is and does in their community. They engaged in the practice of transforming by cross-cutting boundaries and bringing multiple groups together in emergent new directions to enable intergroup reinvention. As a result, they have created inspiring results not only for their organizations but also for the broader communities they serve.

The reinvention that has resulted from cross-cutting boundaries is perhaps most evident as you walk in the door of any of the nine branches of the LCCU. What you'll notice almost immediately are the brightly colored flags that hang from the ceiling, representing not just the Latino countries but many others as well. John tells us that in hindsight, the only thing he would do differently is to change the name of the credit union to reflect its broader purpose. What has happened is that the credit union has gone beyond serving the Latino community and now serves a much more diverse membership that includes a large and growing number of Asian, African, and European immigrants. Members are encouraged to bring the flags of their countries and hang them from the ceiling of *their* credit union so that they feel at home when they walk in the door. Through the practice of transforming, LCCU and its board of directors reinvented the concept of a credit union and created one that represents a variety of nationalities, races, and stakeholder groups.

The three men and their organizations have collaboratively created an alternative future that allows and encourages their diverse racial communities to learn and grow together. John believes the attitude that "white folks can't be trusted" has been challenged as a result of the boundary spanning work these three men and their respective organizations have accomplished. He believes the work they have done has paved the way for future collaborations across boundaries in the community. Today, these three groups continue to work together to support one another and help one another grow and succeed. Where there was once a limiting border, there are now limitless possibilities for innovative and collaborative endeavors.

Realizing the Nexus Effect

By envisioning boundaries as frontiers rather than borders, John Herrera, Linwood Cox, and Jim Blaine were able to create the Nexus Effect: the limitless possibilities and inspiring results that groups can achieve together above and beyond what they could achieve on their own. LCCU has been successful beyond what anyone predicted or even dreamed was possible. Although many thought giving loans to poor people and immigrants could not be done or was simply bad business, the success of LCCU is proof of what can happen when leaders think and act beyond boundaries. A decade after it opened its doors, LCCU's results are indeed inspiring, and the possibilities for the future are boundless.

LCCU has grown to include nine branches in North Carolina and reports $91 million in assets. It financed over $200 million worth of home and car loans in the last 10 years and continues to grow at a rate of almost 800 new members a month. LCCU now serves the needs of low-wealth families and immigrants from many diverse communities. It continues to be the fastest-growing credit union in the United States and is poised to be the financial institution of choice for an increasingly prosperous and rapidly growing immigrant community.

However, the energy John Herrera and many others created at the nexus between groups isn't limited to the present. Once a Nexus

Effect is created in which groups collide, intersect, and link, the energy is sustainable and expansive. This energy ripples outward well beyond its original source. Within the United States, LCCU now serves as a model for other states. Leaders from Oregon to Georgia and from Vermont to Texas are learning from John and others at LCCU how to replicate this model within their own states. U.S. Treasury Secretary Timothy Geithner invited LCCU to Washington, D.C., for a meeting to explore strategies to strengthen community development financial institutions across the country. Yet as we look to the future, perhaps the most exciting new opportunity will unfold in a building just a few blocks from where the credit union first opened its doors a decade ago.

Lured in large part by the inspiring and ongoing collaborations between the credit unions and community development institutions in Durham, North Carolina, Muhammad Yunus, winner of the 2006 Nobel Peace Prize, is on the verge of opening one of its charter U.S. operations for Grameen America within the community. With its origins in Bangladesh, the Grameen Bank revolutionized the "microlending" movement as a way to provide funding for more than 7.6 million impoverished people to start small businesses. It now has branches in 81,343 villages around the world, and Yunus envisions serving a million low-income entrepreneurs across the United States, including those in John, Jim, and Linwood's community. With an expanding network of financial resources available to their customers, the future is inspiring for LCCU, Self-Help, SECU, the NCMSC, and the people they serve.

Once a Nexus Effect is created in which groups collide, intersect, and link, the energy that is created extends far beyond its original source. As this energy moves upward and outward, new frontiers are discovered and old borders fade away. We see this happening in the inspiring boundary spanning leadership of John Herrera as well as in the stories of other leaders described in this book. We hope these stories have inspired you to take action and create a plan for resolving your own unique Nexus Challenge.

Solving Your Nexus Challenge

In this book we've described six boundary spanning practices for realizing new opportunities and inspiring results at the nexus between groups. We believe that these six practices, which are grounded in CCL research, will prove helpful in solving a wide range of challenges that require collaboration across groups, including yours. That said, only you will be able to determine the specific practices and tactics to use in your unique situation. This final activity is designed to enable you to capture your key insights and identify the next steps for solving your Nexus Challenge. In Chapter 1, you identified a specific challenge that can be solved only by leading across boundaries. We returned to your Nexus Challenge in the reflection questions at the end of each of the six practice chapters. Let's pull all the pieces together by *discerning* your challenge, *assessing* the current state, and, finally, *taking action*.

To complete this activity, you will need to turn back to the following pages (or go to www.spanboundaries.com)

- Initial description of your Nexus Challenge: Chapter 1, page 36
- Buffering: Chapter 4, page 102

- Reflecting: Chapter 5, page 123
- Connecting: Chapter 6, page 147
- Mobilizing: Chapter 7, page 167
- Weaving: Chapter 8, page 194
- Transforming: Chapter 9, page 217

Discern: Understanding the Nature of Your Nexus Challenge

The American philosopher John Dewey once said: "A problem is half-solved if properly stated." In Chapter 1, you completed several steps in order to state your Nexus Challenge and give it a specific headline. Before assessing your challenge and taking action, it is important to revisit the way you described it. Now that you've read the book, would you change or expand upon the four questions you answered in Chapter 1? Specifically, consider the following:

1. *What is your Nexus Challenge?* Would you now describe your challenge differently? Are any changes in your headline needed?
2. *Why is it a challenge?* Has your reason for listing this as a significant challenge changed? Beyond organizational structures and systems, can you now identify any deeper issues in human relationships that need to be addressed?
3. *How will you navigate this challenge?* Has your thinking about how you need to address this challenge changed in any significant way?

4. *What if you were to solve this challenge?* Are there any shifts in your thinking in terms of the outcomes that can be realized if you successfully solve this challenge?

Assess: Capturing the Current State

Recall that at the end of each of the six practice chapters, you were asked to rate your team or organization. Now transfer your six ratings into the space provided in Figure 10.1.

Figure 10.1 Ratings.

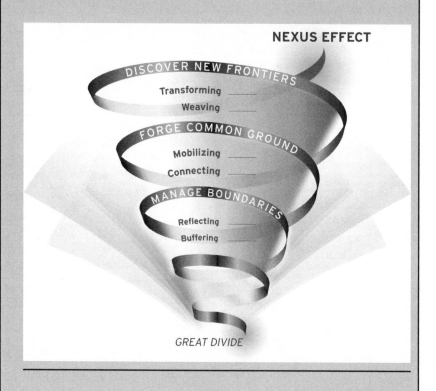

When you reflect on your ratings, what stands out for you? What patterns do you notice? What practice has the highest rating? The lowest? Does anything surprise you? As no two challenges are the same, we would expect significant variation in ratings from leader to leader. For some, the managing boundaries practices—reflecting and buffering—will have the highest ratings. For others, all six will be high, though we wouldn't expect anyone to have all 10s. For yet others, all six will be low.

Now consider what these ratings may mean for your unique Nexus Challenge. Because the six practices of boundary spanning leadership are never complete, we use the image of a spiral to suggest the notion of movement: forward and upward but sometimes backward and downward. Where groups collide, intersect, and link, the potential for the Nexus Effect is there, but so is the potential for a Great Divide. The six practices are not simply "tasks" that you do once and check off your list. Rather, to solve your Nexus Challenge or any challenge that requires creating direction, alignment, and commitment across groups, you will need to create an environment where these practices can take place repeatedly over time. You will find that you continuously must lead groups upward, toward greater intergroup collaboration, and toward the Nexus Effect. That said, solving your Nexus Challenge begins with the first step. Below are several final questions to enable you to identify the specific actions you will take next.

Act: Identifying Your Next Steps

Recall that each practice chapter ends with the following question: What is one idea, tactic, or new insight you've learned that you could apply to your Nexus Challenge? In Table 10.1, we provide an action-planning table. Here you can transfer your responses for each practice in the space provided and write down resources and dates you'll need to consider when taking your next steps.

Table 10.1 Your Nexus Challenge Action Plan

Boundary Spanning Practice	Tactic, Idea, or Insight	Resources Needed	Timeline
Buffering			
Reflecting			
Connecting			
Mobilizing			
Weaving			
Transforming			

What other actions can you take beyond those listed above? For additional inspiration, here are several questions to consider. If your answers spark any new ideas, add them to your Nexus Challenge action plan.

1. In the Discern section above, you considered whether the way you would describe your Nexus Challenge has changed in any notable way after reading this book. If the description of your challenge has changed, does this suggest any additional actions you would like to take?

2. In Appendix B, we provide a summary table of specific actions for each practice organized by the five boundary dimensions: vertical, horizontal, stakeholder, demographic, and geographic. In reviewing this table, are there any additional actions you'd like to take?

3. In the Assess section above, you captured the ratings you gave to your team or organization for all six practice outcomes. In reviewing your highest and lowest ratings, does this suggest any additional actions you'd like to take?

You now have identified the next steps for resolving your Nexus Challenge. The tools and approaches you have read about in this book will help you not only to address your current challenge but also to prepare for an increasingly collaborative future. We appreciate that the journey ahead won't be easy. But as the stories of the leaders described in this book convey, the opportunity for inspiring results are many when leaders span boundaries. The ever-changing world we live in will present more and more opportunities for collaboration as well as conflict at the nexus between groups. What possibilities may the future bring for transforming today's limiting borders into tomorrow's limitless frontiers? We close by considering this question in the Epilogue.

TOWARD AN INTERDEPENDENT, COLLABORATIVE FUTURE

Citizens who cultivate their humanity need an ability to see themselves not simply as citizens of some local region or group but also, and above all, as human beings bound to all other human beings by ties of recognition and concern. ... Issues from business to agriculture, from human rights to the relief of famine, call our imaginations to venture beyond narrow group loyalties and consider the reality of distant lives.

—Martha C. Nussbaum: *Cultivating Humanity: A Classical Defense of Reform in Liberal Education* (Harvard University Press, 1997)

Throughout history, humans have lived and worked in groups and have survived and flourished by collaborating with others. Today, advancing technology, changing global demographics, and accelerating globalization have expanded the scale of human collaboration to encompass every corner of the world. We collaborate because the challenges we face in business and society are interdependent: They can be solved only by groups working productively together. However, it is also true that our potential for collaboration remains largely unrealized. The world may be boundless and flat, but we remain bounded and confined by powerful limits.

What if the efforts of the boundary spanning leaders you've encountered throughout this book *became fully realized* in the years ahead? This is the question we set out to explore in this Epilogue. We'll return to the stories one last time to imagine what is ultimately possible when leaders transform limiting borders into limitless new frontiers. But first, let's take a look at the landscape for leadership in the years ahead.

Though we acknowledge that we lack a clairvoyant vision of the future, this much is clear: The need for spanning vertical boundaries between levels; horizontal boundaries between functions; stakeholder boundaries across a vast array of customers, suppliers, and communities; demographic boundaries in working with every type of human diversity imaginable; and geographic boundaries across distance and regions will only intensify.

As reported by the 128 senior executives who participated in our Leadership at the Peak study, facilitating greater collaboration across horizontal boundaries is the most persistent challenge that leaders face today. Looking ahead, our expectation is that the challenge of horizontal boundaries will be matched by equally relentless challenges in leading across geographic, demographic, and stakeholder boundaries. As organizations expand their footprint to all corners of the world, employ an increasingly diverse talent pool, and seek new competitive advantage through complex interorganizational alliances, joint ventures, and partnerships, the six boundary spanning practices detailed in this book will become the everyday work of leadership. The need to bridge, span, and reach across boundaries in human relationships will only strengthen as our world flattens.

Depending on how you look at it, these realities can be seen as headaches to avoid or exciting opportunities to seize. In this book, we've clearly sided with the latter view, and so have the leaders we've profiled in these pages. Each has created a nexus between groups to achieve new possibilities and inspiring results above and beyond what groups could achieve on their own. Where do their stories go from here? Through their efforts, what new opportunities for problem solving could arise? What alternative futures could be not just imagined but realized? What if the inspiring leaders we've highlighted in the book were able to sustain and build on the positive energy they created through the Nexus Effect? Just imagine what would happen if . . .

What if Joe Pettit and Zanele Moyo work together to create a more psychologically safe environment for their colleagues in a postapartheid South African organization. What if Joe convinces other members of the senior management team that the racial tensions beneath the surface at Insurance Incorporated are an important issue to address head on? What if Zanele continues to speak out courageously on behalf of her black women colleagues? Imagine that these conversations spread and there is a growing realization that deeply embedded tensions across groups are creating counterproductive results. Imagine that the Great Divide representing black and white culture within Insurance Incorporated is transformed from a limiting border to a frontier offering new opportunity.

Insurance Incorporated recognizes that black and white clients view insurance differently: Each group values something different in a policy. What if Insurance Incorporated identifies the unique insurance needs in both cultures and uses that knowledge to offer customized policies to black and white South Africans? Market share grows by leaps and bounds over the competition, and Insurance Incorporated becomes the insurer of choice across South Africa. When leaders span boundaries, intractable challenges can be transformed into bottom-line results and inspiring solutions.

What if the next generation of leaders in Chatham County follows in Rick Givens's footsteps and continues to foster respect between immigrants and nonimmigrants in Chatham County, North Carolina? Imagine that in the near future a special congressional panel is formed to craft a pivotal legislative policy on immigration and contacts Chatham County leaders for guidance. The community has become a model for improving relations between immigrants and nonimmigrants. As a result, Chatham County leaders now play a critical role in efforts to span boundaries between immigrants and nonimmigrants in communities across the United States. The pending legislation fuels a heated debate in which borders are secured and battle lines are drawn. Yet this time, in part inspired by the alternative future created in Chatham County, the discussion and debate serve to improve understanding across groups on all sides of the issue. The seeds of respect that flourished in Chatham County continue to grow, encouraging citizens and government leaders to think and act beyond current borders. Ultimately, groups on all sides coalesce around a new approach to immigration that fully takes into account the complexities of the issue. When leaders span boundaries, the most vexing problems can be tackled and creatively resolved.

What if the members of the cross-sector task force take what they learned from Daniel Sutton about linking people and building trust and apply it in their own spheres of influence? Imagine that this creates a multiplier effect by rapidly expanding the network of relationships between business executives, environmentalists, and government leaders. This connected and collaborative leadership network then aligns around a goal of becoming a carbon-neutral city. They boldly move forward on a number of cutting-edge green energy initiatives. The city's economy rapidly diversifies, and at the same time, air quality and the natural environment flourish. A dream becomes realized when the city is recognized as the first carbon-neutral urban center in the world. When leaders span boundaries, direction, alignment, and commitment can be created to accomplish and sustain a compelling vision.

What if Lenovo fully realizes its potential to create the world's most innovative PCs, with leading market positions in both developed and emerging economies? What if the tactics used by leaders at Lenovo lead to a fundamental rethinking of how to merge organizations with different cultures? Building on the example set by Lenovo, imagine that leaders in future mergers don't just manage the alignment of operational systems but also actively lead the creation of a new organizational culture and identity. When leaders span boundaries, new sources of value—physical, human, financial— can be discovered at the intersection of different values, experiences, and expertise. Furthermore, what if the Lenovo success story inspires other creative and exciting East-West partnerships? The possibilities for collaboration are limitless, ranging from new economic policies to new art forms, from advances in holistic medicine to fusion cuisine, and from transnational business alliances to efforts to create a more just, safe, and peaceful planet. When leaders span boundaries, today's borders between East and West and North and South can become the source for tomorrow's innovative frontiers.

What if CRY's vision is fulfilled: an India in which every child, regardless of birth and circumstances, is truly equal? Imagine CRY's vision becoming not just a guiding principle but a call for action in nations around the world. As written in the 1989 United Nations charter for children's rights, every child born in the twenty-first century is guaranteed a right to survival, protection, development, and participation. This possibility is audacious in its reach, but so is CRY's belief about what groups can achieve together above and beyond what they can achieve on their own. In Ingrid's words, "All it takes is communities becoming aware of their rights and coming together to ensure them." When leaders span boundaries, alternative futures can be created that are as inspiring as they are necessary.

What if Mark Gerzon and countless other leaders on all sides of the energy debate continue to cross boundaries of interest and ideology in pursuit of emerging possibilities? No global issue more vividly conveys the reality that "we are all in it together now" than climate change and energy security. Imagine that as leaders bring people and groups together in new directions around this challenge, identities begin to shift in noticeable and positively transformative ways. Imagine this fuels an awakening in which, in Mark's words, people "transcend partial, fragmented identities and embrace a wider, more integral vision of the planet." When this occurs, collaborative solutions regarding energy sustainability become not just viable but fully realizable. What if this in turn inspires a new generation of leaders to reach across, bridge, and span boundaries on challenges ranging from developing innovative technologies, to responding to natural disasters, to global literacy and poverty erad-ication? What if our human potential for collaboration *becomes fully realized*?

Throughout history, it is where groups collide, intersect, and link that we've discovered new frontiers in physics, science, business, engineering, medicine, the arts, and culture. The pace of societal change and progress is breathtaking. Perhaps now we stand at the precipice of the last, great final frontier: our relationships with one another. In a world that spans boundaries, so too must leadership.

Therein lie the challenge and the opportunity of a more interde-pendent, collaborative future.

A PPENDIX A

ABOUT THE RESEARCH

The information presented in this book is based largely on the experiences of actual leaders who participated in two research projects. The first project, Leadership Across Differences, was a multiyear global research initiative based at the Center for Creative Leadership (CCL). This project was conducted across six world regions, building a database that includes over 2,800 survey responses, 289 interviews, and a wide range of secondary data such as media reports and organizational communications from around the world. The second project involved collecting data from 128 senior executives who participated in CCL's Leadership at the Peak program. These projects are described in greater detail below.

Leadership Across Differences

The Leadership Across Differences (LAD) project began in 2001 and continued through 2008. The goal of the research was to address the following question: What are the leadership processes by which organizations create shared direction, alignment, and commitment across groups of people with very different histories, perspectives, values, and cultures?

A Global Collaboration Effort

LAD was a multiphase project that involved four major stages. During *stage 1*, we conducted an extensive review of the literature and interviews in multiple sectors around the world. We then integrated those two knowledge streams to develop a theoretical framework that served as our guide for future data collection. In *stage 2*, we developed instruments in concert with a panel of international research advisors to measure key constructs in the framework. We then expanded our data collection efforts and refined the framework by gathering data from six regions to maximize variation in cultural values: Africa, Asia, Europe, Middle East, North America, and South America. *Stage 3* involved the development of tools and techniques to assist leaders in their work across differences. *Stage 4* involved the dissemination of the knowledge, tools, and techniques that emerged from our work.

The project was a highly collaborative endeavor that involved a team of faculty members from the Center for Creative Leadership and international researchers and practitioners widely recognized for their work in the areas of diversity, intercultural relations, and global leadership. The CCL faculty members provided a balanced perspective on both learning (research and development) and teaching (application and instruction). The international team members were selected on the basis of their individual contributions to the organizational sciences and collectively brought varied perspectives and expertise to bear on the research. We also found it critically important to have in-country collaborators assist in both data collection and interpretation. Those collaborators were able to illuminate for the larger group things such as cultural values, contextual variables (e.g., historical, legal, political, and societal), and organizational practices that helped shape the team's interpretation of the data, particularly the qualitative data collected during interviews.

Our Data Collection Strategy

Survey data were collected from over 2,800 individuals representing a variety of organizational levels and functions and types of organizations (e.g., corporate, nonprofit, social sector). Data were collected in 12 countries: Brazil, France, Germany, Hong Kong, India, Japan, Jordan, Scotland, Singapore, South Africa, Spain, and the United States. On the basis of interviews conducted during the first stage of the project and in collaboration with international scholars versed in research methodology, four scenarios were crafted to describe unique situations involving tension between social identity groups that require leadership to span boundaries. The four scenarios focused on different social identity groups, including gender, race, religion, and immigration status. Respondents were asked to read the scenario and then evaluate the effectiveness of a number of different leadership strategies that could be used to bridge intergroup boundaries. Surveys were either paper-based or administered online, depending on the context and preference of the organization.

An *organizational assessment* was conducted for each data collection site. It involved an extensive interview with one or more human resource managers or organizational development professionals. Each interview lasted for 60 to 90 minutes and provided us with information about organizational practices and policies that were meant to address issues of identity, difference, and fairness.

The data that most informed the information provided in this book came from 289 *interviews* that lasted anywhere from one to three hours. Subsets of the overall interview database were analyzed, depending on the nature of the research question and the quality and focus of the information provided by the interviewee. In the sections below, we explain our data collection methods and then provide information about the analyses conducted.

Interviewing Those in the Trenches

In stage 1 of the LAD research project, we collected interview data from 50 individuals in 11 different countries: Bali, Germany, Israel, Mozambique, Saudi Arabia, Singapore, South Africa, the United Kingdom, the United States, Zambia, and Zimbabwe. We identified the sample first by collaborating with interviewers versed in the practice of leadership development in multicultural settings and then by asking the interviewers to identify a sample of people who were likely to have experienced or witnessed social identity conflicts in the workplace. The interviewees held a variety of occupations in corporations, social service organizations, hospitals, and schools and were employed at all levels of the organizational hierarchy. We interviewed both individuals who held formal leadership positions within an organization and individuals with no formal leadership authority to examine the challenge leaders face in managing social identity conflict from a variety of different perspectives.

In stage 2 of the LAD research project, we collected interview data from 239 individuals in 11 countries: Brazil, France, Germany, Hong Kong, India, Jordan, Singapore, South Africa, Spain, the United Kingdom, and the United States. We made several changes in our sampling strategy for the second round of interview data collection. We required a minimum of 10 interviewees per organization and made a concerted effort to obtain data from individuals who varied on a number of different factors (gender, race, level in the organization, etc.). We also attempted to maximize cultural variation in our sample to examine whether similar types of events occurred in different cultural contexts, and we included both for-profit and nonprofit organizations.

In both rounds of interview data collection, we used a semistructured interview protocol to gather data. Although some of the protocol questions were modified through the years as more data were collected, the central questions used to identify negative and positive cross-boundary interactions remained very similar. The central question in the protocol used to identify a negative event was as follows:

I would like you to think about a time or an event in which you became strongly aware of the fact that people from different social groups were working together, and they fell short of their best—the groups were at odds with one another. There may have been misunderstandings and there may have even been outright tension and conflict. Tell me a story about this time. What happened? How could you tell the groups were not working well together?

The central question used to elicit information about exemplary boundary spanning leadership and a positive event was as follows:

I would like you to think about a time or an event in which you became strongly aware of the fact that people from any of the different social groups you've talked about were working together. Can you tell me about a time in your history in this organization in which these social groups worked together at their best? This may have been a time in which members of these groups created a shared direction of where they were going, or they aligned their roles and actions, or they felt a common sense of commitment to what they were trying to accomplish.

The protocol also included sample probing questions that interviewers could use to gather additional information about the socio-historical-cultural context, the history of the identity groups involved, the circumstances leading to the conflict, and if/how it was resolved.

Interviewers included both members of the research team and in-country research collaborators. Before gathering data, we asked the in-country research collaborators who were conducting interviews to review a guide prepared by the research team that included both practical suggestions for conducting an effective interview and recommendations for probing and soliciting the critical information needed to address our research questions. We followed up with a phone conversation to answer questions and provide further guidance on data collection. In general, we trained interviewers to establish rapport during the interview and then use a critical incident approach to identify events that had resulted in social identity conflicts.

We took several steps during the interview data collection process to develop trust with interviewees and attempt to obtain rich and candid qualitative data. For example, we assured interviewees that the data would be kept confidential and that no one in their organization would receive feedback. For each organization, we did provide some aggregate information as a form of reciprocation for providing the data, but the feedback was general and was focused on survey results rather than information obtained from the interviews.

All interviews were recorded with permission, and those conducted in a language other than English were translated into English for the data analysis. Collectively, members of the LAD research team reviewed all 289 interview transcripts. Individually, after reading each transcript, researchers responded to a series of questions developed by the research team that were intended to summarize key events and leadership strategies that emerged during the interviews. Researchers then worked in pairs to share their responses to and interpretations of the qualitative data, and together they generated a summary memo for each interview. Further analyses therefore involved both the interview transcripts and summary memos. More information about the methodological and analytical procedures used in our research is provided in a 2009 article published in the journal *Human Relations* (see the reference list at the end of this appendix).

Identifying Triggers

A subset of the full interview database was used to identify triggers. A total of 134 interviews met the criteria established by the research team to qualify as a triggering event. Two researchers independently read the interviews and then engaged in a process to develop and refine a codebook that was used to identify and code triggers within the data. A second team consisting of three additional researchers independently coded the data to evaluate interrater agreement. Thus, a team of five researchers was involved in analyzing the qualitative data. What emerged from this analysis was a typology involving four common types of triggers or "events involving two or more people from different social identity groups that ignite a replication of societal-based identity threat in an organization." These triggers pose a serious challenge for boundary spanning leaders and are described in detail in Chapter 3 of this book.

Identifying Boundary Spanning Practices

The interview data proved useful in identifying types of triggers but also helped the LAD team identify a variety of practices leaders use to create direction, alignment, and commitment across boundaries. Another analysis team consisting of six researchers reviewed 164 of the interview transcripts and summary memos, this time searching for themes that identified leadership practices. Using a literature review conducted in stage 1 of the LAD project, the team identified four theoretical approaches or practices that can be used to support effective intergroup collaborations (decategorization, recategorization, subcategorization, and cross-cutting). The research team used the extensive literature in this area to develop a codebook that was similar in development process and design to the one developed for analyzing triggers. Using this codebook, the team reviewed the data to evaluate how often and in what form these theoretical approaches were used by leaders in the organizations involved in our study. At the same time, the researchers made note of other leadership practices described in the interview data that did not fit within the four strategies identified in the literature.

On the basis of this analysis work, the team was able to make several general conclusions about leadership across differences. We concluded that leaders do engage in some form of the four types of leadership practices identified in the literature; however, the use of these practices in actual organizations is complicated by the many intervening variables that leaders must contend with that are missing in a laboratory setting. Other practices also emerged from the analysis. Two broad categories of leadership practices that fell into the "other" category stood out for the research team: boundary spanning (mediating, sensitizing) and boundary management (gatekeeping). As a result, the research team returned to the literature to examine theoretical and empirical work related to boundary spanning and boundary management.

The heart of this book—the six boundary spanning leadership practices described in Chapters 4 through 9—stems from the work that was conducted on leadership strategies as part of the broader LAD project. Many of the leadership stories in these chapters come directly from the interviews we conducted, and our early conceptualizations of the six practices originated from the analysis of the LAD interviews. However, even after engaging in years of data collection and analysis with our fellow LAD researchers, we felt that it was important to gather even more data to gain a clearer picture of the types of boundaries leaders must learn to span and the possibilities that await those who do. Thus, we gathered additional survey data from leaders participating in one of CCL's leadership training programs designed specifically for people with executive-level roles and responsibilities.

Leadership at the Peak

The second CCL research project involved participants from Leadership at the Peak, a program at CCL designed for senior executives who have more than 15 years of management experience, have worked in the top three tiers of their organizations, and have leadership responsibility for 500 or more people. Admission to the program is by application only. From 2008 to 2009, participants in the Leadership at the Peak program were asked to complete a survey intended to gather information on a variety of boundary spanning topics. Survey questions dealt with pressing trends and challenges, the role of leadership in spanning boundaries, and the types of boundaries leaders face in attempting to create direction, alignment, and commitment. A total of 128 program participants completed an electronic survey (75 percent were male, and 25 percent were female). The majority of respondents (60 percent) worked at the senior vice president or director level. Chief executive officers or presidents accounted for 32 percent of the sample, and the remaining 8 percent held titles such as vice president and plant manager.

Findings from this study informed the thinking behind this book in two primary ways. First, it reinforced our belief that leading across boundaries is critically important as well as challenging. As described earlier in the book, 86 percent of the senior executives reported that it was "extremely important" for them to work effectively across boundaries in their current leadership roles. Yet only

7 percent of those executives believed they were currently "very effective" at doing that: a gap of 79 percent between perceived importance and effectiveness of boundary spanning capability. These leaders are seasoned, high-performing executives working in some of the most respected companies in the world. The wide discrepancy the executives reported affirmed what we learned in our analysis in the LAD study as well as our observations in working with leaders in the field: Boundary spanning leadership is an issue that merits attention.

The other primary finding concerns the identification of the five types of boundaries that leaders today must bridge, span, and collaborate across. In the survey, we included the following open-ended question: What are the key types of boundaries you have to work across in your current role? A total of 181 examples of boundaries were mentioned across all survey participants. On average, the executives were able to cite at least one type of boundary, and some described up to four types. In analyzing the data, we found examples of five dimensions of boundaries: horizontal, vertical, stakeholder, demographic, and geographic. This finding, as well as other trends reported by the executives, formed the basis for the information provided in Chapter 1.

The Nexus Effect Emerges

The data gathered from the Leadership Across Differences project and the Leadership at the Peak survey shaped the basic structure and content of the book. However, as we progressed along the path of our writing journey, new ideas emerged and old ideas began to take new shape and assume meaning. As we immersed ourselves more deeply in the topic of boundary spanning leadership, a vision of limitless possibility and inspiring results at the nexus between groups began to emerge. What happens when leaders transform limiting borders into limitless new frontiers? As we sought to understand the outcomes of boundary spanning leadership more deeply, the idea of the Nexus Effect slowly took shape. Along with several of our CCL colleagues, we interviewed and spoke with one last set of exemplary boundary spanning leaders, ones who were recognized for their ability to bring groups together across boundaries to achieve significant and lasting results. Those leaders included Mark Gerzon, president and founder of the Mediators Foundation; John Herrera, founder of the Latino Community Credit Union; and His Excellency Ong Keng Yong, former secretary general of ASEAN (Association of Southeast Asian Nations). Those individuals provided critical insights into the possibilities that can emerge when leaders learn to span boundaries. The qualitative data we gathered during these interviews are highlighted in Chapters 4 to 10.

The Journey Continues

Overall, the data gathered to support the conclusions drawn in this book involved a decadelong journey. It involved collaborations between over 50 researchers from around the world, the gathering of survey and interview data across six world regions, and the unique opportunity to learn from hundreds of leaders who experienced firsthand the promise and the peril of leading across boundaries.

As authors, we have had the unique privilege to distill this journey into the pages and chapters that constitute this book, yet the journey continues. We believe that the ideas and practices of boundary spanning leadership will only multiply in importance as we progress into the twenty-first century. We provide below a list of publications from the LAD project that are relevant to the information provided in this book, written by the core members of the LAD research team: Kathryn Cartner, Maxine Dalton, Rachael Foy, Bill Gentry, Sarah Glover, Michael Hoppe, Ancella Livers, Belinda McFeeters, Vijayan Munusamy, Patty Ohlott, Marian Ruderman, Joan Tavares, Todd Weber, Jeffrey Yip, Lize Booysen, and David Dinwoodie.

References for the LAD Research

Chrobot-Mason, Donna, Marian N. Ruderman, Todd J. Weber, and Chris Ernst. "The Challenge of Leading on Unstable Ground: Triggers That Activate Social Identity Faultlines." *Human Relations* 62:1763–1794, 2009.

Chrobot-Mason, Donna, Marian N. Ruderman, Todd J. Weber, Patricia J. Ohlott, and Maxine A. Dalton. "Illuminating a Cross-Cultural Leadership Challenge: When Identity Groups Collide." *International Journal of Human Resource Management* 18:2011–2036, 2007.

Dalton, Maxine, and Donna Chrobot-Mason. "A Theoretical Exploration of Manager and Employee Social Identity, Cultural Values, and Identity Conflict Management." *International Journal of Cross Cultural Management* 7:169–183, 2007.

Ernst, Chris, Kelly M. Hannum, and Marian N. Ruderman. "Developing Intergroup Leadership." In *The Center for Creative Leadership Handbook of Leadership Development*, 3rd ed., edited by Ellen Van Velsor, Cynthia D. McCauley, and Marian Ruderman. San Francisco: Jossey-Bass, pp. 375–404, 2010.

Ernst, Chris, and Jeff Yip. "Boundary Spanning Leadership: Tactics to Bridge Social Identity Groups in Organizations." In *Crossing the Divide: Intergroup Leadership in a World of Difference*, edited by Todd L. Pittinsky. Boston: Harvard Business School Press, pp. 87–91, 2009.

Ernst, Chris, and Jeffrey Yip. "Breaking Down Boundaries in the Climate Debate: A Case Study of Mark Gerzon." *Leadership in Action* 29(3):12–16, 2009.

Ernst, Chris, and Jeffrey Yip. "Bridging Boundaries: Meeting the Challenges of Workplace Diversity." *Leadership in Action* 28(1):3–6, 2008.

Gentry, William, Lize Booysen, Kelly M. Hannum, and Todd J. Weber. "Leadership Responses to Gender-Based Tension: A Comparison of Responses between the US and South Africa." *International Journal of Cross-Cultural Management* (accepted for publication).

Glover, Sarah, and Kelly Hannum. "Learning Respect: Showing and Earning Esteem Is Crucial for Leaders." *Leadership in Action* 28(4):3–7, 2008.

Hannum, Kelly M. *Social Identity: Knowing Yourself, Leading Others.* Greensboro, NC: Center for Creative Leadership, 2007.

Hannum, Kelly M. "Branching Out: Social Identity Comes to the Forefront." *Leadership in Action* 28(1):7–11, 2008.

Hannum, Kelly M., Belinda B. McFeeters, and Lize Booysen. *Leading across Differences: Cases and Perspectives.* San Francisco: Pfeiffer, 2010.

Hoppe, Michael H. "Bridging the Identity Gap." *Leadership in Action* 24(3):14–15, 21, 2004.

Ohlott, Patty J., Donna Chrobot-Mason, and Maxine A. Dalton. "Collision Courses: When Social Identity Leads to Conflict." *Leadership in Action* 24(3):8–11, 24, 2004.

Ruderman, Marian, and Donna Chrobot-Mason. "Triggers of Social Identity Conflict." In *Leading across Differences: Cases and Perspectives,* edited by Kelly M. Hannum, Belinda B. McFeeters, and Lize Booysen. San Francisco: Pfeiffer, pp. 81–86, 2010.

Ruderman, Marian, Donna Chrobot-Mason, and Todd J. Weber. "Identity Crisis: Recognizing the Triggers of a Growing Type of Conflict." *Leadership in Action* 27(3):3–8, 2007.

Ruderman, Marian, Sarah Glover, Donna Chrobot-Mason, and Chris Ernst. "Leadership Practices across Social Identity Groups." In *Leading across Differences: Cases and Perspectives,* edited by Kelly M. Hannum, Belinda B. McFeeters, and Lize Booysen. San Francisco: Pfeiffer, pp. 95–114, 2010.

Ruderman, Marian, and Vijayan Munusamy. "Know Thyself." *Concepts & Connections* 15(2):1–4, 2007.

Yip, Jeffrey. "Sense and Sensibility: A Conversation with Ong Keng Yong." *Leadership in Action* 27(3):19–20, 2007.

Yip, Jeffrey, Chris Ernst, and Michael Campbell. "Boundary Spanning Leadership: Mission Critical Perspectives from the Executive Suite." Center for Creative Leadership. http://www.ccl.org/leadership/pdf/research/BoundarySpanning-Leadership.pdf (accessed April 7, 2010).

Yip, Jeffrey, Serena Wong, and Chris Ernst. "The Nexus Effect: When Leaders Span Group Boundaries. *Leadership in Action* 28(4):13–17, 2008.

Yip, Jeffrey, Edward Twohill, Chris Ernst, and Vijayan Munusamy. "Leadership in Faith-Based Nonprofits." *Nonprofit Management and Leadership* 20(4): 461–472, 2010.

APPENDIX B

BOUNDARY SPANNING LEADERSHIP SUMMARY TABLE

Table B.1 outlines specific actions leaders can take to enact each boundary spanning practice in accordance with each of the five boundary dimensions. The table is for illustrative purposes, and many additional actions could be used, depending on the context and the situation. Moving from top (managing boundaries) to bottom (discovering new frontiers), the actions create the conditions for increasing levels of intergroup collaboration, which in turn can lead to increasing the potential for solving problems, developing innovative solutions, and creating transformational change.

Table B.1 Boundary Spanning Leadership Summary

			Managing Boundaries		
	Vertical Boundaries (Hierarchical Levels and Ranks)	Horizontal Boundaries (Functions, Units, and Disciplines)	Stakeholder Boundaries (Partners, Suppliers, Customers, Communities)	Demographic Boundaries (Gender, Age, Culture, Religion, Ethnicity, Education, Ideology)	Geographic Boundaries (Locations, Regions, Languages, and Markets)
Buffering— monitor and protect the flow of information and resources across groups to *define boundaries* and build intergroup safety.	During times of organizational crisis, remind people of proper communication channels to ensure critical information flows across levels effectively and accurately.	Prepare a team "charter" of roles and responsibilities. Share it with others in the organization so they understand the amount of work your group can effectively manage.	Specify "nonnegotiables" or "rules of engagement" that specify how your team and an external team will interact during a joint venture.	Sponsor affinity groups within your organization (women, Hispanics, etc.) so that nondominant groups have an opportunity to network and share experiences with their own group members.	Build a "buffer" between your team and headquarters if agendas are competing. Create a document that summarizes your team deliverables and get written buy-in and agreement from HQ.
Reflecting— represent distinct perspectives and encourage knowledge exchange across groups to *understand boundaries* and foster intergroup respect.	Initiate a meeting with senior management so that you can advocate upward the innovative ideas generated by your employees.	Invite leaders from other units to your team meetings so they can discuss how each unit can help the other to solve pressing organizational problems.	Arrange "field trips" for your team to visit client sites or customer markets. Ask them to take photos and document what they observe as it relates to an organizational initiative or strategy.	When an issue comes up that involves race, gender, or religion, consider making it a "teachable moment." Let everyone have a chance to share and learn about their differences and unique perspectives.	Encourage international business travelers to add an extra day to their trip to hit the streets, experience the culture, and learn about the local market. Ask them to share their observations at a team meeting upon return.

Forging Common Ground

Connecting—link people and bridge divided groups to suspend *boundaries* and build intergroup *trust*.	Host an outdoor lunch picnic to bring people together from different levels of the organization. Ask everyone to "share a blanket" with people they don't get to spend time with regularly.	Set up some comfortable chairs and a whiteboard in the connector wing between two departments to encourage informal, collaborative conversations across functions.	Rotate meetings with a key vendor between your site and theirs. When visiting their site, request time for "putting names with faces" by having your team walk around and meet people in their organization.	Mix it up outside the office. Get people of different generations, races, or nationalities together for a sporting event.	Reserve the first 15 minutes of your bimonthly global videoconference for relationship building. Spend time sharing personal milestones, news, or updates of interest.
Mobilizing—craft common purpose and shared identity across groups to *reframe boundaries* and develop intergroup *community*.	Establish "skip level" meetings for your staff to have conversations with your manager about higher organizational goals and strategy.	Following an organizational merger, get people from the same functions in the two organizations together—have them craft a compelling mission about a new business opportunity that everyone can rally behind.	Articulate a goal that your organization and another organization can partner around in order to beat a common competitor in the marketplace.	Identify a core set of organizational values that are inclusive and motivating for all demographic groups.	Install common organizational symbols, wall hangings, and icons in all your offices that build community and represent "your organization at its best" anywhere in the world.

(continued)

Table B.1 (continued)

Discovering New Frontiers

	Vertical Boundaries	Horizontal Boundaries	Stakeholder Boundaries	Demographic Boundaries	Geographic Boundaries
Weaving—draw out and integrate group differences within a larger whole to *interlace boundaries* and advance intergroup *interdependence*.	Debrief a successful organizational accomplishment by bringing groups together across levels to discuss what factors created the "win" from their unique vantage points.	When divisions are in conflict over an issue, help them articulate the source of their differences and then explore ways to creatively reconcile them for the overall good of the organization.	Integrate the unique strengths of your organization and an organization in a different sector (e.g., nonprofit, government agency) to solve a shared problem in your community.	Bring different demographic groups together to talk about market needs and trends within their respective groups, and how the organization could create new products to serve them.	Develop "glocal" solutions—draw and integrate *global* best practices within your company and *local* market knowledge to envision new products, services, or internal processes.
Transforming—bring multiple groups together in emergent, new directions to cross-cut boundaries and enable intergroup *reinvention*.	Bring members of your network together who represent vastly different levels from top to bottom. Facilitate a dialogue about "how they see things in the business" and explore an unconventional idea that arises from the conversation	Host "alternative future conversations." Invite anyone in the organization to attend; provide no agenda other than to imagine the ideal, transformed organization five years from now.	Strike a small-scale partnership with your no. 1 competitor. Explore new, collaborative frontiers that could be discovered together.	Create action learning teams with "maximum diversity" (e.g., age, gender, race, culture, education, personality differences) to develop business plans of entirely new markets or services than your organization currently offers.	Get the whole system in the room. Bring together a large cross-section of key leaders from around the world once a year to envision "game-changing" opportunities.

APPENDIX C

WHERE TO GO NEXT: CCL RESOURCES FOR BOUNDARY SPANNING LEADERSHIP

L eadership across boundaries is challenging, in part because it requires both individual and collective change. This book has focused on raising your awareness of the need for and possibilities of boundary spanning leadership. At the Center for Creative Leadership (CCL), we also recognize that leadership is not defined exclusively by an individual's role. Organizations—businesses, agencies, communities, schools, governments—also must develop a collective leadership capacity if boundary spanning work is to take place in a widespread and sustainable way.

CCL's Organizational Leadership Practice focuses on identifying and developing individual leadership capabilities; improving team, group, and organizational effectiveness; and developing the ability to create direction, alignment, and commitment throughout an organizational system. Increasingly, this work includes helping our clients meet the challenges and opportunities of spanning vertical, horizontal, stakeholder, demographic, and geographic boundaries.

For leaders seeking to improve their organization's ability to work across boundaries intentionally and systematically, CCL offers several avenues for building on the ideas in this book. When an organization's leadership strategy calls for building new collaborative boundary spanning capabilities, it can invest in three areas: talent systems, leadership culture, and applied learning systems.

Below, we briefly explain how talent, culture, and learning systems relate to boundary spanning leadership. Additional tools, activities, white papers, and articles are available through our Web site, www.spanboundaries.com.

Talent Systems

Leadership talent involves an organization's ability to continuously attract, develop, and retain people with the capabilities needed for current and future organizational success. Talent systems thus can be thought of as the work of designing and implementing the strategies and development processes needed for talent sustainability.

Career development approaches in organizations traditionally focus on preparing leaders for vertical advancement to higher levels of leadership responsibility. Career ladders, fast-track programs, and development focused on leading up and down the organizational hierarchy are common. But to develop individuals' boundary spanning capabilities, career development pathways need to look less like a vertical ladder and more like a zigzag that crosses over vertical, horizontal, stakeholder, demographic, and geographic boundaries. CCL uses the term *boundary-crossing assignments* to define the rich experiences and powerful opportunities for learning that leaders encounter when they engage in cross-boundary assignments, roles, and tasks.[1] Assignments such as working in a different function, managing a joint venture, and taking an expatriate assignment provide leaders with opportunities to deepen their collaborative boundary spanning skills and broaden their organizational perspectives.

Although improving the organizational mechanisms for developing boundary spanning capability is relevant to leaders at all levels, CCL research suggests that the greatest need lies with middle management. Not only do middle managers have roles that increasingly will demand boundary spanning work, they are preparing to shift to senior-level jobs.

In the Leadership at the Peak study, 92 percent of the 128 senior executives believed that the ability to collaborate across boundaries became more important as they moved from middle- to senior-level management. With each increase in level, there are more boundaries to span, a greater emphasis on cross-enterprise coordination, and an increased focus on bridging the organization with the external environment. Success at senior organizational levels requires a critical shift in mindset from leading *within* the boundaries of the function to leading the function *across* organizational boundaries in the context of the larger business strategy and vision.

In the same study, 91 percent of senior executives said boundary spanning was important for middle managers. But they reported that only 19 percent of middle managers are effective in working across boundaries, a gap of 72 percent between perceived importance and effectiveness.

An effective leadership talent approach should, among other things, provide employees with developmental experiences that allow them to work and lead across all five boundaries and not assume that boundary spanning capabilities will emerge once a manager is placed in a senior position. An organization's talent efforts should include the following questions:

- What competencies must be developed if we are to be an effective boundary spanning organization?
- What experiences and support should be provided to improve boundary spanning capabilities among our employees?
- How does the organization recognize and reward managers and teams for engaging in collaborative work?

The answers will vary by organization; however, CCL's experience has shown that certain assignments, as well as coaching and applied learning systems, are effective strategies for developing boundary spanning leadership.

Leadership Culture

Leadership culture refers to the web of individual and collective beliefs and practices in organizations for producing the outcomes of direction, alignment, and commitment. Many organizations are in some stage of a culture shift, moving away from being dependent on a few leaders at the top to becoming a culture in which many leaders throughout the organization collaborate and enact change.

The goal of leadership culture work is to build capability for new ways of working purposefully and actively. It allows for new thinking, beliefs, tools and processes that will result in organizational success. As the need for boundary spanning leadership increases and the practice becomes more complex, an organization must evolve its leadership culture so that it won't systematically reject efforts to work more effectively across vertical, horizontal, stakeholder, demographic, and geographic boundaries.

At CCL, we work with senior leadership in organizations to clarify their leadership culture and determine the gap between the culture they have and the culture they need. Our research finds that organizations tend to fall into one of three categories, or levels, of leadership culture (see Figure C.1).[2]

An organization's leadership culture directly affects the way people respond to the challenge and opportunities of working across boundaries. Generally, interdependent leadership cultures have stronger boundary spanning capabilities than do other organizations. As the leadership culture becomes more interdependent, reaching across, bridging, and collaborating across internal and external boundaries will become an increasingly natural way to get work done. That said, the six boundary spanning practices can be applied in all leadership cultures.

In fact, as leaders, teams, and entire organizations experiment and develop new capabilities in each of the boundary spanning practices, the culture of the organization develops toward greater collaboration and interdependence as well. For instance, buffering and reflecting may be the primary practices in a dependent leadership culture. This is the case because the outcomes associated with these practices—intergroup safety and respect—are primary values in more authoritative dependent cultures. Yet as people in the organization engage in additional practices, for example, connecting or

Figure C.1 Leadership cultures.

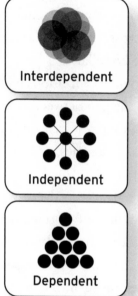

Interdependent leadership cultures
view leadership as a collective activity that requires
mutual inquiry, learning, and a capacity to work with
complex challenges.

Independent leadership cultures
assume that leadership emerges as needed from
a variety of individuals based on knowledge
and expertise.

Dependent leadership cultures
hold only people in positions of authority
responsible for leadership.

mobilizing, the leadership culture begins to shift from dependent to independent and eventually toward interdependent. To develop increased boundary spanning capabilities, organizations also must understand and intentionally develop their leadership culture in ways that enable the six practices to manifest and thrive.

Applied Learning Systems

Applied learning systems are leadership development approaches that involve learning from challenging real-work experiences. More than 30 years of CCL's Lessons of Experience research has consistently found that there are five types of developmental experiences across cultures and contexts: challenging work assignments, developmental relationships, adverse situations, course work and training, and personal experience.[3] Of these, significantly more lessons are learned from challenging work assignments (such as an increase in scope of responsibilities, initiatives that require creating change, and stakeholder engagement activities) than from any other type of event. In light of this finding, CCL's applied learning systems seek to develop leadership at its most powerful source—in the course of work itself.

Applied learning approaches are uniquely suited to the fundamental challenges underlying boundary spanning leadership, requiring leaders to create direction, alignment, and commitment across boundaries in service of a higher vision or goal. For example, CCL's Action Development methodology is a type of applied learning approach that integrates working on real strategic change goals while simultaneously developing the types of leadership capabilities described in this book. Leaders in Action Development initiatives engage collaboratively in cross-boundary teams to advance a strategic goal while receiving intensive support for individual and organizational development. In working interdependently across organizational boundaries, leaders shift from internal to external awareness of the environment and learn to lead from a more integrated understanding of the organization. Action Development enhances not just individual boundary spanning capabilities, but also the intergroup outcomes of safety, respect, trust, community, interdependence, and reinvention needed to foster wide-scale collaboration to help organizations adapt to change.

In closing, CCL's Organizational Leadership Practice accelerates organizational strategy by unlocking leadership potential. When your organizational strategy calls for building new collaborative boundary spanning capabilities and when talent systems, leadership culture, and applied learning systems are aligned in ways that support those efforts, your organization will be well positioned to succeed today and meet tomorrow's challenges.

CCL Development Initiatives and Programs

CCL faculty members are available for speaking engagements and to conduct workshops, programs, and initiatives that address boundary spanning leadership. Learn more by visiting the Center for Creative Leadership Web site at www.ccl.org or contact a client services advisor:

CCL-Americas: +1 336 545 2810
CCL-Europe, Middle East, Africa: +32 (0) 2 679 09 10
CCL-Asia-Pacific: +65 6854 6000

NOTES

Introduction

1. Chris Ernst and Jeffrey Yip, "Boundary Spanning Leadership: Tactics to Bridge Social Identity Groups in Organizations." In *Crossing the Divide: Intergroup Leadership in a World of Difference*, edited by Todd L. Pittinsky. Boston: Harvard Business School Press, 2009, pp. 89–99.

2. Boundary spanning has a long tradition in organization theory. Although the concept has focused on spanning structural and information boundaries in organizations, we address the role of leadership in spanning intergroup boundaries. See Howard Aldrich and Diane Herker's classic article "Boundary Spanning Roles and Organization Structure," *Academy of Management Review* 2(2):217–230, 1977. In the more recent literature, Deborah Ancona and her colleagues at MIT have conducted pioneering work examining how leaders and teams operate beyond traditional boundaries. See Deborah Ancona and Henrik Bresman, *X-Teams: How to Build Teams That Lead, Innovate, and Succeed*. Boston: Harvard Business School Press, 2007.

3. To learn more about CCL's approach and philosophy concerning leadership and leadership development, see E. VanVelsor, C. D. McCauley, and M. N. Ruderman (eds.), *The Center for Creative Leadership Handbook of Leadership Development*, 3rd ed. San Francisco: Jossey-Bass, 2010. To read CCL's foundational article on defining leadership in terms of direction, alignment, and commitment, see W. H. Drath, C. McCauley, C. J. Palus, E. Van Velsor, P. M. G. O'Connor, and J. B. McGuire, "Direction, Alignment, Commitment: Toward a More Integrative Ontology of Leadership." *Leadership Quarterly* 19:635–653, 2008.

4. M. B. Brewer, "The Social Self: On Being the Same and Different at the Same Time." *Personality and Social Psychology Bulletin* 17:475–482, 1991.

Chapter 1

1. Jeffrey Yip, Chris Ernst, and Michael Campbell, "Boundary Spanning Leadership: Mission Critical Perspectives from the Executive Suite." A Center for Creative Leadership Organizational Leadership White Paper, 2009.
2. See Appendix A for more details on this study. Go to the section titled "Leadership at the Peak."
3. In seminal work conducted within General Electric and other organizations, Ron Ashkenas and colleagues identified four types of organizational boundaries: vertical, horizontal, external, and geographic. See Ron Ashkenas, Dave Ulrich, Todd Kick, and Steve Kerr, *The Boundaryless Organization: Breaking the Chains of Organizational Structure*. San Francisco: Jossey-Bass, 1998.
4. Elizabeth Mannix and Margaret A Neale, "What Differences Make a Difference? The Promise and Reality of Diverse Teams in Organizations." *Psychological Science in the Public Interest* 6(2):31–55, 2005.
5. Marian Ruderman, Sarah Glover, Donna Chrobot-Mason, and Chris Ernst, "Leadership Practices across Social Identity Groups." In *Leading across Differences: Cases and Perspectives*, edited by Kelly Hannum, Belinda McFeeters, and Lize Booysen. Hoboken, NJ: Wiley, 2010, pp. 105–112.
6. International Labour Office, *Global Employment Trends Brief*, January 2007.
7. "2009 World Population Data Sheet." Population Reference Bureau, http://www.prb.org/Publications/Datasheets/2009/2009wpds.aspx (accessed February 12, 2010).
8. Maxine Dalton, Chris Ernst, Jennifer Deal, and Jean Leslie, *Success for the New Global Manager: How to Work across Distances, Countries, and Cultures*. San Francisco: Jossey-Bass-Wiley, 2002.
9. Medard Gabel and Henry Bruner, *Global INC: An Atlas of the Multinational Corporation*. New York: New Press, 2003.
10. James K. Glassman, "Playing the China Card." *Kiplinger's Personal Finance*, September 2009, pp. 18–21.
11. See Nancy J. Adler, *From Boston to Beijing: Managing with a Worldview*. Cincinnati: Thomson Learning, 2002. See also Schon Beechler and Mansour Javidan, "Leading with a Global Mindset." *Advances in International Management* 19:131–169, 2007.
12. We expect that while nearly all leaders must address issues related to the five boundary types, the extent and variety of boundaries will vary according to organizational sector as well as job level, function, region, and other variables. For example, it is possible that vertical boundaries were given less priority in our study with senior executives because of their position in the organizational hierarchy. It stands to reason that issues of level and rank may be less relevant for leaders sitting at the top of the hierarchy. That said, in our consulting work with organizations and in a smaller online survey conducted

with a cross-section of mid-, senior-, and executive-level leaders working in the Americas, Asia, and Europe, we found essentially the same frequency patterns. That is, horizontal boundaries were identified nearly three to one as being the most important type of boundary to lead across, followed by geographic, stakeholder, vertical, and demographic, respectively.

Chapter 2

1. Marilyn B. Brewer, "The Social Self: On Being the Same and Different at the Same Time." In *Intergroup Relations: Essential Readings*, edited by Michael A. Hogg and Dominic Abrams. New York: Psychology Press, 2001, 245–253.
2. Henri Tajfel, "Social Categorization," English version of "La Categorisation Sociale." In *Introduction a la Psychologie Sociale*, edited by Serge Moscovici, vol. I. Paris: Larousse, 1972.
3. This activity is adapted from one presented in Taylor Cox and Ruby L. Beale, *Developing Competency to Manage Diversity: Readings, Cases & Activities*. San Francisco: Berrett-Koehler, 1997.
4. Stella M. Nkomo and Marcus M. Stewart, "Diverse Identities in Organizations." In *The SAGE Handbook of Organization Studies*, 2nd ed., edited by Stewart R. Clegg, Cynthia Hardy, Thomas B. Lawrence, and Walter R. Nord. London: Sage, 2006, pp. 520–540.
5. Marilynn B. Brewer and Rupert J. Brown, "Intergroup Relations." In *The Handbook of Social Psychology*, 4th ed., vol. 2, edited by Daniel. T. Gilbert, Susan. T. Fiske, and Gardner Lindzey. New York: McGraw-Hill, 1998, pp. 554–595.
6. Clayton Alderfer's seminal writing on intergroup dynamics examines the notion of boundary permeability and the importance of strengthening group identity as a necessary precondition for successful cross-boundary work. See Clayton P. Alderfer, "An Intergroup Perspective on Group Dynamics." In *Handbook of Organizational Behavior*, edited by Jay W. Lorsch. Englewood Cliffs, NJ: Prentice-Hall, 1987, pp. 190–222.
7. Peggy McIntosh, "White Privilege and Male Privilege: A Personal Account of Coming to See Correspondences through Work in Women's Studies." In *Gender Basics: Feminist Perspectives on Women and Men*, 2nd ed., edited by Anne Minas, 2nd ed. Belmont, CA: Wadsworth, 1993, pp. 30–38; Kecia M. Thomas and Donna Chrobot-Mason. "Group-Level Explanations of Workplace Discrimination." In *Discrimination at Work: The Psychological and Organizational Bases*, edited by Robert L. Dipboye and Adrienne Colella. Mahwah, NJ: Lawrence Erlbaum Associates, 2005, pp. 59–84.
8. *A Class Divided*, videocassette directed by William Peters (1986; Alexandria, VA: PBS, 2003). http://www.pbs.org/wgbh/pages/frontline/shows/divided.
9. Henri Tajfel and John C. Turner, "The Social Identity Theory of Intergroup Behavior." In *Psychology of Intergroup Relations*, edited by Stephen Worchel and William G. Austin. Chicago: Nelson, 1986, pp. 7–24.

10. Henri Tajfel, Michael G. Billig, R. P. Bundy, and Claude Flament, "Social Categorization and Intergroup Behavior." *European Journal of Social Psychology* 1(2):149–178, 1971; John F. Dovidio, Samuel L. Gaertner, and Betty A. Bachman, "Racial Bias in Organizations: The Role of Group Processes in its Causes and Cures." In *Groups at Work: Theory and Research*, edited by Marlene. E. Turner. Mahwah, NJ: Lawrence Erlbaum Associates, 2001, pp. 415–444; John F. Dovidio, Nancy Evans, and Richard B. Tyler, "Racial Stereotypes: The Contents of Their Cognitive Representations." *Journal of Experimental Social Psychology* 22(1):22–37, 1986.
11. Anne Tsui and Barbara A. Gutek, *Demographic Differences in Organizations: Current Research and Future Directions*. Lanham, MD: Lexington Books, 1999.
12. S. Alexander Haslam, *Psychology in Organizations: The Social Identity Approach*. London: Sage, 2001.
13. John C. Turner, "The Analysis of Social Influence." In *Rediscovering the Social Group: A Self-Categorization Theory*, edited by John. C. Turner, M. A. Hogg, P. J. Oakes, S. D. Reicher, and M. S. Wetherell. Oxford: Blackwell, 1987, pp. 68–88.
14. Michael A. Hogg, "A Social Identity Theory of Leadership." *Personality and Social Psychology Review* 5:184–200, 2001.
15. Todd L. Pittinsky and Stefanie Simon, "Intergroup Leadership." *Leadership Quarterly* 18:587–605, 2007.

Chapter 3

1. The boys had not met previously, yet they shared many characteristics. They were all white and from similar sociocultural backgrounds, with the same level of education.
2. The camp counselors were actually researchers and part of the experiment.
3. Gordon Willard Allport, *The Nature of Prejudice*, 25th anniversary ed. Reading, MA: Addison-Wesley, 1979.
4. Thomas F. Pettigrew and Linda R. Tropp, "A Meta-Analytic Test of Intergroup Contact Theory." *Journal of Personality and Social Psychology* 90:751–783, 2006.
5. At various points in time, the researchers asked the boys to make judgments about the other group. Thus, in addition to observing the boys' behavior toward one another, they gathered data on the stereotypes used to refer to the out-group. All the data they gathered, both objective and subjective, pointed to the same conclusion: Because the Eagles and the Rattlers were in competition with each other, their feelings toward the other group had become increasingly negative.
6. Walter G. Stephan and Cookie W. Stephan, "Intergroup Anxiety." *Journal of Social Issues* 41(3):157–175, 1985.
7. Although Bart Hunter is a fictional character, the incident described in this story is based on actual events portrayed in a *Denver Post* story titled "Colorado Plant and Somali Workers Fight over Prayer" by Ivan Moreno, September 12, 2008.

8. Dora C. Lau and J. Keith Murnighan, "Demographic Diversity and Faultlines: The Compositional Dynamics of Organizational Groups." *Academy of Management Review* 23:325–340, 1998.

9. Donna Chrobot-Mason, Marian R. Ruderman, Todd Weber, and Chris Ernst, "The Challenge of Leading on Unstable Ground: Triggers That Activate Social Identity Faultlines." *Human Relations* 62(11):1763–1794, 2009.

10. Our work is the first of its kind, so additional types of triggers are likely to be identified in the future.

11. Matthew L. Sheep, Ellaine C. Hollensbe, and G. E. Kreiner, "Tearing Fabric or Weaving Tapestry? Discursive Interplay of Culture and Organizational Identities." Paper presented at the 69th Annual Academy of Management Meeting, Chicago, 2009; Peter J. Boyer, "A Church Asunder: The Episcopal Tradition Confronts a Revolt." *New Yorker*, April 10, 2006.

12. We found many examples in the LAD data in which leaders like Bart were unprepared for how quickly a particular incident grew in size and scope as more and more people became involved. We noticed that once a trigger occurred in the workplace, one of two things was likely to follow: either the situation died down because those involved chose to avoid conflict or felt powerless to do anything, or the conflict escalated as the threat to identity increased. If those involved in the situation were unable to find common ground or reach a resolution on their own, they often got other people involved in an attempt to make their voice heard with the hope that change would occur. If this failed, the conflict escalated further as outsiders such as the media, the union, or legal representatives got involved. If after all this, the groups were unable to find common ground, we discovered that things did eventually settle down, but the underlying tension and distrust between the groups remained, making it more likely that a future trigger would erupt even more quickly, causing groups to pull apart farther than before. See Terrell A. Northrup, "The Dynamic of Identity in Personal and Social Conflict." In *Intractable Conflicts and Their Transformation*, edited by Louis Kriesberg, Terrell A. Northrup, and Stuart J. Thorson. Syracuse, NY: Syracuse University Press, 1989, pp. 55–82.

  Researchers define conflicts that stem from identity differences as "intractable identity conflicts." Such conflicts are very difficult to resolve because distrust is high and group safety is threatened. In-group–out-group differences become exaggerated, and thus, finding common ground is a significant challenge. See Marlene Fiole, Michael G. Pratt, and Edward J. O'Connor, "Managing Intractable Identity Conflicts." *Academy of Management Review* 34:32–55, 2009.

13. Stephen Young, "Micro-Inequities: The Power of Small." *The Workforce Diversity Reader*, Winter 2003, pp. 88–95.

14. Mathew J. Pearsall, Aleksander P. J. Ellis, and Joel M. Evans, "Unlocking the Effects of Gender Faultlines on Team Creativity: Is Activation the Key?" *Journal of Applied Psychology* 93:225–234, 2008.

15. David Migoya, "EEOC: Swift Acted with Bias." *Denver Post*, September 1, 2009, business section.

16. CCL, "Tension Triggers: What Sets Off Identity Conflict?" *Leading Effectively* e-newsletter, July 2005. For additional tools to identify fault lines and potential triggers in your workplace, see Kelly M. Hannum, Belinda B. McFeeters, and Lize Booysen, eds., *Leading across Differences: Cases and Perspectives*. San Francisco: Pfeiffer, 2010.
17. More objective measures confirmed that negative stereotypes and attitudes toward the other group diminished.

Chapter 4

1. Some of the details in this story are also presented in a case study. See Lize Annie Eliza Booysen and Stella Nkomo, "The Tea Incident Case Study: Lessons in Social Identity Tensions, Diversity and Social Identity Conflict Management." *International Journal of Diversity in Organizations, Communities, and Nations* 7(5):97–106, 2007.
2. Samer Faraj and Aimin Yan, "Boundary Work in Knowledge Teams." *Journal of Applied Psychology* 94:604–617, 2009.
3. Lisa is a fictional character.
4. Christian Homburg and Matthias Bucerius, "Is Speed of Integration Really a Success Factor of Mergers and Acquisitions? An Analysis of the Role of Internal and External Relatedness." *Strategic Management Journal* 27:347–367, 2006.
5. Lynda Gratton, Andreas Voigt, and Tamara J. Erickson, "Bridging Faultlines in Diverse Teams." *MIT Sloan Management Review* 48(4):22–29, 2007.
6. Todd L. Pittinsky and Stefanie Simon, "Intergroup Leadership." *Leadership Quarterly* 18:587–605, 2007.

Chapter 5

1. Ned Glasock, "Mexico Trip 'Humbling' for Official." *News & Observer*, February 16, 2000, p. A1.
2. This trip was led by Winifred Ernst, wife of author Chris Ernst, and Millie Ravenel, the director of the Center for International Understanding. For more information about the Center, go to their website: http://ciu.northcarolina.edu. For additional information about Rick Given's story, see Bill Ong Hing, *Deporting Our Souls: Values, Morality, and Immigration Policy*. Cambridge and New York: Cambridge University Press, 2006.
3. NPR morning edition, October 23, 2006, Jennifer Ludden, "Policymakers Get Cross-Border View of Immigration."
4. This is the first in a two-part series on NPR. The other story is "N.C. Officials Learn from Mexico Visits," October 24, 2006, by Jennifer Ludden. This also was on the NPR morning edition.
5. Ned Glasock, "Mexico Trip 'Humbling' for Official." *News & Observer*, February 16, 2000, p. A1.
6. "Chatham Rejects Immigration Program." *News & Observer*, January 13, 2009.

7. C. Marlene Fiol, Michael G. Pratt, and Edward J. O'Connor, "Managing Intractable Identity Conflicts." *Academy of Management Review* 34:32–55, 2009.
8. C. Marlene Fiol, Michael G. Pratt, and Edward J. O'Connor, "Managing Intractable Identity Conflicts." *Academy of Management Review* 34:32–55, 2009.
9. Rothman proposes a four-step strategy (antagonism, resonance, invention, and action) called the ARIA framework. Jay Rothman, *Resolving Identity-Based Conflict in Nations, Organizations, and Communities*. San Francisco: Jossey-Bass, 1997.
10. J. Rothman and M. L. Olson, "From Interests to Identities: Towards a New Emphasis in Interactive Conflict Resolution." *Journal of Peace Research* 38(3):289–305, 2001.
11. DriveTime is case study illustrated in a CCL report. See Cynthia D. McCauley, Charles J. Palus, Wilfred H. Drath, Richard L. Hughes, John B. McGuire, Patricia M. G. O'Connor, and Ellen Van Velsor, *Interdependent Leadership in Organizations: Evidence from Six Case Studies*. Greensboro, NC: Center for Creative Leadership, 2008.
12. To learn more about powerful questions, as well as to see comprehensive examples of types of powerful questions, see C. Ernst and A. Martin, *Critical Reflections: How Groups Can Learn from Success and Failure*. A Center for Creative Leadership Guidebook, 2006. See also, Charles J. Palus and David M. Horth, *The Leader's Edge: Six Creative Competencies for Navigating Complex Challenges*. San Francisco: Jossey-Bass, 2002.
13. Researchers call this phenomena the out-group homogeneity effect. For more information, see Todd D. Nelson, *The Psychology of Prejudice*. Boston: Allyn & Bacon, 2002.
14. C. Marlene Fiol, Michael G. Pratt, and Edward J. O'Connor, "Managing Intractable Identity Conflicts." *Academy of Management Review* 34:32–55, 2009.
15. "Sheriff's Position: Quiet Ruth Sheehan," *News & Observer*, February 2, 2009, p. B1.

Chapter 6

1. The story of Daniel Sutton and the cross-sector task force is a composite of several organizational examples.
2. Thomas F. Pettigrew and Linda R. Tropp, "A Meta-Analytic Test of Inter-group Contact Theory." *Journal of Personality and Social Psychology* 90:751–783, 2006.
3. The psychological process is known as decategorization. For a review, see Norman Miller and Marilynn M. Brewer, "Beyond the Contact Hypothesis: Theoretical Perspectives on Desegregation." In *Groups in Contact: The Psychology of Desegregation*, edited by Norman Miller and Marilyn. M. Brewer. New York: Academic Press, 1984, pp. 281–302.
4. Chris Ernst and Jeff Yip, "Boundary Spanning Leadership: Tactics to Bridge Social Identity Groups in Organizations." In *Crossing the Divide: Intergroup*

Leadership in a World of Difference, edited by Todd L. Pittinsky. Boston: Harvard Business School Press, 2009, 89–99.
5. Michael J. Muller, "Participatory Design: The Third Space in HCI." In *The Human-Computer Interaction Handbook: Fundamentals, Evolving Technologies and Emerging Applications*, 2nd ed., edited by Andrew Sears and Julie A. Jacko. New York: Erlbaum Associates, 2008, pp. 1061–1083.
6. Jade Chang. "Behind the Glass Curtain." *Metropolis* magazine, article posted June 19, 2006. http://www.metropolismag.com/story/20060619/behind-the-glass-curtain (accessed February 12, 2010).
7. Richard L. Hughes and Chuck J. Palus, "The Development of Effective Collaboration in Organizations." Connected Leadership Project white paper. Greensboro, NC: Center for Creative Leadership.
8. Nicholas Negroponte, *Being Digital*. New York: Vintage Books, 1995.
9. Rob Cross and Robert J. Thomas, "How Top Talent Uses Networks and Where Rising Stars Get Trapped." *Organizational Dynamics* 37(2):165–180, 2008.

Chapter 7

1. Rebecca Buckman, "Not East or West." *Forbes*, article posted November 27, 2008, http://www.forbes.com/forbes/2008/1222/050.html (accessed February 12, 2010).
2. J. Yip, S. Wong, and C. Ernst, "The Nexus Effect: When Leaders Span Group Boundaries." *Leadership in Action* 26(6):3–7, 2008.
3. Sumantra Ghoshal and Lynda Gratton, "Integrating the Enterprise." *MIT Sloan Management Review* 44(1):31–38, 2002.
4. The psychological process is known as recategorization because it attempts to regroup and reorganize people under a common category. For a review, see S. L. Gaernter and J. F. Dovidio, "Reducing Intergroup Bias." In *Motivational Aspects of Prejudice and Racism*, edited by Cynthia Willos-Esqueda. New York: Springer, 2007.
5. Jeffrey Yip, Edward Twohill, Chris Ernst, and Vijayan Munusamy, "Leadership in Faith-Based Nonprofits." *Nonprofit Management and Leadership*, 20(4), 461–472, 2010.
6. Charles J. Palus and David M. Horth, *The Leader's Edge: Six Creative Competencies for Navigating Complex Challenges*. San Francisco: Jossey-Bass, 2002.
7. Stephen Denning, *The Springboard: How Storytelling Ignites Action in Knowledge-Era Organizations*. Woburn, MA: Butterworth-Heinemann, 2001.
8. Stephen Reicher, S. Alexander Haslam, and Nick Hopkins, "Social Identity and the Dynamics of Leadership: Leaders and Followers as Collaborative Agents in the Transformation of Social Reality." *Leadership Quarterly* 16:547–568, 2005; S. Alexander Haslam, Stephen Reicher, and Michael Platow, *The New Psychology of Leadership: Identity, Influence, and Power*. New York: Psychology Press, 2008.

Chapter 8

1. Jeffrey Yip, Serena Wong, and Christopher Ernst, "The Nexus Effect: When Leaders Span Group Boundaries." *Leadership in Action* 28(4):13–17, 2008.
2. John B. McGuire and Gary B. Rhodes, *Transforming Your Leadership Culture*. San Francisco: Jossey-Bass, 2009.
3. The psychological process is known as subcategorization. See Miles Hewstone and Rupert Brown, "Contact Is Not Enough: An Intergroup Perspective on the Contact Hypothesis." In *Contact and Conflict in Intergroup Encounters*, edited by M. R. C. Hewstone and R. J. Brown. Oxford: Blackwell, 1986, pp. 1–44.
4. An initial version of this story appeared in Jeffrey Yip, Serena Wong, and Chris Ernst, "The Nexus Effect: When Leaders Span Group Boundaries." *Leadership in Action* 28(4):3–7, 2008. This is an extended version based on an interview conducted with Mechai Viravaidya after the original article was published.
5. Etienne Wenger, Richard McDermott, and William M. Snyder, *Cultivating Communities of Practice*. Boston: Harvard Business School Press, 2002.
6. Michelle A. Marks, Leslie A. DeChurch, John E. Mathieu, Frederick J. Panzer, and Alexander Alonso, "Teamwork in Multiteam Systems." *Journal of Applied Psychology* 90:964–971, 2005.

Chapter 9

1. John McGuire, Charles Palus, William Pasmore, and Gary Rhodes, "Transforming Your Organization," Organizational Leadership White Paper, 2010.
2. Margaret Jenkins is a character based on several events, including Chris's personal experience in facilitating a series of dialogues between two competing associations in his neighborhood.
3. Chris thanks his CCL colleagues Bill Drath, David Horth, and Chuck Palus for helping uncover these distinctions through their conversations. For further discussion on developing more interdependent approaches to leadership such as the transforming practice, see Drath, Palus, and McGuire, "Developing Interdependent Leadership." In *The Center for Creative Leadership Handbook of Leadership Development*, 3rd ed., edited by E. Van Velsor, C. D. McCauley, and M. N. Ruderman. San Francisco: Jossey-Bass, 2010, pp. 405–428.
4. Marilynn M. Brewer, "Managing Diversity: The Role of Social Identities." In *Diversity in Work Teams*, edited by Sharon E. Jackson and Marian N. Ruderman. Washington, DC: American Psychological Association, 1995, pp. 47–68.
5. Barbara Benedict Bunker and Billie T. Alban, *The Handbook of Large Group Methods: Creating Systemic Change in Organizations and Communities*. San Francisco: Jossey-Bass, 2006.
6. This story is derived from an interview conducted with Mark Gerzon in 2009 that first was written about in Chris Ernst and Jeffrey Yip, "Breaking Down

Boundaries in the Climate Debate: A Case Study of Mark Gerzon." *Leadership in Action* 29(3):12–16, 2009.

Chapter 10

1. From *Merriam-Webster's Collegiate Dictionary*, 11th ed.: (1) connection, link; (2) a connected group or series; (3) center, focus.
2. The concept of the Nexus Effect was first described in Jeffrey Yip, Serena Wong, and Christopher Ernst, "The Nexus Effect: When Leaders Span Group Boundaries." *Leadership in Action* 28(4):13–17, 2008.

Appendix C

1. See Chapters 2 and 13 in Cynthia D. McCauley, Ellen Van Velsor, and Marian N. Ruderman (eds.), *The Center for Creative Leadership Handbook of Leadership Development*, 3rd ed. San Francisco: Jossey-Bass, 2010.
2. John B. McGuire and Gary B. Rhodes, *Transforming Your Leadership Culture*. San Francisco: Jossey-Bass, 2009.
3. See Chapter 2 in Cynthia D. McCauley, Ellen Van Velsor, and Marian N. Ruderman (eds.), *The Center for Creative Leadership Handbook of Leadership Development*, 3rd ed. San Francisco: Jossey-Bass, 2010.

INDEX

ABOUT THE AUTHORS

Chris Ernst is a senior faculty member at the Center for Creative Leadership (CCL). His work focuses on developing boundary spanning leadership in individuals, organizations, and broader communities to help them thrive in an interdependent world.

Currently, Chris is a core faculty member in CCL's Organizational Leadership Practice, chartered to develop talent systems, leadership culture, and applied learning systems to advance organizational strategy and unlock leadership potential. Previously, Chris served in an expatriate capacity as Research Director, Asia-Pacific, with responsibility for the start-up of CCL's Research and Innovation group in Singapore.

As a researcher, Chris is a recognized authority in advancing collaborative approaches to leadership. His research has been published in articles, book chapters, the popular press, and another coauthored book titled *Success for the New Global Manager: How to*

Work across Distance, Countries and Cultures (Jossey-Bass/Wiley). Chris co-led the Leadership Across Differences project, a program of research across six world regions that formed the knowledge foundation for this book.

As a practitioner, Chris has served in multiyear expatriate roles in Asia and Europe, manages and leads multicultural teams, and designs and facilitates leadership interventions in diverse cultural and organizational contexts. Alongside his CCL colleagues, he continues to translate the ideas in this book into modules, tools, and applications to help solve client challenges.

By integrating research knowledge with real-world experience, Chris seeks to create innovative leadership solutions for organizations and communities worldwide. Chris has a Ph.D. in industrial and organizational psychology from North Carolina State University.

Donna Chrobot-Mason is an associate professor in psychology at the University of Cincinnati and Director of the Center for Organizational Leadership. Her work is focused on the intersection of two fields, diversity and leadership, to better understand the challenges and opportunities that exist in leading a diverse workforce.

Donna has been teaching courses in organizational psychology, diversity, and leadership for over 12 years. As center director, she spanned boundaries to create a cross-disciplinary research team that examines leadership from a variety of theoretical and methodological perspectives.

As a researcher, Donna has presented at nearly 50 conferences, coauthored five book chapters, and published 12 peer-reviewed articles in journals such as *Human Relations, International Journal of Human Resource Management, Journal of Organizational Behavior,* and *Group and Organization Management.* Donna also serves on three editorial review boards for leading management journals.

Donna began her career as a practitioner in human resources at the Xerox Corporation. She also consulted with numerous organizations to evaluate diversity climate and develop training programs. Her skill as a diversity scholar and passion for applied research landed her an invitation to join the Leadership Across Differences project at CCL, eventually leading to the partnership that created this book.

As an applied scholar, Donna seeks to examine practical problems scientifically and then translate the findings so that they have meaning and value for those leading within a diverse workplace. Donna has a Ph.D. in applied psychology from the University of Georgia.

ABOUT THE CENTER FOR CREATIVE LEADERSHIP

The Center for Creative Leadership (CCL®) is a top-ranked global provider of executive education that unlocks individual and organizational potential through its exclusive focus on leadership development and research. Founded in 1970 as a nonprofit educational institution, CCL helps clients worldwide cultivate creative leadership—the capacity to achieve more than they imagined possible by thinking and acting beyond boundaries—through an array of programs, products, and other services. Ranked in the Top 5 Worldwide in executive education by *BusinessWeek* and the *Financial Times*, CCL is headquartered in Greensboro, North Carolina, with campuses in Colorado Springs, Colorado; San Diego, California; Brussels, Belgium; and Singapore. Its work is supported by more than 450 faculty members and staff.

ABOUT THE CENTER FOR ORGANIZATIONAL LEADERSHIP

The Center for Organizational Leadership at the University of Cincinnati (http://www.artsci.uc.edu/orgleadership/) brings together diverse disciplines involved in the study of organizational leadership. Researchers at the center investigate how leaders can effectively bridge boundaries to foster individual, group, and organizational performance. The center enables students to develop leadership competencies, produces high-quality scholarship, and partners with organizations to enhance leadership practices.